RETRIEVING THE HUMAN

SUNY series, Philosophy and Race
Robert Bernasconi and T. Denean Sharpley-Whiting, editors

RETRIEVING THE HUMAN

Reading Paul Gilroy

Edited by
Rebecka Rutledge Fisher
and
Jay Garcia

SUNY PRESS

Published by State University of New York Press, Albany

Printed in the United States of America

For information, contact State University of New York Press, Albany, NY
www.sunypress.edu

Production by Jenn Bennett
Marketing by Michael Campochiaro

Library of Congress Cataloging-in-Publication Data

Retrieving the human : reading Paul Gilroy / edited by Rebecka Rutledge Fisher and Jay Garcia.
pages cm. -- (SUNY series, philosophy and race)
Includes bibliographical references and index.
ISBN 978-1-4384-5276-0 (paperback : alk. paper)
ISBN 978-1-4384-5275-3 (hardcover : alk. paper) 1. Gilroy, Paul 2. Race relations. 3. Racism. 4. Blacks—Social conditions. 5. Great Britain—Race relations. 6. United States—Race relations. I. Fisher, Rebecka Rutledge II. Garcia, Jay, 1972-
HT1521.R458 2014
305.8—dc23

2013037615

10 9 8 7 6 5 4 3 2 1

Contents

Introduction

Twenty years have elapsed since the publication of Paul Gilroy's *The Black Atlantic*, a work that returned to the archives of New World slavery and post-slavery, and countered prevailing understandings of modernity through a focus on "race," transnational intellectuals, and music. Gilroy's projects after *The Black Atlantic* have expanded upon his earlier theorizations of the complex networks of cultural and intellectual exchange he sees at work across black diasporic locales. The post–*Black Atlantic* corpus, as it were, is significant for many reasons, including its more explicit connection to the writings of Frantz Fanon, the intellectual genealogy of "human rights" it identifies and seeks to expand, and its reexamination of metropolitan cultures in which long-standing patterns of race hierarchy have mutated yet continue to figure in ongoing postcolonial predicaments and everyday encounters. *Retrieving the Human: Reading Paul Gilroy* brings historical perspectives to bear on Gilroy's corpus even as it considers the distinctive features of his current projects. Its premise emerged from a lecture given by Gilroy on the campus of the University of North Carolina at Chapel Hill in 2007. Seven scholars from around the country were invited to write and speak on any aspect of Gilroy's oeuvre with which they had become intellectually engaged or by which they had been influenced. Each was asked to use his or her own site of intellectual engagement with Gilroy's writings as a point of departure.

Richard King and Dennis Dworkin, in keeping with their perspectives as historians, undertook critical readings in Gilroy's intellectual biography, examining each of his major works in succession. Their essays appear together, along with that of the postcolonial critic Anthony Alessandrini, in part 1, "Theories in Motion: Roots and Routes." In King's case, Gilroy's intellectual roots and routes form the occasion for an essay on the stakes at work in Gilroy's continuously evolving thought. In his essay "Traditions, Genealogies, and Influences: Gilroy's Intellectual Roots and Routes," King considers Gilroy as a thinker whose vision of the "Black Atlantic" and the world stresses shifts, borrowings, and hybridities, and thus he sees the dominant influences on Gilroy's thought as multiple and overlapping from the start. One can easily identify a Western Marxist–Frankfurt approach, King argues, but Gilroy also makes use of an anti-imperialist analysis derived from Hannah Arendt's *The Origins of Totalitarianism* and has recently drawn upon aspects of Freudian theory. As King points out, a further tension exists between Gilroy's debts to British cultural studies and the influence of African American thought and culture, between cultural sociology and the history of ideas, between postcolonial and New World orientations. Finally, King maps with nuance a movement in Gilroy's thought between high cultural theories and popular cultural sources. In his contribution to this volume, King explores the various strands of Gilroy's intellectual history, how they interact with one another, and whether one seems to predominate above the others. He makes a convincing case for Gilroy as a thinker who is best described as part of a "diasporic" intellectual tradition that encompasses extraordinary figures. Of the diasporic thinkers pertinent to Gilroy's work, the presence of W. E. B. Du Bois, Frantz Fanon, and Richard Wright certainly makes itself felt. Even so, among all these thinkers, for King, Gilroy is arguably the most versatile and wide-ranging, for his thought is not to be exclusively identified with the European, African, North American, or Caribbean strands in modern social critique, but in fact navigates routes that transgress their limits.

Dworkin, for his part, demonstrates how Gilroy's sometimes renegade thought pushed at the boundaries of British cultural studies. In chapter 2, "Paul Gilroy and the Pitfalls of British Identity," Dworkin situates Gilroy's recent analysis of contemporary Britain in its intellectual and political setting, emphasizing the entanglement of British intellectual life and Gilroy's work as a critic and intellectual. Gilroy's *Postcolonial Melancholia*, written in the aftermath of the September 11th attacks and the Anglo-American invasion of Iraq, challenges the growing ethnic absolutism and cultural nationalism in contemporary Britain and the West more broadly. Gilroy's critique of contemporary Britain is a potent affirmation and defense of multiculturalism, cosmopolitanism, and transnationalism at a time when all of these are threatened by essentialist notions of national identity and unbridgeable cultural difference. Yet as Dworkin reminds us, *Postcolonial Melancholia* also builds upon Gilroy's earlier engagements with "the Condition of England" question. Dworkin underscores the ways in which Gilroy's more recent work resonates with arguments that Gilroy has been making since he was a graduate student at the Birmingham Centre for Contemporary Studies in the late 1970s, building on theoretical/political openings found in the Centre's collectively authored *Policing the Crisis* (1978). These arguments have been important to cultural studies; they have simultaneously been significant within discourses of decline and identity in contemporary Britain. Gilroy's concomitant attention to "structure" and "agency," his focus on modes of dominance and resistance, his privileging of history and counterhistory, and his exploration of the politics of representation all suggest vital connections with both British cultural studies and the discourse of decline. Drawing upon and traversing the cultural studies tradition, Gilroy's recent work, Dworkin argues, addresses the political culture of contemporary Britain from distinctive transnational and multicultural perspectives.

Other scholars examine the relationship between Gilroy and his intellectual models. Such is the impetus behind Anthony Alessandrini's essay on the intellectual filiation at work between Gilroy and Frantz Fanon. In chapter 3, "'Enough of This Scandal': Reading Gilroy through Fanon, or Who Comes after Race?" Alessandrini demonstrates the ways in which Gilroy's body of work has made its way along an interesting route in its engagement with humanism—that is, "humanism" both as concept and strategy. One of the more striking transitions from *The Black Atlantic* to *Against Race* and *Postcolonial Melancholia*, Alessandrini points out, is the move from what might be seen as a highly critical but nevertheless sympathetic investigation of the legacies of the Enlightenment in the earlier work to the repeated invocations of "planetary humanism" and "strategic universalism" in his more recent books. This move, Alessandrini argues, is coterminous with Gilroy's increasingly close and complex reading of Frantz Fanon. Fanon was not a key intellectual figure in the genealogy of *The Black Atlantic* that Gilroy set out in his earlier work. By the time of *Against Race*, however, Gilroy introduces Fanon in the early pages of the book as the figure "whose work frames these concerns." Given that Gilroy's double project is simultaneously to expose the complicity of humanist thinking (as well as other aspects of the Enlightenment project) with colonialism, slavery, and racialism, while at the same time working toward a transformed concept of humanism as part of an antiracist and anticolonial political strategy, the link to Fanon, who made a similar sort of call for a "new humanism" almost fifty years ago, is perhaps to be expected, Alessandrini writes. The more interesting point comes out of an examination of the ways in which Gilroy draws upon Fanon's work in articulating his vision of planetary humanism even as he distances himself from certain aspects of Fanon's own reformulation of humanism—in particular, what Gilroy refers to (in *Postcolonial Melancholia*) as Fanon's "youthful flirtations with an existentialist understanding of human agency." By contrast, Gilroy's stated goal is to place his "radically nonracial humanism" upon a "more stable foundation than those provided by . . . Fanon's phenomenological, existential, and psychoanalytical interests." So it is instructive to move back to Fanon's complex and agonized engagement with humanism throughout his diverse body of work in order to provide a framework for assessing Gilroy's planetary humanism. When we encounter Gilroy through Fanon, Alessandrini insists, we may be in a better position to appreciate the specific political strategy that is articulated through the notion of planetary humanism, which is to provide revisionist content for antiracist thinking and action. In this sense, the shared strategy of Gilroy and Fanon resonates more than a bit with the project that Michel Foucault referred to as "the critical ontology of ourselves." What the strategic humanisms of Gilroy and Fanon share with Foucault's project, Alessandrini argues, is an orientation toward "the history of the present." In the case of Gilroy and Fanon, the orientation is specifically toward a radically nonracial future, with an awareness that this future will only come through the sort of antiracist acts that their own notions of humanism are intended to frame and enable. Gilroy's "radically nonracial humanism," in other words, must not be seen as a case of wishful thinking but rather as a strategy for nurturing a nonracial future, not by declaring us "beyond race" but precisely by the urgency of antiracist thinking and action as the starting point for contemporary criticism.

Paul Gilroy's essay along with Jonathan Boyarin's response to it together constitute the second part of the book, "Retrieving the Human: Two Scholars in Dialogue." Central to this particular dialogue, Gilroy's "Multiculturalism and the Negative Dialectics of Conviviality" also serves as the volume's touchstone, for all of the writers respond to its thought in some way. In it, Gilroy addresses a range of subjects, including the currency of human rights discourse, the problem of the undoing of postcolonial approaches in the humanities, and recent theoretical reassessments of the concentration camp as a modern form. As he engages the work of such writers as Giorgio Agamben, Michel Foucault, Frantz Fanon, Hannah Arendt, and Primo Levi, Gilroy considers the evasion of histories of racism and racial hierarchies within debates about human rights and multiculturalism. For Gilroy, the current critical dialogue on human rights and multiculturalism drowns out histories of racism through "esoteric academic specialisms," effectively rendering illegitimate any commentary that would "de-nature race." His answer to this particular intellectual moment is an antiracist pedagogy that revives rather than circumvents the idea of the "human," and thereby reworks the genealogy of human rights by attending to histories of racial hierarchy and colonial statecraft. Gilroy closes his intervention in contemporary debates by returning to African American critical thought, an area of scholarly inquiry within which he has long held an important place. He summons the words of David Walker, Frederick Douglass, Ida B. Wells, and others to indicate an alternative account of the emergence of "human rights"—an account that seeks to restore the possibilities of critical humanism in what he calls our "age of rendition."

Jonathan Boyarin, a scholar of religion, engages Gilroy on this very topic, and his essay includes a compelling and direct (at times a point-by-point) response to "Multiculturalism and the Negative Dialectics of Conviviality." In chapter 5, "For a Dialogue with Paul Gilroy," Boyarin contends that Gilroy's essay may be read as a manifesto for rights in the name of a humanity that is shared but not bare. For Boyarin, Gilroy seeks to articulate a notion of that humanity as freed from the reified hierarchies of a racism forged in the adventure of colonialism abroad and genocide in the European cosmopole but still constituted within human history rather than merely posited in terms derived from Aristotelian analytics. The project is extraordinarily ambitious and is by all means one to be cheered and fostered, Boyarin allows. Perhaps like any manifesto, however, it implicitly holds certain truths to be self-evident. In his response, Boyarin points to several moments in the essay where such givens appear to limit the rhetorical force of Gilroy's argument in its current iteration and where further interrogation in the spirit of an antiracist, critical humanism promises to make multiculture and the negative dialectics of conviviality even more powerful resources within Gilroy's future-oriented criticism.

Part 3 of the collection, "Debating the Human in Everyday Spaces," includes three essays and an interview with Gilroy. The essays by Ranu Samantrai, Jay Garcia, and Tavia Nyong'o present alternative conceptualizations and critical rereadings of Gilroy's work. In chapter 6, "Sedentary and Mobile Poetics: Paul Gilroy and the Aesthetics of Postcolonial Theory," Samantrai takes Paul Gilroy's broadly noted celebration of mobility as an instance of postcolonial theory's debt to modernism—to the great modern thinkers certainly, especially among them Marx, but also to the icon of the city in modernist aesthetics. As is well known, English cities have been transformed since the mid–twentieth century by the migrations of peoples from former colonies.

But if urban settings are celebrated as shifting sites replete with political potential, in the popular imagination the national essence has retreated to the haven of the countryside. Always dependent on the aestheticization of land and people, English racial discourse is currently drawing again on the rural aesthetic to represent the nation as an organic and threatened geobody. But, preoccupied with the icon of the city as the setting for the innovations of cosmopolitan, hybrid cultures, postcolonial theorists leave undisturbed the reenchantment of the countryside as the privileged repository of Englishness, according to Samantrai. She situates Gilroy's urban aesthetic against the push of English racial discourse and the pull of the modern city, arguing that Gilroy's reliance on the urban as the necessary setting of the Marxist account of historical change limits our understanding of contemporary racial discourse. Importantly, however, Gilroy does not leave this question unaddressed, for he takes it up in his discussion of the images that figure prominently in *Black Britain*, a work described in the interview with Gilroy that concludes the present book.

Jay Garcia's "Dynamic Nominalism in Alain Locke and Paul Gilroy" examines complementary arguments and critical strategies in the work of Gilroy and that of the African American intellectual Alain Locke. Locke's criticism, centrally invested in the historicizing of racial ideology and alert to the authoritarian potential of all forms of race thinking, in many ways prefigures the arguments against "race" and racism that emerge in Gilroy's work, which has long been known to begin with the refusal of absolutist thinking in the analysis of racial ideology and of racial formation. According to Garcia, investigating Gilroy's arguments in relation to Locke's early-to-mid–twentieth century writings brings to the fore the common concerns and remarkably congruent lines of inquiry pursued by both critics. He concentrates on how Gilroy's recent cultural inquiry reprises and reworks Locke's prior efforts in three key ways. First, Gilroy presses the analysis of "race" even more dramatically than in his earlier work into the domain of the political, much as Locke's work set out to rid "race" of apolitical or prepolitical valences. Second, Gilroy's claims on behalf of the anticolonial humanism of the Second World War and postwar eras converge with Locke's own writings from those periods. And third, Gilroy's insistence on approaching racial hierarchy and ideology through a paradigm of dynamic nominalism recalls Locke's complex use of "race" in his advocacy of "culture-citizenship." Gilroy has increasingly distanced himself from paradigms organized primarily around US race politics and has veered away from W. E. B. Du Bois's concept of "double-consciousness," in particular, as a valuable contemporary critical lens. At the same time, he continues to focus upon black American letters throughout his work. Garcia shows how Gilroy's intellectual affinities with Locke provide an indispensable critical purchase on his recent interventions.

In "Black Humanitarianism," Tavia Nyong'o turns to Gilroy's treatment of black involvement in the celebrity-humanitarian complex in *Against Race* (2000) and addresses Gilroy's subsequent call, in *Postcolonial Melancholia* (2005), to reshape mainstream debates over "human rights" by harnessing the analytical import of historical struggles of black peoples over "the right to be human." Considering Gilroy's transcoding of Hannah Arendt's conception of a "right to have rights," the essay tracks an itinerary of "race" and the human through subsequent commentators on Arendt, including Giorgio Agamben and Jacques Rancière. It then turns from this post-Enlightenment philosophical trajectory to weigh, as Gilroy has encouraged scholars to do, the self-fashioning agencies of black popular culture as a counter-culture to modernity. In particular it considers the musical legacy of The Fugees, a Haitian, Haitian American, and African American hip hop band, in terms of how the figure of the refugee, as Agamben and Arendt both argue, radically transfigures the ideal-type of citizen, releasing its contained liberatory energies. Employing both musical and visual analysis, the essay argues for moments of internal tension in the contemporary humanitarian appeal—centering on the relief effort in the wake of the 2010 Haitian earthquake—moments that deconstruct the seemingly smooth assimilation of black star power into the celebrity-humanitarian complex. Reversing dominant critical practice, Nyong'o's argument proceeds by unveiling a deep genealogical link between blackness and light: the icon of the halo. The troping of blackness, black people, and Africa as haloed—that is, as shrouded in uncreated light—is irreducible to the seeming analogues of the Enlightenment or racial whitening. Rather, as Nyong'o points out, the halo, and the associated phenomenon of spiritual or secular "glorying," illuminates a central problem for black humanitarianism: does it achieve the goals of a "planetary humanism" that Gilroy has called for? Or does it consolidate the huge gulfs in wealth, well-being, and power that have been celebrity's historical occasion?

The interview transcribed here—"A Dialogue on the Human: An Interview with Paul Gilroy"—was moderated by Rebecka Rutledge Fisher in January 2007, and included questions posed by graduate students from the University of North Carolina at Chapel Hill and Duke University, whose incisive questions regarding race, gender, religion, music, conviviality, and the post-9/11 "War on Terror" provided Gilroy ground upon which to further illuminate features of his work. The book's final essay, an afterword written by John McGowan, responds to pivotal issues raised by the contributors. The refusal to elide racial hierarchies and the history of empire marks all of the component parts of *Retrieving the Human: Reading Paul Gilroy.* The collection also attends to what Richard Wright called "a sense of the inexpressibly human." Yet rather than attempt to fill that category with self-evident content, we instead offer Gilroy's work and several responses to that work as opportunities to return to the "human" and "human rights" in particular in the current conjuncture. Our premise is that such opportunities are necessary and benefit from rethinking from within the black critical tradition. As a recurrent and ever more complex project in the excavation and reworking of that tradition, Gilroy's work represents one of the major critical contributions of the twentieth and twenty-first centuries.

The editors thank John McGowan for his assistance and encouragement throughout the production of this collection. Sandy Darity, Larry Grossberg, and Maya Winfrey also offered sound advice during various phases of the project.

Part I

Theories in Motion

Roots and Routes

1

Traditions, Genealogies, and Influences

Gilroy's Intellectual Roots and Routes

RICHARD H. KING

Paul Gilroy first came to intellectual prominence with the publication of *The Black Atlantic* (1993). Though always working against the grain of received opinion, Gilroy's work has shown a general consistency of theme and concern, from its initial focus on British society and culture in *'There Ain't No Black in the Union Jack'* (1987) and *Small Acts* (1993) to a much broader focus in *The Black Atlantic* (1993), a visionary exploration of the cultural connections linking the peoples of the African diaspora. With *Between Camps* (2000), Gilroy advocated a "planetary humanism" and "cosmopolitanism" to counter what he saw as a resurgence of racism and a new sort of generic fascism, ostensibly shorn of its disreputable historical associations. *After Empire* (2004) narrowed the focus to the cultural implications of the post-imperial status of Britain, while his most recent book, *Darker than Blue* (2010), moves back out to the black Atlantic to consider the crisscrossing claims of commercialism, cosmopolitanism, and citizenship within a broader cultural context.[1]

Yet the continuities in Gilroy's work are definitely there. A suspicion of the viability or validity of nation, ethnicity, and race has been present from the beginning, as has his opposition to the idea that cultural configurations map neatly onto the boundaries of contemporary nation-states. Gilroy has always been very adept at using high theory to illuminate popular culture. In particular, he has focused on black popular music, roughly post-1960s vintage, as the main evidence for the existence of a shared culture among people of African descent in the Atlantic world. Finally, Gilroy's predominant emphasis has fallen upon the workings of expressive culture rather than upon politics or economics, even though he has increasingly felt compelled to address the political implications and occasionally the economics of the cultural phenomena that he is exploring.

Since Gilroy's work is so intellectually ambitious, I focus here on four particular clusters of problems in his intellectual biography. The first involves the British sources of Gilroy's thought, in particular his relationship to cultural Marxism via the Birmingham Centre for Contemporary Cultural Studies. Second, I want to explore the issues raised by his claim that the black Atlantic is a "counterculture of modernity," particularly the idea of modernity as the working out of "racialized reason and terror" as experienced by members of the African diaspora (and the Jewish diaspora). Then, I analyze his treatment of race and racism, as reflected in the relationship between politics and culture, citizenship and cosmopolitanism, in *Between Camps* and much of his later work. Finally, though Gilroy has rightfully assumed a place beside W. E. B. Du Bois as a canonical figure in the black Atlantic intellectual tradition, an unresolved tension in his thought is the relationship between culture and politics. As Lucy Evans among others has observed, Gilroy has shown a "troubling tendency to privilege culture over politics."[2]

The Anxiety of Influence

It is easy to minimize the impact of British cultural Marxism, particularly in the United States, on the 1960s and 1970s. Yet figures such as literary critics Richard Hoggart and Raymond Williams, historian E. P. Thompson, and sociologist Stuart Hall all exerted a powerful influence on trans-Atlantic debates about mass and popular culture, the making of "working-class culture" and "youth culture," as well as the uses of high culture to define the nature of the nation.[3] The debate about mass, popular, and high culture emerged among New York intellectuals in the late 1930s, as it did among such British intellectuals as George Orwell, but postwar studies such as Hoggart's *The Uses of Literacy* (1957) and Williams's *The Long Revolution* (1961) rekindled and reoriented the debate on both sides of the Atlantic. Labour/left-wing credentials were more prominent among the British cultural Marxists, while those who spearheaded the debate in America, such as Dwight Macdonald and Clement Greenberg, had a firmer commitment to avant-garde and high modernist artistic expression than their British counterparts. The

British cultural critics tended to focus on culture rather than economics but were less hostile to popular culture and less theoretically oriented than the thinkers of the Frankfurt School in exile in America.[4]

Though Hoggart, Williams, Thompson, and Hall were far from agreement on everything, they did react against orthodox Marxism's economic emphasis and devoted most of their attention to forms of working-class culture and consciousness. First, for example, at the end of his preface to *The Making of the English Working Class* (1963), Thompson apologized for not having dealt with the Scottish and Welsh working classes. Since "class is a cultural as much as an economic formation," he wrote, "I have been cautious as to generalising beyond English experience."[5] Second, a distinctly voluntarist bias marked their brand of Marxism. As Thompson emphasized in his attack on the French structuralist Marxist Louis Althusser, in "The Poverty of Theory" (1978), the proper emphasis of a history of the working class should fall upon agency, not structure; upon political action not impersonal social forces. Finally, this British tradition reversed the Marxist international orientation by underlining the national setting of the working classes. Thus, the British working class, as depicted in the work of these cultural Marxists, emerged as remarkably homogeneous in religious, racial, ethnic, and national terms, as witness Thompson's exclusion of the Scotch and Welsh from his study. Put another way, there seemed to be a genuinely organic British/ English working-class culture to match a vital working-class political tradition.[6]

It was in the context of the second half of the 1970s and the first half of the 1980s that the Birmingham Centre, under the directorship of Anglo-Jamaican Stuart Hall since 1968, shifted its attention from the white English working class to a new, ethnically diverse working class increasingly made up of immigrants from the Caribbean, Africa, and Asia. It was under the influence of Hall, who was in the process of reformulating Marxism to accommodate race and ethnicity as "articulations" of, but still distinct from, class formations, that Paul Gilroy, who earned his PhD at Birmingham, began to write.[7]

What Gilroy came to challenge specifically was Raymond Williams's notion of British working-class culture. Gilroy's startling claim was that thinkers on the cultural left such as Williams sounded eerily similar to the new white racism and "ethnic absolutism" that had gathered momentum since the late 1960s. (This white particularism was often seen to have emerged in the wake of Enoch Powell's infamous "Rivers of Blood" speech in 1968.) Williams, for instance, contrasted a working class grounded in "actual and sustained relationships" with "merely formal" or "legal" forms of national identity.[8] Thus Williams seemed to suggest that the new immigrants could hardly be considered authentic members of the working class, since they did not yet possess "a whole way of life" grounded in the "immediacy of lived experience."[9] In light of such evocations of cultural consensus, what Gilroy most feared was, as Baker et al. put it, the "naturalization of race, ethnicity and nation."[10] Since then, Gilroy has fought against ideas of race and culture grounded in biology and/or rigidly conceived cultural differences. Overall, whether race or ethnicity was emphasized, the upshot was all too often the same—a commitment to group purity and the politics of exclusion.

By now, a consensus seems to exist that Gilroy's critique of the ontology of cultural experience advanced by Williams hit on something. Williams had his own problems with working out the relationship between his working-class Welsh identity and the national identity, particularly at Cambridge where he studied and later taught.[11] It was as though there was no room for another new group to be accommodated within the national identity. Certainly, the rural, culturally Christian and white origins of the British working-class experience were different from the new immigrant population, who were themselves concentrated in the urban areas, particularly London. Nor with the honorable exception of George Orwell did any of the Marxist-oriented cultural critics really deal with the relationship of the British working class to British imperialism or colonialism. This is not to say that they were champions of Imperial Britain, and in fact Thompson's father had been an advocate of Indian independence. But it was difficult to find them making any economic or cultural connections between the working class at home and the colonial workforces that generated the productive capacity of British imperialism.[12]

On the other hand, Gilroy retained much from his precursors as well. Besides the cultural materialism, he also shared their emphasis upon the importance of culture; and he, like them, was drawn particularly to its popular forms of expression. Similarly Thompson's characterization of class as something that emerged in and through political activity was echoed in Gilroy's idea that race was defined by its role in political struggle rather than as a biological or cultural entity. And, like Thompson, the centrality of agency, particularly in cultural and social action, was important to his thought. Finally, Gilroy objected to the view, then and now, that black British culture was one in which "[r]acial subordination [was] the sole factor shaping the choices and actions of Britain's black settlers and their children."[13]

Clearly, Gilroy's overall relationship to Marxism has been a complex one right from the start. While believing that capitalism by nature created conflict between labor and capital, Gilroy contended that it was race that "enable[d] political action" based on the "experience of subordination as well as exploitation" in Britain.[14] Nor did he believe in what he later referred to in *The Black Atlantic* as "the assumptions of occidental progress which Marxism shared,"[15] though he did briefly identify a utopian, visionary, and redemptive promise in black Atlantic culture.[16] Moreover, Gilroy has always rejected Marxism's "productivism," the idea that the existential and even ontological foundations of the self and history are located in the activity of labor. The experience of slavery, which defined the slave merely as *animal laborans* and was the *raison d'être* of the black Atlantic, had discredited that particular anthropological conception of human beings once and for all.[17] Thus, borrowing from Hannah Arendt, we might say that the *work* of creativity and culture, not "the labor metaphysic," stands at the heart of Gilroy's philosophical anthropology.[18]

More generally, though mentioned only in passing in *The Black Atlantic*, Gilroy also jettisoned the orthodox Marxist (and Weberian) notion of the incompatibility of slavery and capitalism. Up to a certain historical point, the latter clearly depended not only on what Max Weber referred to as "formally free labor," but also on slave labor. Gilroy rejected the Marxist-derived notion that slavery was "pre-modern residue,"[19] as historians of slavery in the 1960s and 1970s such as Eugene Genovese claimed. Of course, black Marxists such as W. E. B. Du Bois, C. L. R. James, and Oliver O. Cox had already linked the origins of modern capitalism with racial slavery, while Stuart Hall, as we have seen, was developing the idea of "articulation" to conceptualize the links between class and race in slavery and afterward. In these respects, Gilroy was originally closer to what Cedric Robinson has called "Black Marxism" than to other schools of Marxism.[20]

But, Gilroy's early work was lacking a vocabulary to describe the differences between cultural affiliation and political identity, and this has remained an underexplored aspect of his thought. While precursors such as Raymond Williams used "nation" to refer both to state and culture (a "whole way of life"), there was, and is, another tradition, perhaps more continental, that distinguished the state (legal-political institutions and values) from the nation (ethnic and cultural values). Jürgen Habermas has, for instance, proposed the idea of "constitutional patriotism," that is, loyalty to the political institutions and ideals of a country over loyalty to its cultural, ethnic, and religious traditions.[21] But on the political side of his thinking, Gilroy has tended to identify politics with political organizing and action outside the workings of regular state institutions, without really paying the political sphere the attention that he has devoted to the cultural sphere. Still, Gilroy's idea of culture has never carried the connotation of organic rootedness so central to the other British cultural Marxists. There was obviously some connection between culture and shared experience over time, but Gilroy has done everything he could to make the match between them as complex as possible. Thus throughout his intellectual career Gilroy has had trouble imagining the relationship between a stable political entity and culture, a problem to which I attend throughout this essay.

A New Master Narrative: Death Is a Master . . .

The Black Atlantic has been written about so much and so well that it is difficult to think of a new angle on it. Yet it is still not clear what made the book seem so new and different when it was first published. Historically, the idea of "Atlantic history" or of "the Atlantic world" was by no means new when Gilroy's book was published.[22] The comparative history of slavery involving North America, Britain and France, the Caribbean and Latin America, and Africa flourished in the three decades after World War II. Even before that, the issue of continuity versus rupture between the cultures of West Africa and the New World was intensely debated in the late 1930s and early 1940s, as witness the exchanges between sociologist E. Franklin Frazier, who questioned any meaningful links between the cultures of West Africa and North America, and anthropologist Melville Herskovits, who stressed the cultural continuity between West Africa and Africans in the Western Hemisphere. The debate reemerged in the 1950s and 1960s under the aegis of Négritude, Black Consciousness, and the Black Aesthetic. Then, Robert Farris Thompson used the phrase "the black Atlantic tradition" in his *Flash of the Spirit* (1983), very much following in the footsteps of, and indirectly helping to rehabilitate, Herskovits. All this historical, sociological, and anthropological work clearly prefigured aspects of Gilroy's work in cultural sociology and intellectual history, though Gilroy scarcely mentions this tradition in *The Black Atlantic* and undoubtedly saw it as too close to the Afrocentric approach.[23] He was, however, more sympathetic to the radical spirit of the work of historians Peter Linebaugh and Marcus Rediker, who made "a conceptual unit of the Atlantic" in their social and cultural histories of the workers' Atlantic.

The Black Atlantic was also just what the New Americanists such as Donald Pease had been calling for since the late 1980s—a transnational (not just comparative) approach to race and culture. Nor was Gilroy shy about challenging the exceptionalist assumptions and flirtations with racial politics of

African American scholars and intellectuals, a critique that echoed his earlier attacks on the British cultural Marxists. On the other hand, by expanding the Britain-Caribbean network of black popular music—and it was music that Gilroy took as the central mode of communication within the black Atlantic—and by bringing the United States more prominently into the picture, the scope of the concept of diaspora was widened considerably in *The Black Atlantic*. Indeed, for all his efforts *not* to privilege the African American component, the dominant voices and salient issues in his book tended to be African American in origin.

Still, as several critics have noted, Gilroy didn't actually spend much time on African culture, especially popular culture, in *The Black Atlantic*.[24] Rather he focused on the historical role that Martin Delany, Edward Blyden, and W. E. B. Du Bois played in the creation of consciousness of Africa, as well as exploring themes such as that of the "outsider" in Richard Wright's work and the "slave sublime" in Toni Morrison's. Strangely, Gilroy spent little time with the two works—*Black Power* (1954) and *The Color Curtain* (1956)—in which Wright wrote about Africa and the Third World. Moreover, *The Black Atlantic* is a thoroughly Anglophone book. The non-Anglophone Caribbean, especially Haiti, the homeland of African-oriented culture in the Western Hemisphere, receives short shrift, not to mention the strange omission of Brazil or Spanish-speaking northern Latin America from the discussion. Gilroy never really engages fully with the Francophone architects of Négritude so central to black modernity such as Léopold Sédar Senghor and Aimé Césaire; nor, as he acknowledges, does Frantz Fanon, who rebelled against Négritude, play much of a role in *The Black Atlantic*. (Gilroy does return repeatedly to Fanon's concept of a new humanism in his work after *The Black Atlantic*.) Pan-Africanism as an idea is taken up, but only in passing, even though Gilroy devotes an entire chapter to Du Bois. Admittedly, Gilroy had already included a paragraph or so on Pan-Africanism in *'There Ain't No Black in the Union Jack'* but characterized it there as "inadequate . . . particularly as it can suggest mystical unity outside the process of history or even common culture or ethnicity which will assert itself regardless of determinate political and economic circumstances." It is not necessary to be a champion of, or even an expert on, Pan-Africanism to suspect that this dismissive summary of the concept fails to do it justice. Indeed, where Gilroy's notion of the black Atlantic lacked a strong political dimension, Pan-Africanism tended, if anything, to emphasize the political over the cultural dimension of its vision.[25]

More serious was Gilroy's omission of two large areas of cultural creativity central to the culture of the black Atlantic—its visual arts and its religious life. If Gilroy overemphasizes the importance of music in the construction of the black Atlantic, he radically underplayed its strong tradition in the visual arts, especially its influence on early modernist painting and sculpture of the School of Paris. In the last decade or so, however, the visual culture of the black Atlantic—"Afromodernity"—has received fresh attention. Indeed, the international exhibitions Rhapsodies in Black: Art of the Harlem Renaissance, which opened in 1997 in London, and Afro Modern: Journeys through the Black Atlantic (2010) at the Tate Liverpool went a long way toward confirming and deepening Gilroy's thesis. His work was explicitly a central part of the impetus for the Liverpool show, while he contributed a piece to the 1997 exhibition catalogue that began at the Hayward Gallery in London. What the exhibitions (and accompanying catalogues) made clear was that, as several critics have noted, the "Harlem Renaissance," for instance, loomed large in importance when it was placed in an international nexus of influences and impacts.[26] Similarly, the stature of the visual arts of the modern black Atlantic was augmented by contributions from Haiti and Brazil, not to mention West Africa, as the Liverpool show was at pains to show.

Moreover Brent Hayes Edwards's exploration of the concept of diaspora has revealed certain tensions between it and Gilroy's idea of the black Atlantic. Though one of the chapter titles in *'There Ain't No Black in the Union Jack'* contained the term "diaspora," its meaning there was restricted to the relations of cultural production and transmission between three points in the slave trade—Britain, the Caribbean, and the United States. When *The Black Atlantic* explicitly added Africa itself to the cultural geographical reach of the black Atlantic, at least in theory, the idea was complete. Yet Gilroy has also been wary of using the term "diaspora" since it seems to imply the idea of return to origins and thus is more compatible with the Afrocentric tendency that he (Gilroy) wants to take his distance from. His black Atlantic, on the other hand, was meant to stress movement and hybridity, "routes" not "roots."[27] Edwards also notes, for instance, that the concept of diaspora has historically tended to stress the emergent differences within a people, while Gilroy has also stressed the idea of a common black Atlantic culture.

Appearing a decade after *The Black Atlantic*, Edwards's *The Practice of Diaspora: Literature, Translation and the Rise of Black Internationalism* (2003) explored the literary and intellectual history of Paris at the crossroads of the black Atlantic in the interwar years. His analysis of the institutional and organizational structure of an emerging black Atlantic (African American, Caribbean, and French in conception) helped remedy another omission in Gilroy's work—the organizational infrastructure of the black Atlantic. What Edwards and more recent studies have emphasized is the importance of journals such as *Présence Africaine*, not to mention the 1956 and 1960 International Congresses of Negro Writers and Artists in Paris and then Rome for the emergence of Négritude and more broadly the black Atlantic. At those congresses, diaspora intellectuals brought (back) into being something that Edwards calls the idea of a "black internationalism."[28] Had Gilroy worked through some of this predominantly Francophone material, his original concept of the black Atlantic would have had more historical density and texture to it.

About the varieties of religious experience, observance, and organization in the black Atlantic, it is hard to know where to begin. But clearly the philosophical and metaphysical dimensions of black Atlantic existence can be traced back to the spread of Christianity among the slave population of the hemisphere and the syncretistic combinations that resulted from the cross-fertilization of Christianity and the religions of West Africans as they both arrived in the New World. To be sure, Gilroy has recently explored the importance of Rastafarianism in the music of one of his cultural heroes, Bob Marley. But *The Black Atlantic* never really conveys much sense of the importance of religion, the life of the spirit in its myriad and necessarily hybrid forms, in the life of the black diaspora.[29] Specifically, Gilroy's focus on the post-1960s musical cultures of the black Atlantic needed to be grounded in the persisting force of diasporic religious consciousness. One of the weaknesses, for instance, of Gilroy's discussion of the popular music associated with the (US) Civil Rights movement during and after the 1960s is his failure to emphasize the religious roots of, say, the music of Curtis Mayfield. Thus Gilroy has been reluctant to engage in any serious way with African American history; the historiography of African American slavery would have provided him with an impressive model for understanding complex history of black religion in one prominent region of the black Atlantic.

My wider point here is not that Gilroy never discusses particular religious traditions that feed into the "slave sublime," including the importance of the Fisk Jubilee Singers or the exodus narrative with diasporic Jewry. It is rather that he never explores in any great detail the spiritual underpinnings of the black Atlantic. For instance, if Max Weber's resonant idea of the "disenchantment of the world" captures the spiritual state of modern Western culture, then the black Atlantic, as a "counterculture of modernity," can be seen as part of the effort to "reenchant the world," or at least to protect the realms of the spirit from modernity's relentless rationalization of the world. The spiritual legacy of religion remains, to quote Marx, the "heart of a heartless (modern) world" and not just the "opiate of the masses."

Finally, in reference to historical and methodological matters, *The Black Atlantic* forces the reader to ask just what kind of "thing" the black Atlantic was supposed to be. On the one hand, Gilroy clearly considers it to be an actually existing entity about which empirical claims concerning causes and effects, forces and factors can be made. To that extent his claims about it are open to historical challenge, subject to verification or falsification, and open to arguments from plausibility. And yet, Gilroy's book should also be seen as an extended performative utterance calling into existence the black Atlantic as in: "Let us imagine something I will call the black Atlantic." Put succinctly, the black Atlantic thesis makes a historical claim *and* announces a visionary project. With it Gilroy proposed a condition of possibility (Kant) or a new paradigm (Kuhn) for viewing commonly understood things in a different way. Historically speaking, a question such as how do we know when the black Atlantic came into existence and when it can be said to no longer exist can in principle be answered. But in terms of a visionary or utopian project, something that is constructed *out of* historical materials, the question about its existence is much more problematic. Put in pragmatic terms, the truth value of the concept of the black Atlantic depends on whether it enables people to survive and flourish according to a certain narrative of historical experience and attendant values. The claims that the culture of the black diaspora is future- rather than past-oriented, that it stresses openness and hybridity rather than purity, are clearly wishes disguised as historical statements of fact. Here questions about the future shape of the black Atlantic still need thinking through. Must those positive characteristics be distributed homogeneously or can the black Atlantic include individuals, groups, and ideologies that are not open to the future but stuck in the past, committed to "roots" rather than "routes"? Plurality is a central value of the black Atlantic, but should intolerant groups be tolerated within it?

Another thing that distinguishes *The Black Atlantic* is Gilroy's deliberate use of figures of speech to carry his argument. Such rhetorical sophistication differentiates it from most works of intellectual history or cultural sociology. Though bent on dismantling binary oppositions where possible, he likes to deploy them rhetorically. The "roots/routes" pun is of course central, as is the trope/chronotope of the "ship" as the carrier of the black Atlantic culture, not to mention the characterization of the diasporic tradition in terms of the "changing same," originally a phrase of Amiri Baraka's. Sometimes all this can sound like Jesse Jackson in his rhetorical heyday, but at its best, Gilroy's prose generates a powerful momentum, though its dense texture makes *The Black Atlantic* an impossible book to skim or easily summarize. At times its obliqueness is frustrating, as, for instance, when Gilroy defines the tradition he is addressing as "the nameless, evasive qualities that make these diasporic conversations possible,"[30] a characterization that barely avoids circularity. Though it has endnotes in the usual academic style, *The Black Atlantic* is not finally a neutral work of historical research or value-free social science, since it is, as already mentioned, informed by a strong and often compelling vision.

All that said, what moved *The Black Atlantic* to a different level was Gilroy's placement of a grand narrative of (Western) modernity at its center, but one that departed significantly from the West's own self-understanding. In Gilroy's hands the story "to be passed on" is not one of inevitable progress or the inevitable increase of freedom under modernity; rather it is a story of the emergence of capitalism, with racial slavery, including the horrors of the Middle Passage, at its heart. Indeed, Gilroy's claim is that the very concept of progress through reason was implicated in slavery and racism—"racialized reason and terror"—and they were yoked together in an unholy alliance. As a result the concepts of diaspora and modernity take on an added moral and historical depth and complexity. Simon Gikandi has suggested that, though Gilroy emphasizes the close link between racism and modernity, he stops short of considering the former as "part of the immanent logic of modernity" but rather sees racism as something that contaminated Enlightenment values from the outside, as it were.[31] But this seems to me misplaced, even if correct. How is Gilroy to make use of the secular European tradition that defended the idea of racial equality, if the Enlightenment, for instance, is rejected as complicit in the worst aspects of modernity. Not even Adorno and Horkheimer so ruthlessly rejected the Enlightenment heritage; instead, they considered it dialectically. I will return to this matter latter.

Gilroy's second crucial addition to the notion of modernity was Du Bois's idea of "double consciousness," the sense that diasporic peoples were both inside and outside, part of, but apart from, modern Western culture, at home but never quite. This led Gilroy to make the claim about the people of the African diaspora that has been made about the Jews: in their very marginality, they embodied the essential meaning of modernity. It was now the (former) slaves who were the carriers of a newly emergent culture not the proletariat as in the Marxist historical narrative. Where anthropologists once considered Africans to be *Naturvolker* (primitive) rather than *Kulturvolker* (cultured), they were now the carriers of an irresistible, diasporically inflected version of modern Western culture.

But what I want to focus on as the moral core of Gilroy's narrative of the black Atlantic are the connections he makes between Hegel's master-slave (lordship and bondage) relationship as illustrated in Frederick Douglass's *Narrative* and the story of Margaret Garner that forms the core of Toni Morrison's *Beloved* (1987) and the comparison of the West's two great diasporic peoples—Jews and blacks. By focusing on these paradigmatic responses of slaves to the terror at the heart of slavery, Gilroy wants to claim "the repeated choice of death rather than bondage articulates a principle of negativity" that provides the impetus for "act[s] of cultural creation and affirmation" in the black Atlantic.[32] Gilroy also wants to suggest that Hegel was wrong about the master-slave relationship, since slaves such as Frederick Douglass and Margaret Garner chose to resist their master or his proxies rather than acceding to the threat of death.[33]

Yet I would suggest that the stories of Douglass and Garner follow, rather than contradict, the logic of Hegel's parable of the origins of self and society. In choosing to risk one's life, as Douglass did, or in choosing to sacrifice her children, as Garner did, they ceased to be slaves in a subjective sense. They became free, even though they still bore their chains. In risking their lives (or that of their children), they gained freedom. But Gilroy's wider point about the intimate relationship in the black Atlantic between life and death, terror and creativity is still an important one. It is made even more complexly powerful when we learn that Hegel's thinking about the dialectic of lordship and bondage was, according to Susan Buck-Morss, profoundly influenced by his thinking about the slave uprising Toussaint L'Ouverture led in Haiti in the 1790s that eventuated in independence for Haiti.[34]

Beyond that Gilroy's narrative of modernity linked Jews and people of African descent since both had been subjected to the worst violence modernity had to offer. Gilroy's discussion of the parallels between Jews and blacks took a good bit of intellectual courage in the context of the book's appearance. Stanley Elkin's concentration camp analogy in *Slavery* (1959) was so comprehensively rejected by African American (and white) historians and intellectuals in the 1960s that it was daring for Gilroy to raise the issue at a time when the animosity between blacks and Jews seemed to be, if anything, on the increase.[35] Gilroy was also at considerable pains *not* to compare the relative suffering of the two peoples, since such calculations led to the worst sort of comparative victimhood. Rather, he emphasized that the point of reintroducing a comparative perspective was to learn "about the way modernity operates," not to champion blacks against Jews or vice versa.[36]

Still, some would also question the relevance of the Hegelian master-slave paradigm for modern forms of mass domination—under slavery, the factory systems of the Industrial Revolution, and the camp systems in Germany and the Soviet Union. Where human beings are so demeaned and their selves all but effaced on such an extensive scale over time, the question of the master's desire for recognition and the slave's decision to fight to the death seem beside the point. Hannah Arendt noted something along these lines when, in *The Origins of Totalitarianism* (1951), she suggested that resistance ceased to have any meaning once people were in the camps, since the camps systematically undermined the personal, moral, and legal identity of the inmates; and in that situation, a meaningful existential choice to resist was practically impossible. What went on in the camps was not a struggle for recognition but a struggle to render "superfluous" those who labored for the masters, made all the easier by the "stateless" status of the victims, without the "right to have rights."[37]

Indeed, Arendt's whole point regarding the vulnerability of refugees, stateless people, and minorities to selection, concentration, and even extermination found echoes in the historical experience of the black Atlantic. As Gilroy himself emphasizes in *Darker than Blue* (2010), the history of human rights includes large lacunae, periods of silence, especially during the period of slavery and colonialism and the aftermath of colonialism in the non-European world.[38] Arendt's point concerning "rights" was that the appeal to natural or human rights proved to be ineffectual, cruelly useless, in the years between World Wars I and II. From this, Arendt concluded that what every human needed was "the right to have rights," which was plausible only in a bounded political entity that provided a space of speech, action, and protection. I mention this particularly because Gilroy emphasizes the transnational nature of the black Atlantic culture and in his later works rejects "civil rights" for "human rights." In light of this, questions about what preserves openness and hybridity, what protects civil liberties and even the right to life must be asked. Significantly, in his definition of genocide, Raphael Lemkin included a cultural dimension, but who will nurture or protect cultural rights of and in the black Atlantic?[39]

Finally, in the same year that Gilroy published *The Black Atlantic*, Laurence Thomas suggested that what allowed Jews not only to survive the Holocaust but also to flourish afterwards was their possession of a common "narrative" that made sense of individual and group existence. While Jews had their historically venerable religion, with its sacred texts and institutions, and a common memory, Thomas feared that blacks lacked anything like that: "skin color does not make a narrative."[40] At one level, Gilroy might be sympathetic to this judgment, since he has been so suspicious of race, particularly skin color, as the basis of group identity. Indeed, I would suggest that *The Black Atlantic* be read as Gilroy's heroic effort to create a new cultural narrative for people of the African diaspora to replace the grand narratives of both Afrocentrism and Western modernity.

Is There a "Beyond Race"?

Gilroy's own intellectual roots were recently clarified when he noted that *The Black Atlantic* was modeled on Edward Said's *Orientalism*, while his longest book, *Between Camps*, took as its model Hannah Arendt's *The Origins of Totalitarianism.*[41] This makes it all the more appropriate to invoke Arendt's essay "Organized Guilt and Universal Responsibility" (1945) as a way into Gilroy's book of 2000 and much of his work since then. Writing in the postwar spirit of universalism, she offered the sobering observation that the newly discovered awareness of "the idea of humanity and of the Judeo-Christian faith in the unitary origin of the human race" brought with it a moral burden. In fact some had already rejected the obligation to the point that they had "become more susceptible to the doctrine of race, which denies the very possibility of common humanity." In a time of global expansion and awareness, Arendt continued, "To follow a non-imperialistic policy and to maintain a non-racist faith becomes daily more difficult because it becomes daily clearer how great a burden mankind is for man."[42] Thus the British title of *Origins*, *The Burden of Our Time*, refers not only to the memory of totalitarianism and genocide but also to the moral challenge a concept such as "mankind" (humankind) presents.

Though over a half-century separates Arendt's essay from Gilroy's *Between Camps*, her warnings sound very familiar to those who have read it. Where the traditional "modern" idea of race based on biological characteristics had lost credibility, claimed Gilroy, "new" ideas of race, based not on skin color or physical appearance but on unobservable genetic makeup, have become more appealing. Racism, or what he calls "raciology," leads almost inevitably to a kind of generic or "universal fascism,"[43] the latter being an ideological complex arising out of a lethal mixture of pride, frustration, humiliation, and "anxiety," not to mention what he refers to in *After Empire* as "post-imperial melancholia."[44] In fascism, identity ceases being a flexible self-construction, but, rather, a "thing to be possessed and displayed" and often grounded in a rigid racial or ethnic ideology.[45] The idea of race itself is generated by the ideology of racism. The racist doesn't hate black people, they have certain distasteful characteristics; rather the racist imputes those characteristics to all blacks and thereby creates them as a racial group. The same goes for people of color, whether black or yellow or red.

The symptoms of the fascist ethos are a glorification of the body (both racialized and eroticized); an emphasis on masculinity, brutality, and power; and the cultivation of military values, hierarchy, and usually some form of ethnic or racial purity. It privileges "the image over writing."[46] Indeed, anticipations and premonitions of these neo-fascist ideologies can be seen in what are seemingly harmless public displays of the body powerful among models, actors, and athletes. One of Gilroy's more interesting—and controversial—points in *Between Camps* is to insist that blacks can be just as attracted to fascist or quasi-fascist forms of identity as are white people, a point which Richard Wright made in his essay on *Native Son* back in the early 1940s. Indeed, it is a sign of their modernity that "blacks are not after all a permanently innocent people."[47] Gilroy instances the Garvey movement, aspects of the Nation of Islam, and of the Black Panther Party as exemplifying the fascist mind-set. Finally, Gilroy considers the idea of race as one that has nothing good to be said for it: "The space in which 'races' come to life are a field from which political interaction has been banished."[48] Just as with someone like Susan Sontag, fascism is both a cultural and a political concept for Gilroy.

Though *Between Camps* lacks the relatively tight focus of *The Black Atlantic*, the former does see Gilroy pay more adequate attention to Fanon, Senghor, and Césaire. As veterans of combat in Europe, they realized that what had happened on European soil between 1939 and 1945 was powerfully shaped by the racialization of all aspects of life in the European colonies in Africa and Asia, which was then brought back directly or indirectly to Europe. There, they became "black witnesses to European barbarity"[49] not just in Germany but throughout Europe. It was this historical experience of black soldiers, along with the idea developed by Césaire, Arendt, and Sartre of the "boomerang" effect, that links the horrors of the Holocaust and the racial terror at the heart of the black Atlantic

It should be clear by now that Gilroy's central purpose in *Between Camps* and since has been to demolish the concept of race. But what are the implications of abandoning the idea/language of race? Gilroy spends much of *Between Camps* exploring an alternative, which he names "planetary humanism," which expresses itself in a "cosmopolitan" stance toward the world. Gilroy prefers to avoid the term "global humanism" since "global" has so many negative connotations (as in "globalization"); nor does he want to resurrect "bourgeois" or "liberal" as qualifications on humanism. This older humanism was, following

Fanon, thoroughly discredited by its association with capitalist exploitation, colonial domination, and racialization. As already mentioned, Simon Gikandi suggests that race's role in modernity did not arise from an adventitious association but through an inner complicity.

But Gilroy might have been more systematic in exploring the links between the humanist tradition, including the Enlightenment, and racism. For instance, modern humanism seems to have provided little resistance to the emergence of racist modes of thought in the modern world, while the secularized notion of reason has been used to group individuals hierarchically as often as it has been taken to be a common human capacity. At the same time, the idea of human equality was one of the proudest achievements of the Enlightenment, though its debt to Christianity is probably just as strong, as Winthrop Jordan established in his comprehensive analysis of the history of race in early America in *White over Black* (1968). But, the modern intellectual history of race and racial thinking, at least in the United States, would suggest, for instance, a crucial distinction between equality as a claim about moral standing and as a claim about capacities. Thus, moral equality between races did not necessarily entail equal political and social rights (in the same way that they did not for women and still do not for children) well into the twentieth century in much of the country.

All this might be said to hinge on whether we can talk about some individuals or groups as being more fully human than others. Race was the very crude modern way of making this internal distinction, but the distinction did not have to be, or derive from, biological differences. Cultural and intellectual achievement has sometimes been understood to betoken a fuller humanity, while the notion that human beings are political beings, an Aristotelian view which Arendt also accepted, can be read to suggest that those who lack a polis or a political space of self-government are condemned to a kind of provisional inferiority to those in possession of one. Indeed, the Greek distaste for the Persians and hence the West's asserted superiority to the Orient (and to Africa) had much to do with the West's tradition of self-government in organized states. All this would suggest that sometimes humanism is, and at other times it is not, complicit with assertions of racial or cultural differences among individuals and groups. It is misleading to suggest the answer is all on one side or the other. That is why Gilroy's turn to Fanon for clues as to how to formulate a new humanism that does not simply dethrone the white colonizer (capitalist, bourgeois) and elevate the black colonized (socialist, working class) to a position of supposed superiority is both important and inadequate. Planetary humanism must cast aside the old binary oppositions (white over black / black over white) and move to higher ground, but whether it will have any foundations other than discursive ones is not clear.[50]

Similarly, Gilroy rejects the term "universal"—though he does use the term "strategic universalism" once[51] —for the term "cosmopolitan." In the latter viewpoint, the differences among human communities are not washed out in the name of a universal, but ungrounded, set of values. Rather cosmopolitan people learn to move in and between various cultures and to express "solidarity" with political and cultural struggles "from below and afar."[52] In this sense the cosmopolitan is always "between camps," that is, never allowing him- or herself to be caught in a rigid identity. The longer range goal of cosmopolitanism is to revitalize the "democratic and cosmopolitan traditions that have been all but expunged from today's black political imaginary."[53] Put in other terms, the emphasis over several decades on racial and ethnic exclusivity from former oppressed groups themselves also needs to diminish and be replaced by openness to otherness.

Overall, then, Gilroy's point is that race and ethnicity are self-defeating existential traps, whether imposed from outside or chosen more or less freely. *After Empire* and some of his later essays identify a certain urban British "convivial culture," which has grown up naturally among various immigrant peoples and groups in contrast, he claims, with America where formal political and legal equality is accompanied by, and stands in stark contrast with, racial and ethnic segregation into ghettoes and enclaves. Gilroy also suggests that British ethnic groups relate to each other and to the majority white population in a more relaxed fashion than is the case in the United States. At the same time, sectors of the white British population respond to the loss of empire with a kind of cultural melancholia, as already mentioned.[54]

This may be the case, but it won't be convincing until Gilroy spends more time exploring the historical experience of African Americans since the 1960s, or even before. Where the experience of most black Britons is rooted in a post-1945 context of voluntary immigration into the United Kingdom, the vast majority of black Americans trace their roots back to chattel slavery, almost a century of often violent and always repressive Jim Crow segregation, and a much more arduous Great Migration north than experienced by the "Windrush" generation of immigrants from the West Indies to Britain after World War II. Needless to say, race relations in such two very different settings (with very different demographics) are going to be very different, as will be the ways race is formulated and articulated.

Indeed, the enthusiastic reaction of many Americans to the election of Barack Obama as president should not be forgotten when Gilroy offers evidence of better British intergroup relations by instancing the interethnic composition of the crowds mourning the death of Diana and the testimony of a Briton just released from Guantanamo that he had yearned for Highland Shortbread biscuits during his incarceration. In his recent *Darker than Blue*, Gilroy speaks of the North Atlantic's (United States and United Kingdom) "imperial potency" as now being in "irreversible decline,"[55] while Barack Obama's rise to power signifies America's "success" in giving special rights and privileges to "a privileged caste from racial and ethnic minorities." Indeed, Obama is a "smiling human cipher" in place to mask the war on terror, while African American culture has "been more comprehensively mainstreamed than ever before without yielding any discernible benefit to the vast majority of African Americans."[56] Without denying that Gilroy raises important issues in such polemical statements, the way he handles them (or fails to do so) indicates a baffling political and historical tone deafness.

Of course, this is not to say that Gilroy should not comment on the way race and skin color has underpinned group identity among African Americans. One response to this on his part has been a recent decision to abandon one of the central concepts from *The Black Atlantic*: "double consciousness." In Gilroy's present thinking, "doubleness" is too easily an excuse for maintaining separateness rather than relating across racial and ethnic divisions. In an inclusive planetary humanism, there is no longer any need for, or virtue in, double consciousness. Moreover, the kind of multiple identities that are relatively common in contemporary multicultural societies suggest that the Du Boisian dialectic has outlived its effectiveness.[57]

But opposition to Gilroy's position has come not only from the usual quarters—the Afrocentrists or the Nation of Islam. There are other "progressive" rather than nationalist voices who have also challenged Gilroy's ideas. First, the use of the term "black" arose directly out of the political struggles of the 1960s (circa 1965 to be exact). It simply has too strong a historical pedigree and carries too strong an ideological charge to be easily abandoned just because an outsider urges that it be done.[58] But as philosopher Tommie Shelby has emphasized, the term "black" is the descriptor for African Americans who share a complex set of experiences, traditions, and ideologies arising from a history of racism and oppression. Though white racists may use "black" to refer to fixed biological characteristics or deeply embedded cultural differences, and black radicals frequently essentialize their experience into something that seems unchanging, most Americans, of all races, have largely ceased to use "black" to signify something biological: "African Americans do not seem to care much in social practice about the scientific standing of the concept of race," claim philosophers Lionel McPherson and Shelby.[59] For Shelby, "black" is a complex term of "identification" but not necessarily "identity," a distinction that is central to his thinking on these matters.[60] For Shelby, the term "black" does not pick out unvarying racial qualities that constitute a black identity but refers to a "shared experience with anti-black racism and the joint commitment to ending it" that is "publicly acknowledge[d]."[61] In fact Shelby's essentially defensive emphasis upon antiracism as the basis of group solidarity (*not* group identity) would fit Gilroy's own desire to focus on ending racism, not celebrating race in whatever form.

What then is the problem? Again, at the heart of this controversy is the question of politics, always an underdeveloped area in Gilroy's thought. For Shelby, who has indicated that his remarks are specifically aimed at Gilroy and Kwame Anthony Appiah, it is crucial to distinguish between black "solidarity" (roughly synonymous with identification) and black "identity." Shelby's argument is that solidarity is based on *what* has happened to make a group what it is. It is how "we" choose to appear to the world and to ourselves. Those who claim a black identity, however, *also* claim to share something that says *who* we are as well as *what* we have experienced. Shelby's real interest is in the minimal requirements for social and political action rather than in discussing what constitutes authentic blackness. But, then, Gilroy is not interested in the latter either. Where Shelby and Gilroy part company is that Gilroy seems to think that black politics must be based on an explicit black identity, but such is too dangerous to embrace. Shelby agrees that demanding a shared black identity is dangerous and probably impossible. Indeed, he shrewdly suggests that to try to arrive at a shared racial identity easily leads to fissures and factions that undermine (black) group solidarity.[62] All that is needed for an antiracist politics is identification with a set of experiences, since a shared group identity is difficult, perhaps even undesirable, to achieve. Identification resembles something like a public label, while identity is measured in terms of authenticity and subjectivity.

Despite all this, Gilroy and Shelby might split the difference and come to an agreement. For example, if there is a "black" style of music, then one person who could surely be identified with it is James Brown. But when it came to matters of politics, Brown was a Republican rather than a Democrat like most African Americans. He would surely have seen himself as a "black" singer and proponent of a black identity ("Say It Loud, I'm Black and I'm Proud"), but he disagreed with most other African Americans insofar as he supported the Republican Party. The point is that black cultural identity does entail black political solidarity or vice versa. Surely Gilroy and Shelby could agree that in the public arena of political and social action, racial identity should have no role to play. Racial solidarity/identification should be the glue that makes the group capable of political action, which includes the capacity for entering into alliances with other interest groups to undertake joint action. But in the realm of individual cultural preferences, and private group activities, the cultivation of a black identity, as an ethnic and cultural but not a racial entity, may be valuable. In fact, we can see Gilroy doing this in the cultural preferences and examples he deploys in his work. They are overwhelmingly black. As Simon Gikandi has acutely observed, "racial identity" seems to be "acceptable in expressive culture" for Gilroy, who is obviously no black nationalist politically.[63]

Conclusion

It is difficult to know which direction Paul Gilroy's thought will take. His most recent book offers discussions of the relationship of culture and commerce in the American "car culture," the uneven history of human rights, and the significance of cosmopolitan popular cultural figures such as Bob Marley and Jimi Hendrix. What I have been most concerned with in his work are the tensions between culture and politics, the cultural sphere and the nation-state, and the pernicious effects of racialized politics and culture. But one more element should be added to this cluster of problems, what Gikandi has identified as the close connection Gilroy makes between "rootlessness" and "cosmopolitanism."[64] "Rootlessness" is particularly a problem because my sense is that most people, even in the black Atlantic, do not live lives of rootlessness; and if they find themselves in that situation, they try to remedy it as soon as possible. In sum, they want to have *a world*. It is this impulse to have or to be at home in the world, including not only a cultural but also a political home, that seems to me most in need of addressing in Gilroy's future work.

Notes

1. Paul Gilroy, *'There Ain't No Black in the Union Jack'* (Abingdon: Routledge, 2002 [1987]); *The Black Atlantic: Modernity and Double Consciousness* (London: Verso, 1993); *Between Camps: Nations, Cultures and the Allure of Race* (London: Allen Lane, 2000) (published as *Against Race: Imagining*

Political Culture beyond the Color Line in the United States); *After Empire: Melancholia or Convivial Culture?* (Abingdon: Routledge, 2004) (published as *Postcolonial Melancholia* in the United States); and *Darker than Blue: On the Moral Economies of Black Atlantic Culture* (Cambridge: Harvard Belknap Press, 2010).

2. Lucy Evans, "The Black Atlantic: Exploring Gilroy's Legacy," *Atlantic Studies* 6, 2 (August 2009): 255–68.
3. The major relevant works of these figures are Raymond Williams, *Culture and Society, 1780–1950* (New York: Harper and Row, 1966 [1958]) and *The Long Revolution* (London: Chatto and Windus, 1961); Richard Hoggart, *The Uses of Literacy* (London: Chatto and Windus, 1957); E. P. Thompson, *The Making of the English Working Class* (New York: Vintage, 1963) and *The Poverty of Theory and Other Essays* (London: Merlin, 1978).

   Dennis Dworkin's *Cultural Marxism in Postwar Britain: History, the New Left, and the Origins of Cultural Studies* (Durham: Duke University Press, 1997) is a clear and invaluable overview of this topic. Dworkin's more recent piece on Gilroy emphasizes his links with the Birmingham cultural studies group and also discusses his next to last work, *After Empire*. See "Paul Gilroy and the Cultural Politics of Decline," *Rethinking History* 13, 4 (December 2009): 521–39. Please also see Houston A. Baker Jr., Manthia Diawara, and Ruth H. Lindeborg (eds.), *Black British Cultural Studies: A Reader* (Chicago: University of Chicago Press, 1996), 1–15; Martin Jay, *Songs of Experience* (Berkeley: University of California Press, 2005), chapter 5 (170–215); Gilroy, *'Union Jack,'* 50–53, and *The Black Atlantic*, 5–19.
4. Dworkin, *Cultural Marxism*, 4–5. Actually the cultural debate emerged before and during World War I in the United States. Later, there was some interaction between the New York intellectuals and the Frankfurt School theorists in exile, such as Theodor Adorno and Leo Lowenthal. Former Trotskyist Irving Howe was also an American participant in the debate. Trinidadian Trotskyist C. L. R. James's *American Civilization*, written in the 1940s and early 1950s, was not published until 1993. See Thomas Wheatland, *The Frankfurt School in Exile* (Minneapolis: University of Minnesota Press, 2009).
5. Thompson, *The Making of the English Working Class*, 13.
6. The ambiguity here between British and English as qualifiers arises from the fact that Raymond Williams was of Welsh rather than English origins. Interestingly, Thompson's emphasis upon class culture was used by social and cultural historians of slavery in the United States in the 1960s

and 1970s to bolster the idea that there had been a vital, and oppositional, slave culture there and that it had survived the end of slavery in the form of a strong African American culture. Here the work of John Blassingame, Eugene Genovese, and Herbert Gutman was essential in undermining older claims about the pathology of slave culture suggested by Gunnar Myrdal and Stanley Elkins.

7. See the introduction to *Black British Cultural Studies*, Stuart Hall, "Race, Articulation, and Societies Structured in Dominance," 16–60, and "New Ethnicities," 163–72, in the same volume. Gilroy's undergraduate major at Sussex University had been in American Studies, which he remembers was one place where race was talked about. The two members of the faculty Gilroy mentions in this connection, Cora Kaplan and George Rehin, were both Americans teaching at Sussex. See Max Farrar, "Paul Gilroy in Conversation," *darkmatter: in the ruins of imperial culture*, 7 May 2007, http://www.darkmatter101.org/site/2007/05/07/paul-gilroy-in-conversation/.
8. Quoted in Gilroy, *'There Ain't No Black in the Union Jack,'* 51.
9. See Jay, *Songs of Experience*, 211. E. P. Thompson also criticized Williams's "whole way of life" phrase for its neglect of class and power struggles within the national culture and suggested rather that the social landscape be seen in terms of a "whole way of struggle." Dworkin, *Cultural Marxism*, 102.
10. *Black British Cultural Studies*, 4.
11. See Donald M. Nonini, "Race, Land, Nation: A(t)-tribute to Raymond Williams," *Cultural Critique* 41(Winter 1999): 158–83; and especially Francis Mulhern, "Culture and Society, Then and Now," *New Left Review* 55 (January–February 2009): 1–8 http://www.newleftreview.org/?view=2760.
12. Dworkin's *Cultural Marxism* has only two small references to matters having to do with imperialism/colonialism.
13. Gilroy, *'There Ain't No Black in the Union Jack,'* 201.
14. Ibid., 30.
15. Gilroy, *The Black Atlantic*, 128.
16. Ibid, 38–39, 50. This is perhaps the only explicitly utopian moment in Gilroy's early work. Ultimately, what this culture promised was the overcoming of the modernist separation of "truth, goodness, and beauty," a distinctly German formulation of the separation of values spheres in modernity. But he seems to hold to this vision for its utopian potential rather than as the inevitable destination of the historical process.

17. See Gilroy, *'There Ain't No Black in the Union Jack,'* 268, 305–07; *Small Acts* (London: Serpent's Tail, 1993), 36; *The Black Atlantic*, 40.
18. See Hannah Arendt's distinction between "labor" and "work" in *The Human Condition* (Chicago: University of Chicago Press, 1958). According to Arendt, work creates lasting objects, such as works of art, while labor, with its connotations of physical toil, blunts human action and creativity. C. Wright Mills's phrase "labor metaphysic" turns up in "The New Left (1960)," in *Power, Politics and People*, ed. Irving Louis Horowitz (New York: Oxford University Press, 1963), 256.
19. Gilroy, *The Black Atlantic*, 49.
20. Cedric Robinson, *Black Marxism: The Making of the Black Radical Tradition* (Chapel Hill: University of North Carolina Press, 2000 [1983]).
21. The post-Westphalian ideal in the modern European political tradition has been the culturally homogeneous nation-state. Hannah Arendt made much of the distinction between nation and state in her historical sketch of the "decline of the nation-state and the end of the rights of man" in *The Origins of Totalitarianism* (Cleveland, OH: Meridian, 1958), chapter 9. For Arendt the triumph of the cultural nation over the rights-protecting state was a historical tragedy. See also Jürgen Habermas, *A Berlin Republic* (Lincoln: University of Nebraska Press, 1997). By distinguishing so clearly between the political and the cultural but also by privileging the former over the latter, Habermas both echoed and inverted the valorization of the German distinction between "culture" (the particular, organic, authentic, and rooted) and "civilization" (the formal, institutional, and legal).
22. For a mainstream overview of this historiography, see Bernard Bailyn, *Atlantic History: Concepts and Contours* (Cambridge: Harvard University Press, 2005). In general, Bailyn gives cultural and intellectual history a relatively minor place in the historiography of the Atlantic and pays practically no attention to the African contribution to the cultural history of the Atlantic.
23. Robert Farris Thompson, *Flash of the Spirit* (New York: Vintage, 1984 [1983]), 3. For the study of comparative slavery, see early works such as Frank Tannenbaum, *Slave and Citizen* (Boston: Beacon Press, 1992 [1947]) and, of course, Stanley Elkins, *Slavery* (Chicago: University of Chicago Press, 1959). For a discussion of the Frazier-Herskovits exchange, see Richard H. King, *Race, Culture and the Intellectuals, 1940–1970* (Washington and Baltimore: Wilson Center / Johns Hopkins University

Press, 2004), 133–34. Strangely, Gilroy doesn't mention or acknowledge Thompson in *The Black Atlantic* nor does Thompson mention Herskovits but one time, and without any wider discussion in *Flash of the Spirit*.

24. There is a considerable critical literature on *The Black Atlantic* and related matters. For this piece, I have found useful the following: Ronald A. T. Judy, "Beside the Two Camps: Paul Gilroy and the Critique of Raciology," *Boundary 2* 28, 3 (Fall 2001): 207–16; Simon Gikandi, "Race and Cosmopolitanism," *American Literary History* 14, 3 (Fall 2002): 593–615; Christine Chivallon, "Beyond Gilroy's Black Atlantic: The Experience of African Diaspora," *Diaspora* 11, 3 (2002): 359–82; Angela McRobbie, "Black and Not-Black: Gilroy's Critique of Racialized Modernity," *The Uses of Cultural Studies* (London: Sage, 2005), 39–60; Gunvor Simonsen, "Moving in Circles: African and Black History in the Atlantic World," *Nuevo Mundo Mundos Nuevos* (2008): 1–12, http://nuevomundo.revues.org/index42303.html; and Neil Roberts, "Paul Gilroy's Postcolonial Melancholia," *Shibboleths* 2, 2 (June 2008), http://www.shibboleths.net/2/2/Roberts,NeilReview.pdf.
25. Gilroy, *'There Ain't No Black in the Union Jack,'* 208.
26. Joanna Skipwith (ed.), *Rhapsodies in Black: Art of the Harlem Renaissance* (Berkeley and London: University of California Press, 1997). The exhibition was selected by African American art historian Richard Powell and British photographer David Bailey; Tanya Barson and Peter Gorschlueter (eds.), *Afro Modern: Journeys through the Black Atlantic* (London: Tate Gallery, 2010). Gilroy was involved in the planning of this Liverpool exhibition.
27. Gilroy, cited in Brent Hayes Edwards, "The Uses of Diaspora," *Social Text* 66, 19, 1 (Spring 2001): 63; see Chivallon, "Beyond Gilroy's Black Atlantic," 359–60. The notion of return is central to what she calls the "classical" view of diaspora and refers primarily to the use of the concept in the history of the Jewish people.
28. Brent Hayes Edwards, *The Practice of Diaspora: Literature, Translation and the Rise of Black Internationalism* (Cambridge: Harvard University Press, 2003).
29. Gilroy, *Darker than Blue*, 101–19. To be fair Gilroy had occasionally mentioned Rastafarianism in his work of the 1980s.
30. Gilroy, *The Black Atlantic*, 194.
31. Gikandi, "Race and Cosmopolitanism," 597, 606. In fact, Gikandi's penetrating article is directed mainly at Gilroy's *Between Camps*. His more

general criticism of Gilroy is that he tends to equate cosmopolitanism with exposure to the European tradition alone. As Gikandi notes, when Zora Neale Hurston went to Haiti or George Padmore spent time in the United States, this did not seem to add to their cosmopolitanism in the way that Du Bois's time in Germany did (600).

32. Gilroy, *The Black Atlantic*, 68. The discussion of the lordship and bondage relationship is found, of course, in Hegel's *Phenomenology of Spirit*.
33. Gilroy, *The Black Atlantic*, 63.
34. Susan Buck-Morss, *Hegel, Haiti, and Universal History* (Pittsburgh: University of Pittsburgh Press, 2009). Because Hegel's exploration of the master-slave relationship is so powerful in its capacity as a story of the origins of self and society, it is easy to forget that it not only can but also must be read as a profound exploration of the logic of slavery and freedom as historical phenomena. Buck-Morss also suggests that Gilroy is wrong in claiming that Douglass's account contradicts Hegel's.
35. Gilroy also noted that distinguished European analysts of anti-Semitism such as Zygmunt Baumann and Emmanuel Levinas avoided the comparison as well (see *The Black Atlantic*, 213–14).
36. Gilroy, *The Black Atlantic*, 217. For instance, Stanley Crouch rejected *Beloved* as a "blackface holocaust novel." Gilroy did not accept Crouch's judgment of Morrison's novel, but he did suggest that it deserved careful refutation.
37. See Arendt, *The Origins of Totalitarianism*, 2nd edition (Cleveland, OH: Meridian, 1958), 437–59, 296, 298.
38. Gilroy, *Darker than Blue*, 60, 72.
39. Seyla Benhabib, "International Law and Human Plurality in the Shadow of Totalitarianism: Hannah Arendt and Raphael Lemkin," *Constellations: An International Journal of Critical and Democratic Theory* 16, 2 (2009): 331– 50.
40. Laurence Thomas, *Vessels of Evil* (Philadelphia: Temple University Press, 1993), 202.
41. Farrar, "Paul Gilroy in Conversation."
42. Hannah Arendt, "Organized Guilt and Universal Responsibility," *Essays in Understanding, 1930–1954* (New York: Harcourt Brace and Company, 1994), 131.
43. Gilroy, *Between Camps*, 225.
44. Gilroy, *After Empire*, 133.
45. Gilroy, *Between Camps*, 103.

46. Ibid., 225–37, 156.
47. Ibid., 237. See Richard Wright, "How 'Bigger' Was Born," *Native Son* (New York: Harper and Row, 1940).
48. Ibid., 41.
49. Ibid., 93. For a recent collection addressing this "boomerang" effect, see Richard H. King and Dan Stone (eds.), *Hannah Arendt and the Uses of History: Imperialism, Nation, Race, and Genocide* (New York and London: Berghahn Books, 2007), and Michael Rothberg, *Multidirectional Memory: Remembering the Holocaust in the Age of Decolonization* (Stanford: Stanford University Press, 2009).
50. See Ivan Hannaford, *Race: The History of an Idea in the West* (Washington and Baltimore: Wilson Center Press / Johns Hopkins University Press, 1996), and King, *Race, Culture and the Intellectuals*, 119.
51. Gilroy, *Between Camps*, 326.
52. Gilroy, *After Empire*, 89.
53. Gilroy, *Between Camps*, 356.
54. See Gilroy, "From a Colonial Past to a New Multiculturalism," *The Chronicle of Higher Education* (January 7, 2005): B7–B10.
55. Gilroy, *Darker than Blue*, 175.
56. Ibid., 173. The motivations gleaned from the (usually) young men of Islamic background in Britain involved in planning or executing home-grown terrorist plots offer little support for the idyllic account Gilroy offers of British hospitality toward different cultures, races, and faiths. In fact, a report on equality and fairness in Britain in mid-October, 2010, established that a higher percentage of minorities were in prison in Britain than in the United States.
57. Gilroy, "From a Colonial Past"; Gilroy, *Darker Than Blue*, 152–53.
58. The introduction to Baker et al. (eds.), *Black Cultural Studies* includes a brief but lucid account of the historical importance of racially inflected language for African Americans.
59. Lionel McPherson and Tommie Shelby, "Blackness and Blood: Interpreting African American Identity," *Philosophy and Public Affairs* 32, 2 (2004): 187.
60. Shelby, "Foundations of Black Solidarity: Collective Identity of Common Oppression," *Ethics* 112, 2 (January 2002): 237, 263.
61. McPherson and Shelby, "Blackness and Blood," 184.
62. Tommie Shelby, "Collective Identity or Common Oppression," *Ethics* 112, 2 (January 2002): 250.

63. Gikandi, "Race and Cosmopolitanism," 612. Philosopher Eddie Glaude wants to retain an idea of black identity in politics in order to stress its emergence through political action. This avoids the essentialization that Shelby, Glaude, and Gilroy all are opposed to. See Glaude, *In a Shade of Blue: Pragmatism and the Politics of Black America* (Chicago: University of Chicago Press, 2007), 55–57. See also James T. Kloppenberg, *Reading Obama: Dreams, Hopes, and the American Political Tradition* (Princeton: Princeton University Press, 2010), 230.
64. Gikandi, "Race and Cosmopolitanism," 609.

2

Paul Gilroy and the Pitfalls of British Identity

DENNIS DWORKIN

Introduction

Paul Gilroy's *Postcolonial Melancholia* (2005) (published as *After Empire: Melancholia or Convivial Culture?* in the United Kingdom) represents a major contribution to understanding and critiquing the political culture of contemporary Britain. Written in the aftermath of the September 11th attacks and the Anglo-American invasion of Iraq, the book challenges the growing ethnic absolutism and cultural nationalism in contemporary Britain and the West more broadly. Speaking from an explicit position of "agonistic, planetary humanism,"[1] Gilroy argues that "an obsessive repetition of key themes—invasion, war, contamination, loss of identity—and the resulting mixture" has produced "an anxious, melancholic mood"—"part of the cultural infrastructure of the place, an immovable ontological counterpart to the nation-defining ramparts of the white cliffs of Dover."[2] To overcome this melancholy state, he advocates political soul searching: a historical analysis of the British Empire, the brutalities and atrocities committed in its name, and the racial hierarchies that were among its legacies. While Gilroy is critical of the siege mentality of the dominant cultures, he likewise sees shifts in popular culture that give reason for optimism. What he describes as a culture of conviviality, while not constituting formal political groups or organizations, represents forms of "spontaneous tolerance and openness." In this culture, race has become "ordinary," providing a twist on a formulation made by Raymond Williams more than fifty years ago.

Gilroy's critique of contemporary Britain is a potent affirmation and defense of multiculturalism, cosmopolitanism, and transnationalism at a time when they are threatened by essentialist notions of national identity and unbridgeable cultural difference. Yet *Postcolonial Melancholia* builds on earlier engagements with (what might only partially be called in jest) "the Condition of England" question. The book has resonances of arguments that Gilroy has been making since he was a graduate student at the Centre for Contemporary Studies at the University of Birmingham in the late 1970s, first in *The Empire Strikes Back: Race and Racism in 70s Britain* (1982) and subsequently in *'There Ain't No Black in the Union Jack': The Cultural Politics of Race and Nation* (1987), a text that he began as his dissertation. Pushing forward the theoretical/political opening found in the Centre's collectively authored *Policing the Crisis*, Gilroy argued that late-twentieth-century British racism was founded on discourses of cultural difference, which cast blacks as permanent outsiders. Not only had such thinking become a central feature of new-right ideology, but it had subtly infiltrated left-wing perspectives as well, including the cultural studies and cultural Marxist tradition from which Gilroy's own thinking had emerged.

In making this critique, Gilroy aligned himself with black Atlantic intellectual and political traditions, traditions that, in a sense, he did just as much to produce as to explore, most famously in *The Black Atlantic: Modernity and Double Consciousness* (1993). Yet if in one respect Gilroy situated himself within a diaspora tradition, distancing himself from his British intellectual roots, at another level his thinking represented a continuation and extension of the cultural Marxist and cultural studies tradition from which his thinking emerged.[3] Gilroy simultaneously analyzed and critiqued dominant discourses, ideologies, and apparatuses of no less than E. P. Thompson, Raymond Williams, and, notably, Stuart Hall while highlighting forms of resistance and opposition that were challenging and transforming them. Gilroy might not have allied himself with Marxist or cultural materialism, as the founders of the cultural studies tradition had, but he regarded language and discourse as contradictory material forces, subject to power relationships, which both shaped human action and were shaped by it.

Gilroy's work has been critical to the development of cultural studies, but his interventions have also been important to broader discussions involving decline and identity in contemporary Britain. Here, grappling with the loss of empire, post–World War II migrations, a precarious world role, relative—if not absolute—economic decline, European integration, and devolution and the potential breakup of the United Kingdom has produced a small publishing industry. Answering the questions "Who are the English?" and "Who are the British" has become a national passion among journalists, pundits, political writers, ideologues, and cultural commentators. Gilroy suggests that such self-reflection, particularly when coupled with its soul mate in contemporary discussions, "heritage," represents signs of a deeper malaise: "the widespread desire to elevate Englishness into an ethnicity, and the impulse to recast Britishness so it acquires an almost racial resonance."[4]

Writing some fifty years ago, Raymond Williams sought to free culture from attempts by cultural conservatives and orthodox Marxists to channel it in specific directions. In his words:

> My own view is that if, in a socialist society, the basic cultural skills are made widely available, and the channels of communication widened and cleared, as much as possible has been done in the way of preparation, and what then emerges will be an actual response to the whole reality, and so valuable.[5]

Writing in a very different context but with a similar spirit, Gilroy advocated opening up discursive spaces of "Englishness" and "Britishness," ossified and immobilized by essentialized notions of culture. "Culture can never for me," he wrote, "be frozen in the way that this anxious pursuit of identity demands. To seek to fix culture is a problem because if we arrest its unruly motion we ossify it. Culture then becomes a dead specimen behind glass, to be contemplated rather than engaged."[6] Like Williams, Gilroy was interested in opening up the channels. He was less concerned with identity politics than the politics of identity and culture.

There is something unquestionably dismal about the "discourse of decline" that has intermittently percolated through British intellectual and political culture: the obsession with decay, the submission to second-rate status, the endless rounds of self-recrimination and finger pointing, and the efforts to pin on certain groups blame for cultural and political degeneration. But such discussions also potentially suggest revitalization and regeneration, new identity spaces and emerging cultural formations. Few writers have been as important to this process of potential renewal as Paul Gilroy. He has stood decline discourses on their head, seeing imperial decline and collapse as providing the ground for an open and diverse society and culture. Rather than mourn the decline of "Englishness" and "Britishness," as conservative critics have tended to do, Gilroy sees an opportunity to broaden and rejuvenate their meaning. By placing Gilroy's arguments in their intellectual, cultural, and political setting, in other words, their historical context, we gain a better appreciation of the nature of his achievement.

Rereading Cultural Studies

In *The Black Atlantic*, Gilroy argues that the development of cultural studies "from an ethnohistorical perspective requires more than just noting its association with English literature, history, and new left politics." He, most importantly, has in mind the need for examining the role of cultural perspectives in producing "images of their racialised others as objects of knowledge, power, and cultural criticism."[7] In this section, I take Gilroy's suggestion seriously, looking at the formative years in British cultural studies in relationship to debates on identity, race, and national belonging. I situate these arguments in relationship to discourses of decline that have been inseparable from them. Gilroy's interrogation of cultural studies, while he was a graduate student, was not only important for the trajectory of that field of work, but it enabled a cultural politics that had ramifications for broader national and transnational political discussions.

Discourses of decline have almost always been a component of British cultural Marxism and cultural studies. At roughly the same time that E. P. Thompson was publishing *The Making of the Working Class* (1963), the classic text of "history from below," he was likewise embroiled in a heated dispute with the editor of *New Left Review* (Thompson 1965), Perry Anderson, whose "Origins of the Present Crisis" (1965) took as its point of departure debates on postwar British decline. Britain was being rapidly overtaken by Common Market competition, its share of world trade plummeting to 15 percent. (It stood at 33 percent in 1900.) A spate of books and articles—exemplified by the Penguin series What Is Wrong with Britain?—analyzed the country's stagnation and debated solutions for its revival. Thompson disputed Anderson's contention that British decline was rooted in its original failure to produce a bourgeois revolution, but their exchange established a new left discourse that took as its point of departure Britain's decline as an imperial and economic power.

The new-left writer Tom Nairn was in the forefront of recognizing the relationship between decline, the British crisis, and national identity, notably in *The Break-Up of Britain* (1977). Written at the height of the 1970s crisis, Nairn's dissection of a troubled political culture was a prophetic analysis of the structural forces that threatened the unity of the United Kingdom as a discursive force in that very fragmentation. An important component of Nairn's analysis was his portrayal of the enigmas of Englishness. While the national aspirations of the "Celtic Fringe" were expressed in terms that echoed those of numerous nationalist movements, discourses of Englishness trod no such path. "The English," in his words, "are too vague and mixed-up to fit a nationalist stereotype." "Too internally differentiated for the vulgar measurements of nationalism" and diluted by the demands of Empire, Englishness had achieved a "faltering iconography."[8] The result was that English identity vacillated between myths of "the semi-divine Constitution and the Mother of Parliaments" and the racism of little Englanders such as Enoch Powell, who famously prophesized that "rivers of blood" were the inevitable result of recent emigration.

British cultural studies, as it developed at the Birmingham Centre for Contemporary Cultural Studies in the 1970s under the directorship of Stuart Hall, developed in an intensifying atmosphere of crisis frequently represented as an intensification of decline. At one level the crisis was economic—a depressed economy accompanied by high unemployment and inflation, culminating in an emergency loan negotiated between the Labour government and the International Monetary Fund in 1976. At another level it consisted of multiple challenges to the British state: two miners' strikes, Scottish and Welsh nationalist calls for devolution or outright separation, the Northern Irish political crisis, and emerging new social movements. The crisis produced, and was in part produced by, virulent forms of nationalism and racism, spurred on by the emergence of the new Right. Racism in Britain was by no means new, but its level of intensity and politicization nationally was unprecedented.

Stuart Hall and his team of researchers at the Centre for Contemporary Cultural Studies in *Policing the Crisis* located the roots of the British crisis at the level of the state, regarded it as being connected to the end of empire, and saw antagonism toward blacks and other emigrants as symptomatic of a deeper malaise. The impetus for the book was a divisive criminal case involving a group of black youth who attacked a white working-class man in Handsworth, a multiracial and working-class neighborhood in Birmingham. The fact that these young men committed the crime was not at issue, but their sentences were excessive, and the case helped precipitate the apparently spontaneous mugging scare that surfaced in the early 1970s. Hall and his colleagues situated the case in a broader ideological context and argued that it was symptomatic of a British crisis rooted in postwar decline. As they wrote: "Britain participated in the world-wide capitalist boom, but more slowly and hesitantly than her major rivals. The long imperialist inheritance, coupled with the ancient nature of her industrial infrastructure and the slow rate of technological innovation, set her at a striking disadvantage. In economic terms, she was a third-rate post-imperial, not a first-rate new capitalist power."[9]

These broad historical perspectives underpin the book's analysis of the mugging scare. Hall and his colleagues argued that the mugging scare was a consequence of a prolonged and intricate process of ideological preparation in which the state and the media deployed fears of race, crime, and youth to create a "moral panic." They regarded this ideological mobilization in the context of the collapse of the social-democratic consensus that underpinned British politics since World War II. They understood the current historical moment in terms of a Gramscian hegemonic crisis and that the emergent right-wing "authoritarian populism" connected with Thatcherism was the most likely victor. Hall and his colleagues suggested that, even though blacks in Britain were labeled as immigrants and hence outside British culture, their historical experience was, in fact, shaped by the British Empire. Blacks were thus at the center—rather than the periphery—of British history. They shared with others of the black diaspora a common African connection, yet their experience was informed by a specifically British context as well. Blacks were predominantly of the working class. However, some of their deepest conflicts were with white workers. In an influential argument, Hall argued that class experience of blacks was mediated by racial categories.

Paul Gilroy's early work explored the theoretical and political opening created by *Policing the Crisis*. Unlike Hall, who was born in Jamaica and came to Britain to study at Oxford as a Rhodes Scholar in 1951, Gilroy was born in London. By the time he came to the Birmingham Centre as a graduate student, he had already studied as an undergraduate the traditions of Caribbean and African American intellectual and cultural practice that became the inspiration of works such as *The Black Atlantic*. Thatcher's electoral victories in 1979 and 1983, the Falklands War, the brief experiment of a progressive Greater London Council, the disarray of the Left, and the intensification of racial conflict boiling over in the riots of 1981–1982, provided the context for Gilroy's work during this period. Nationalism, racism, identity, crisis, and decline are interwoven themes in both the collectively produced *The Empire Strikes Back* and Gilroy's own *'There Ain't No Black in the Union Jack,'* where he wrote:

> The process of national decline is presented as coinciding with the dilution of once homogeneous and continuous national stock by alien strains. Alien cultures come to embody a threat which, in turn, invites the conclusion that national decline and weakness have been precipitated by the arrival of blacks. The operation of banishing blacks, repatriating them to the places which are congruent with their ethnicity and culture, becomes doubly desirable. It assists in the process of making Britain great again and restores an ethnic symmetry to a world distorted by imperial adventure and migration.[10]

A central dimension of Gilroy's argument was that the articulation of racial and national discourses had become a central feature of British political culture. In contrast to late-nineteenth-century British racism, which was based on biological hierarchy, its late-twentieth-century equivalent was founded on cultural differences, which cast blacks as permanent outsiders. In Gilroy's words, "black settlers and their British-born children are denied authentic national membership on the basis of their 'race' and, at the same time, prevented from aligning themselves within the 'British race' on the grounds that their national allegiance inevitably lies elsewhere."[11] For Gilroy, not only had such thinking become a central feature of new Right ideology, but it had also shaped left-wing political ideas as well. When those on the Left sought to reclaim the signifier "Britishness" from their conservative opponents in the aftermath of the Falklands War, they left its racial and imperial dimension unexamined. "The possibility," wrote Gilroy, "of politically significant connections between nationalism and contemporary racism is either unseen or felt to be unworthy of detailed discussion. More importantly, the types of subjectivity which nationalisms bring into being and put to work pass unquestioned. The problem has become how socialists can (re)possess them from the right."[12] This critique did not apply only to left-wing political efforts to reclaim patriotism in the wake of Thatcherism's colonization of it following the 1982 Falklands War with Argentina. It extended as well to the cultural studies and cultural Marxist tradition of the Birmingham Centre. In an important critique of the theoretical development of British cultural studies and cultural Marxism, Gilroy suggested that scholars such as Eric Hobsbawm, E. P. Thompson, and Raymond Williams were oblivious to the consequences of left-wing patriotism:

> Nationhood is not an empty receptacle which can be simply and spontaneously filled with alternative concepts according to the dictates of

> political pragmatism. The ideological theme of national belonging may be malleable to some extent but its links with the discourses of classes and "races" and the organizational realities of these groups are not arbitrary. They are confined by historical and political factors which limit the extent to which nationalism becomes socialist at the moment that its litany is repeated by socialists.[13]

Gilroy might have been more sensitive to the historical context in which Thompson's and Hobsbawm's left-wing patriotisms surfaced: the 1930s and 1940s Popular Front forged in opposition to European fascism. Yet when such a perspective continued to be espoused in the transformed context of post-war migrations, when what counted as British cultures was being remapped, it proved deeply problematic. They were not intentionally racist, but their efforts at recouping nationalism were implicitly founded on notions of ethnic absolutism and essentialist and fixed notions of national identity, and thus had racist and exclusionary consequences in the very different political situation of the 1980s. In essentializing national identity, these left-wing writers ignored the importance of local, regional, and transnational dimensions of peoples' identity, critical to any democratic politics of the Left in an increasingly globalized world.

'There Ain't No Black in the Union Jack' was a critique of the dominant political culture and cultural studies, and it sought to rethink ethnicity, race, and national belonging in relationship to a broader politics of the Left. That critique was part of an antiracist politics that, among other things, helped establish discursive spaces for blacks in Britain as "black Britons." As Gilroy stated: "Blacks born, nurtured and schooled in this country are, in significant measure, British even as their presence redefines the meaning of the term."[14] Their relationship to the dominant culture was one of "cultural syncretism," defined by diasporic and transnational traditions and experiences. In Gilroy's words:

> Analysis of the political dimensions to the expressive culture of black communities in Britain must reckon with their position within international networks. It should begin where fragmented diaspora histories of racial subjectivity combine in unforeseen ways with the edifice of British society and create a complex relationship which has evolved through various stages linked in different ways to the pattern of capitalist development itself.[15]

In effect, Gilroy simultaneously critiqued the ideologies of the dominant bloc and articulated modes of opposition and resistance to them. He might have critiqued cultural Marxism and British cultural studies for their oblivion to the politics of race and nation, but the form of his argument was very much within these traditions. Like Thompson, Williams, and (of course) Hall, Gilroy's mode of analysis simultaneously paid attention to structure and agency. Like others in this tradition, he simultaneously embraced the phrase that the patron saint of British cultural Marxism, Antonio Gramsci, selected for the masthead of the newspaper *L'ordine nuovo*: "pessimism of the intellect, optimism of the will."

History Debates

We can better appreciate Gilroy's critical position in the 1980s, and its subsequent development in the decades that followed, by considering his intervention in the debates on history's role in primary and secondary education. The debates were occasioned by proposals initiated by the Thatcher government and implemented in modified form by the administration of John Major. Their goal was to create a mandatory and uniform history curriculum in English and Welsh schools as part of a broader curricular reform, the most significant overhaul of education in Britain since the 1940s.

The "History Debate" was part of a more wide-ranging cultural and political struggle over national identity. In public culture the renewed enthusiasm for history was discernible in the growth of "heritage industries," which, in the historian Raphael Samuel's words, "ha[ve] contrived to make the idea of 'Englishness' aesthetically and visually appealing at the very moment when, with the collapse of industry and withdrawal from Empire, it appears politically and economically bankrupt."[16] It was the cultural critic and scholar Robert Hewison who most famously argued that, rather than manufacturing goods, Britain was producing heritage, which he connected to Britain being "gripped by the perception that it is in decline." In his words:

> The heritage industry is an attempt to dispel this climate of decline by exploiting the economic potential of our culture, and it finds a ready market because the perception of decline includes all sorts of insecurities and doubts (which are more than simply economic) that make its products especially attractive and reassuring. Looking at a

> Laura Ashley catalogue, it is possible that we imagine ourselves living in a museum already.[17]

Also important in this context is the work of Patrick Wright, a graduate of the Birmingham Centre, whom Gilroy described as the "most acute observer" of "the morbidity of heritage."[18] Wright's *On Living in an Old Country* (1985), among other things, analyzed the various organized efforts at preserving English artifacts, landscapes, and country houses in the name of a pure and authentic nationhood. In terms that recalled Gilroy, Wright argued that the heritage movement was part of a complex cultural formation whereby the class and multicultural conflicts of the present were collapsed into an eternal, static national essence. "Abstracted and redeployed," he wrote, "history seems to be purged of political tension; it becomes a unifying spectacle, the settling of all disputes. Like the guided tour as it proceeds from site to sanctioned site, the national past occurs in a dimension of its own—a dimension in which we appear to remember only in order to forget."[19]

That history should be a subject of public debate at all was remarkable. As Juliet Gardiner observed, "less than a decade ago there was a very real possibility that history could cease to be a mainstream subject in British education at all."[20] The renewed interest, however, did not arise simply from a love for the past: it represented an effort to create secure borders for a British identity that conservatives perceived as being under siege by a multicultural other and European integration. In Samuel's words:

> If there is a single issue which has made history into a front-line subject and propelled it into the arena of public debate, it is the question of what it means, in the present day, to be British. In recent decades, the national question has emerged, or re-emerged, as a storm-centre of British politics, most obviously in relation to New Commonwealth immigration and settlement, and Britain's membership of [*sic*] the EEC.[21]

The movement to create a national curriculum, with history as a major focal point, developed from the convergence of several strands of new right intellectual and political activism: the Hillgate Group, the Social Affairs Unit, and the Centre for Policy Studies prominent among them. Intellectuals who produced the *Salisbury Review* played a critical role in laying the ideological groundwork. Roger Scruton—the journal's editor, chief spokesperson, and a writer in newspapers and the popular press—sought to rejuvenate a common culture (which he viewed as being) under threat from immigrants and migrants. The right-wing belief that history was central to the renewal of English/British political culture came to be held by the most powerful political actors. Margaret Thatcher recalled that the "hardest fought battle" in connection to the national curriculum was over history. "No amount of imaginative sympathy for historical characters or situations," she wrote, "can be a substitute for the initially tedious but ultimately rewarding business of memorizing what actually happened."[22] She made clear what she meant by "what happened" as her biggest objection to the initial draft for the history curriculum was that it did not have enough on Britain.

Following the passage of the Educational Reform Act of 1988, the National History Working Group, chaired by Commander Saunders Watson, began to plan the history curriculum. The Group consisted of history teachers in primary and secondary schools, academics, authors, a director of education, and the secretary of the Institute for Historical Research.[23] Between the time that the committee first met and the publication of its final report in April 1990, a debate raged among academics, teachers, politicians, political writers, and journalists. It was Raphael Samuel who was in the forefront of galvanizing discussion, debate, and action among left-wing historians. At a History Workshop in 1990, he brought together a group of historians and educators, the majority of whom resisted history's role in the new national curriculum.

Samuel's numerous essays in the mainstream press as well as his intervention at the 1990 History Workshop are notable for their spirited defense of a wide-ranging notion of history, particularly "history from below" or "people's history." Samuel lumped together the "heritage baiting" of left-wing cultural critics and the attacks by conservative intellectuals on the method of historical empathy taught in the schools. He acknowledged that people's history had too often ignored its imperial dimension and that conservative intellectuals supportive of the Thatcher/Major government's efforts at reforming the history curriculum had been more passionate about history's centrality than the labor intellectuals and governments of the sixties. Yet he not surprisingly found the kind of history that they wanted to resurrect and the high politics on which it was founded as narrow and outmoded. Samuel represented history as being continually in flux, subject to constant argument, open to shifting perspectives, and capable of being interrogated from multiple points of view.

An important dimension of Samuel's argument was that British history needed to be opened up to European and global perspectives, and he recognized that any rethinking of history in the schools must take into account the increasing numbers of people from black and Asian backgrounds in Britain.

At the same time, he defended national history per se: "Yet history, whether we like it or not, is a national question and it has always occupied a national space. . . . Nor can the history of minorities escape it, since it is in relations of opposition to majorities that minorities are defined."[24]

Gilroy's intervention, "Nationalism, History and Ethnic Absolutism" (1990) more than any other (among those subsequently published), challenged not only conservative critics but left-wing historians such as Samuel as well. His paper, and ensuing article, articulated views that he already expressed and also conveyed new directions in his thinking. Rejecting the title of the session in which his paper was to be presented, British History: For or Against, Gilroy sought to shift the debate from "national history" to "nationalism," and he addressed the links between racism, nationalism, and nationalist historiography. In terms recalling his earlier critique in *'There Ain't No Black in the Union Jack,'* he reiterated his view that it was not only the new Right that was guilty of forms of English cultural nationalism; new left historians also had envisioned the people from a nationalist perspective. In his view, the conflict over history in the national curriculum masked the implicit consensus shared by historians on both sides of the political divide. Advocating going beyond either affirming or rejecting national history, Gilroy argued for an alternative that, he candidly admitted, was connected to his own complex identity as a black Briton:

> I think we need a new line of thought that goes beyond either/or ism into a different conceptual logic or supplementarity. In its simplest form, this might turn on the alternative couplet both/and. I make no apology for the fact that this shift in my own thinking arises from a desire to be recognized as being both black and English in addition to everything else that I am.[25]

Gilroy's passionate plea to overturn the binary oppositions underpinning ethnic absolutism gains added poignancy when it is recalled that his remarks at the History Workshop conference were made (as he himself mentioned) in the midst of the international crisis provoked by Salman Rushdie's *Satanic Verses*. It resulted from the fatwa issued by Ayatollah Khomeini, supreme leader of Iran, calling for the murder of the author and his publishers, and it was largely conducted as a narrowly defined and polarizing "clash of civilizations." Liberal defenders of Rushdie championed free speech, and Islamic fundamentalists defended the Iranian leader's defense of Islam in the wake of

Rushdie's "desecration" of it. Edward Said suggested that such binary oppositions simply ignored the proliferation of cultural hybridity in a globalized world and the complex and contradictory experience of migrations. In a spirit that recalls Gilroy's theoretical/political practice, Said wrote: "There is no pure, unsullied, unmixed essence to which some of us can return, whether that essence is pure Islam, pure Christianity, pure Judaism or Easternism, Americanism, Westernism."[26]

Significantly, Gilroy did not just call for a "different conceptual logic," he began to sketch it out. On the one hand, it meant rewriting British history from a transnational perspective so that "it ceases to be recognizably British at all."[27] On the other hand, he admitted that "somewhere between the local and the global there must be a place for that nation state [*sic*] and indeed for the myths and dreams of national or ethnic collectivity that condition our political predicament even as the relationship between the local and the global is itself transformed."[28] Such attitudes, contradictory as they may in fact be, tell us something about Gilroy's complex relationship to Englishness/Britishness, his simultaneous roots in multiethnic Britain and the cultures of the African diaspora. Gilroy's means of achieving "both" was by exploring the black Atlantic world:

> It contains a fluid and dynamic cultural system that escapes the grasp of nation states and national conceptions of political and economic development. The writers and political thinkers generated within the black Atlantic tradition have produced a rich body of work in which reflection on nationality, hybridity, independence, syncretism and self-determination have been acknowledged as central political and philosophical questions for something like two hundred years.[29]

Thus, in the "History Debate," Gilroy challenged the understanding of the national, the assumed ground of most historical writing. Gilroy rethought black and British history from a transnational perspective, viewed nationhood as part of the politics of signification struggle and Britain's borders as porous and permeable, subject to flows and counterflows, caught in a web of global connections. In doing so, Gilroy carved out a theoretical and political space whereby the black experience spilled over national borders, simultaneously challenging and redefining what constituted those borders. Conservative efforts to revise the national curriculum were rooted in British decline and a rearguard action to set up barricades around narrow notions of Englishness/

Britishness. Gilroy's intervention subverted discourses of decline, envisioning new potentialities and possibilities. Such insights would be more fully developed in Gilroy's influential book *The Black Atlantic.*

Postcolonial Melancholia

Gilroy's *Postcolonial Melancholia*—his most sustained meditation on contemporary Britain since the 1980s—was produced in what was, in many respects, was a transformed historical context. It was written in the aftermath of the events of September 11th, the Anglo-American invasion of Iraq, and rising anxieties in Europe and the United States over what was stigmatized as Islamic fundamentalism and terrorism. If a notable focal point of the book is contemporary Britain, it is Britain in a global context. At certain points what is said about Britain could equally pertain to either North America or Western Europe, and, indeed, the end of the book fuses Gilroy's analysis of Britain and Europe. In *Postcolonial Melancholia*, Gilroy moves effortlessly between being a black European and a critic of American imperialism and popular culture, achieving a multidimensional, multilayered, and cosmopolitan analysis. It is appropriate for a world where simultaneously national boundaries are increasingly blurred and where national fortresses are being hastily erected in modular fashion.

Britain's unique handling of global challenges forms an important segment of Gilroy's book. His representation and critique of contemporary British cultural politics is inflected by the continued salience of discourses of decline and a preoccupation with defining Englishness/Britishness in response to the intensifying assaults of the "Celtic fringe," European integration, asylum seekers, immigration, and British Muslims. This context pervades the debates produced by *The Future of Multi-Ethnic Britain* (2000) or the Parekh Report, which significantly Gilroy analyzes in the preface to *Postcolonial Melancholia*, describing the reaction to the report as "a depressing and deeply symptomatic counteraction."[30] It was commissioned by the Runnymede Trust; produced by a committee of twenty-three prominent academics, journalists, writers, and professionals; and chaired by Bhikhu Parekh, a political philosopher who had been awarded a life peerage. Home Secretary Jack Straw publicly blessed the commission. Despite a wide-ranging analysis and recommendations on numerous subjects, the media and the political Right (sometimes the same thing) focused on the report's few pages analyzing the meaning of British identity, claiming that it equated Britishness with racism.

In fact, what the report argued was that British identity had been historically racialized and that for black and Asian Britons, it was connected to collective memories of imperial domination. It called for widening the scope of—rather than rejecting—Britishness, and it advocated, among other things, making British history germane for a multicultural society.

Defending the report in the *Guardian*, Stuart Hall, a committee member, wrote: "We did say that, historically, the idea of Britishness carried 'largely unspoken racial connotations'—meaning that, in common understandings, the nation is usually imagined as white. . . . We nowhere suggested that this was destined to remain so until the end of time."[31] Yet the Parekh Report was lambasted by right-wing pundits and selectively and tendentiously quoted in conservative-leaning newspapers. Significantly, Straw sought to distance himself and the Blair government from the report's perspective on British identity. "Unlike the Runnymede Trust," he wrote, "I firmly believe there is a future for Britain and a future for Britishness."[32] For Straw, the report's sentiments were symptomatic of the Left's lack of patriotic feeling. "Given the tendency of some of the left to wash their hands of the whole notion of nationhood, it is perhaps not surprising that some people's perception of Englishness and Britishness became a narrow, exclusionary, conservative one. That's a view of Britishness that I don't recognize." In part, Straw's response can be seen as part of New Labour's ongoing efforts at placating middle England. However, his comments should also be seen in relationship to fears over devolution, a resurgence of an ethnically based English nationalism, and anxieties over British Muslims' resistance to the "British way of life."

Despite Gilroy's critique of the founders of cultural studies, his mode of analysis extends rather than rejects the form in which they conceived of historical moments. In *Postcolonial Melancholia*, Gilroy, no less than earlier writers in the cultural studies tradition, simultaneously analyzes the dominant cultural ideologies and discourses that permeate as well as articulate the forms of opposition and resistance that challenge them. Gilroy's analysis of the dominant modes is manifest in one of the most important conceptual leaps forward in his analysis of contemporary Britain. He argues that the nation's historical possibilities are constrained by postimperial or postcolonial melancholia. Gilroy derives his idea of "melancholia" from the German psychoanalysts Alexander and Margarete Mitscherlich, who grappled with post–World II Germans' evasion of their collective responsibility for the Third Reich. Germans, they argued, avoided the reality of a loss of moral legitimacy through a melancholic response that made it impossible for a genuine reconstruction. Extending their argument to postwar Britain, Gilroy argued that Britain's response to imperial decline was a collective loss of memory, the result being an identity crisis and a neurotic preoccupation with heritage, a reference in all probability to the work of Patrick Wright, cited earlier.[33]

In popular culture, this melancholia finds expression in the refrain of "two World Wars and one world cup," a chant favored by fans at international sporting events. For Gilroy, its odd fusion of class and masculinity, war and sports, betrays a deeper historical amnesia. In his words: "It declares that nothing significant changed during the course of Britain's downwardly mobile twentieth century. Under a tattered flag, the precious thin red, white, and blue line remains unbreached . . ."[34] This analysis is particularly germane to World War II—"the finest hour"—despite the fact that most of the citizenry has no longer any firsthand experience of it. The romanticizing of the war goes hand in hand with a nostalgic longing for a society secure in its ethnic and racial homogeneity. "Repairing that aching loss," he writes, "is usually signified by the recovery or preservation of endangered whiteness—and the exhilarating triumph over chaos and strangeness which that victory entails."[35] Gilroy's analysis of the contemporary signification of the war can be extended to the time when it was being fought. As the historian Sonya Rose argues in her important study *Which People's War? National Identity and Citizenship in Britain 1939–1945* (2003): "Heroic, populist and utopian constructions of national identity and citizenship dominated public and political culture during the war years. But these articulations did not have singular meanings—they differed by gender, for example, and were inflected by issues of class difference, the significance both of British imperialism and racial difference as well as regionalism to ideas about the nation, and so on."[36] In short, the idealization of the war, so prominent in contemporary representations, was there from the beginning.

For Gilroy, the political culture's postcolonial melancholy finds expression in the numerous commentaries on Britain's declining fortunes. Gilroy cites Jeremy Paxman's *The English: A Portrait of a People*, whose inquiry into the nature of the English is premised on the widely held view that "something has rotted in England."[37] He also mentions Roger Scruton's *An Elegy for England*, which mourns the loss of cultural cohesiveness brought on by postwar immigration, suggesting that anxieties over immigrants was not so much racist as caused by "the disruption of an old experience of home, and a loss of enchantment which made home a place of safety and consolation."[38] We can easily add to this list. The BBC's soon-to-be political editor Andrew Marr, in the TV series and book *The Day Britain Died* (2000), traveled throughout Britain and found that Britishness meant nothing in Scotland and a mass of confusion south of the border. In his words: "A certain kind of nation-state, with its rituals and hierarchies, its place in the world and its self-assumptions, has certainly slipped away and quietly died when no one was watching."[39] Mark Leonard, of the New Labour think tank Demos, sought in *Britain™: Renewing Our Identity* (1997) to "rebrand" the country's image. In the nineteenth century it had had an "extraordinarily strong external image," he argued. British identity today "has become confused and outdated and, in many parts of the world, decades of relative decline have left the word 'Britain' meaning very little. To anyone living in Britain, it comes as something of a shock to discover just how little 'brand recognition' we have."[40]

In addition to diagnosing the symptoms and roots of postcolonial melancholia, Gilroy makes recommendations for its cure. He believes that a precondition for renewal is confronting Britain's imperial past, which, most importantly, includes grappling with the racial hierarchies that were produced, sustained, and spread by the British Empire. Extending the ideas of the Mitscherlichs to Britain, he writes:

> Before the British people can adjust to the horrors of their own modern history and start to build a new national identity from the debris of their broken narcissism, they will have to learn to appreciate the brutalities of colonial rule enacted in their name and to their benefit, to understand the damage it did to their political culture at home and abroad, and to consider the extent of their country's complex investments in the ethnic absolutism that has sustained it.[41]

What Gilroy says here returns us to his analysis of World War II. He contrasts the fixation with World War II heroism and collective will with the cultural amnesia regarding Britain's numerous violent and bloody twentieth-century wars, all of which were connected to colonial rule. More generally, he suggests that only through a historical accounting of the experience of empire—which penetrated the metropolis as much as the periphery—is it possible to move beyond the deeper malaise afflicting contemporary Britain. In effect, Gilroy views discourses of decline as symptomatic of a paralyzed political culture. Grappling with the imperial past is central to political and cultural renewal.

A central reason that Gilroy advocates such a historical reconstruction is that it provides the groundwork for denaturing race, in his view a precondition for overcoming racism in British political culture. Returning to arguments first prominently featured in *Against Race: Imagining Political Culture Beyond the Color Line* (2000) (published in the United Kingdom as Between

Camps: Nations, Cultures *and the Allure of Race*), Gilroy argues that while racism is, indeed, a historical and material force, and continues to thrive, "race" and "racial hierarchies" are constructs, produced by the very racist dynamic that is supposedly its logical consequence. Gilroy's argument is analogous to those linguistic critics of orthodox Marxism, for whom class consciousness was not ultimately rooted in an objectively verifiable structure: it was produced by language and discourse, that is, it was ultimately a form of representation.[42] Similarly, in terms reminiscent of Stuart Hall and others, Gilroy advocates a discursive understanding of racial categories. "I am disinclined," he writes, "to accept the power of racial divisions as anterior to politics or see them as an inescapable, natural force that conditions consciousness and action in ways that merely political considerations simply cannot match."[43]

The denaturing of race, which involves the historical reconstruction of its production, is then the precondition for its transcendence. Its taken-for-granted status—what Gilroy describes here as "ethnic and racial absolutism"—is at the heart of preserving divisions along racial lines. In making this assertion he has a host of right-wing thinkers in mind. But he also is distancing himself from antiracist thinkers and activists who have been engaged in progressive political struggles yet have tended to invert, rather than displace, these essentialist categories. In the process they have reproduced fixed notions of racial identity. Gilroy admits that imagining a world beyond race is "utopian-sounding," but he passionately defends it. In his words: "Indeed, I would argue that the ability to imagine political, economic, and social systems in which 'race' makes no sense is an essential, though woefully undeveloped part of formulating a credible antiracism as well as an invaluable transitional exercise."[44]

Gilroy understands that a world beyond race is not on the immediate horizon, but he nonetheless locates points of critique and resistance in contemporary Britain that may be regarded as steps toward freeing it from its melancholic condition. Despite the fact that the dominant political culture polices the borders separating native and migrant, white and black, Gilroy argues that "race" (reformulating Raymond Williams's influential understanding of culture) has become "ordinary." As he states it: "Crossracial sex is now no more or less meaningful than multiracial football. White kids routinely speak patois and borrow strategically from Punjabi. Charismatic leaders born in Jamaica can become eloquent mouthpieces of political Islam . . ."[45] In these yet-to-be-fully-understood changes, where "spontaneous tolerance and openness" are marks of "the underworld of Britain's convivial culture," humor manages the "stresses" of multicultural society. Here, Gilroy accords a special position to Sacha Baron Cohen. Cohen's comic character Ali G's playful exploration of racial ambiguities points to the tensions in Britain's multicultural society as well as distancing itself from Britain's melancholic mentality.

Gilroy views Ali G's emergence as one among many signs of a "vibrant, ordinary multiculture," part of, what he describes as, a culture of "conviviality." By "conviviality," he means not the absence of racism but "a different setting" for its "empty, interpersonal rituals, which mean . . . different things in the absence of any strong belief in absolute or integral races." Moreover, "the radical openness that brings conviviality alive makes a nonsense of closed, fixed, and reified identity and turns attention toward the always unpredictable mechanisms of identification."[46] Despite the prolonged malaise and interminable identity crisis of British political culture, Gilroy in the end senses a cultural terrain in flux. Indeed, he argues, that "the subversive ordinariness" of its convivial culture might just provide a model for others. It "might one day teach the rest of Europe something about what will have to be done in order to live peacefully with difference, to manage the hatreds directed against postcolonial and sanctuary-seeking peoples, and to contain the murderous mischief of organized neo-Nazis, ultranationalists and other racist groups."[47] Despite his cosmopolitanism and planetary humanism, Gilroy ultimately sees an emergent culture in Britain in terms that seem almost akin to national pride, although perhaps it is more like a national pride in cosmopolitanism. Nonetheless, Gilroy's optimism about Britain's future provides a stark contrast to his earlier views in the 1980s.

Conclusion

Paul Gilroy has been an influential cultural theorist and scholar, but he has also been important to wider debates concerning decline and identity in contemporary Britain, debates precipitated by decolonization, unprecedented immigration and multiculturalism, relative economic decline, devolution movements, the Northern Irish troubles, and European Union membership. Gilroy's innovative understanding of contemporary Britain as a political culture suffering from postcolonial melancholia builds on some of his earliest published work. Yet *Postcolonial Melancholia* represents a theoretical advance over these earlier explorations. He sees Britain's plight in relationship to recent seismic shifts in the contemporary world and understands it by deploying an array of theoretical insights drawing on European and black Atlantic intellectual sources. Gilroy had been a trenchant critic of the early British cultural studies tradition, but his simultaneous attention to "structure" and "agency," focus on modes of dominance and resistance, privileging of history and counterhistory, and exploration of the politics of representation, suggest vital connections with that tradition as well. Indeed, Gilroy has played a pivotal role in redefining it, stretching it to its limits and beyond, articulating it with other intellectual and theoretical movements and trends. I am not suggesting that Gilroy's thought can exclusively be seen in relationship to the British cultural studies and cultural Marxist tradition, only that it continues to be a crucial dimension of his intellectual and political vision.

In *Postcolonial Melancholia*, Gilroy accords an important position in the history of European reflections on modernity to Baron de Montesquieu's *Persian Letters*. Written from the perspective of two Persian travelers, Montesquieu's satirical text, in Gilroy's view, provides a rare critical perspective on the metropolitan life of France's *ancien régime*. In Gilroy's words: "The social and moral conventions of the day were subjected to the anthropological gaze of a stranger, which aimed to reintroduce France to itself and to suggest that critical knowledge of one's own culture and society can only arise from a carefully cultivated degree of estrangement."[48] What Gilroy says about Montesquieu may be extended to his own critical analysis of the plight of contemporary Britain in *Postcolonial Melancholia*. It represents a counterhistory, written from "a carefully cultivated degree of estrangement." As Montesquieu does for France, Gilroy "reintroduces" Britain to itself.

Notes

1. Paul Gilroy, *Postcolonial Melancholia* (New York: Columbia University Press, 2005), 4.
2. Ibid., 14.
3. Dennis Dworkin, *Cultural Marxism in Postwar Britain: History, the New Left, and the Origins of Cultural Studies* (Durham: Duke University Press, 1997).
4. Paul Gilroy, "Melancholia or Conviviality: The Politics of Belonging in Britain," in *Race, Identity and Belonging: A Soundings Collection*, ed. Sally Davison and Jonathan Rutherford (London: Lawrence and Wishart, 2008), 49.
5. Raymond Williams, *Culture and Society, 1780–1950* (New York: Harper and Row, 1966), 283.

6. Gilroy, "Melancholia or Conviviality: The Politics of Belonging in Britain," 49.
7. Paul Gilroy, *The Black Atlantic: Modernity and Double Consciousness* (London: Verso, 1993), 5.
8. Tom Nairn, *The Break-Up of Britain* (London: NLB, 1977), 292.
9. Stuart Hall, Chas Critcher, Tony Jefferson, John Clarke, and Brian Roberts, *Policing the Crisis: Mugging, the State, and Law and Order* (London: Macmillan Press, 1978), 233.
10. Paul Gilroy, *'There Ain't No Black in the Union Jack': The Politics of Race and Nation* (Chicago: University of Chicago Press, 1992), 46.
11. Ibid.
12. Ibid., 53.
13. Ibid., 55.
14. Ibid., 155.
15. Ibid., 157.
16. Raphael Samuel, "The Schools: Introduction," *History Workshop Journal* 30 (1990): 75–80. See 76–77.
17. Robert Hewison, *The Heritage Industry: Britain in a Climate of Decline* (London: Methuen, 1987), 9–10.
18. Gilroy, *Postcolonial Melancholia*, 100.
19. Patrick Wright, *On Living in an Old County: The National Past in Contemporary Britain* (London: Verso, 1985), 69–70.
20. Juliet Gardiner, "Introduction," in *The History Debate*, ed. J. Gardiner (London: Collins and Brown, 1990), 1–5. See 2.
21. Samuel, "The Schools: Introduction," 76.
22. Margaret Thatcher, *The Downing Street Years* (New York: Harper Collins, 1993), 595.
23. Gardiner, "Introduction," 2.
24. Raphael Samuel, "History, the Nation, and the Schools: Introduction," *History Workshop Journal* 30 (1990): 75–80. See also 127.
25. Gilroy, *'Union Jack,'* 117.
26. Edward Said, "Untitled," in *The Rushdie File*, ed. Lisa Appignanesi and Sara Maitland (Syracuse, NY: Syracuse University Press, 1990), 166.
27. Paul Gilroy, "Nationalism, History and Ethnic Absolutism," *History Workshop Journal* 30 (1990): 114–20. See 119.
28. Ibid., 117.
29. Ibid., 119.
30. Gilroy, *Postcolonial Melancholia*, xi.

31. Stuart Hall, "Comment: A Question of Identity (II)," 15 October 2000, www.guardian.co.uk/uk/2000/oct/15/britishidentity.comment1.
32. Quoted in Alan Travis, "Be Proud to Be British, Straw Tells Left." 12 October 2000. guardian.co.uk/uk/2000/oct/12/race.labour.
33. Gilroy, *Postcolonial Melancholia*, 208–09.
34. Ibid., 108.
35. Ibid., 88.
36. Sonya Rose, *Which People's War? National Identity and Citizenship in Britain, 1939–1945* (Oxford: Oxford University Press, 2003), 24–25.
37. Gilroy, *Postcolonial Melancholia*, 17.
38. Quoted in Gilroy, *Postcolonial Melancholia*, 114.
39. Andrew Marr, *The Day Britain Died* (London: Profile Books, 2000), 209.
40. Mark Leonard, *Britain™: Renewing Our Identity* (London: Demos, 1997), 15.
41. Gilroy, *Postcolonial Melancholia*, 99.
42. Dennis Dworkin, *Class Struggles* (London: Pearson Longman, 2007).
43. Gilroy, *Postcolonial Melancholia*, 33.
44. Ibid., 54.
45. Ibid., 131.
46. Ibid., xv.
47. Ibid., 150.
48. Ibid., 70.

3

"Enough of This Scandal"

Reading Gilroy through Fanon, or Who Comes After "Race"?

ANTHONY ALESSANDRINI

> In recognition of the need for more assertive and wholeheartedly political moods and tactics, we should become prepared to acknowledge the extreme difficulty as well as the great value of moral and political enterprises that require the systematic denaturing of "race" as part of confrontations with the alienated sociality that absorbs the cries of those who suffer by making them sound less human.
>
> —Paul Gilroy, *Postcolonial Melancholia*

> There is nothing ontological about segregation. Enough of this scandal.
>
> —Frantz Fanon, *Black Skin, White Masks*[1]

Paul Gilroy's body of work has made its way along an interesting route in its engagement with humanism. In what follows, I refer to this term with some frequency, so I should make clear at the outset of this essay that here and throughout, I refer to "humanism" both as a concept and as a strategy. One of the notable transitions from Gilroy's earlier work, culminating in *The Black Atlantic*, to his later work in *Against Race* (published as Between Camps in the United Kingdom) and *Postcolonial Melancholia* (published as *After Empire: Melancholia or Convivial Culture?* in the United Kingdom) is the move from what might be seen as a sympathetic but nevertheless highly critical investigation of the legacies of the Enlightenment in Gilroy's earlier work to the active championing of "planetary humanism" and "strategic universalism" in his more recent books. As I argue here, I do not believe that this represents a conceptual change so much as it does a change of strategy, from the seminal "*re*-constructive intellectual labor" that Gilroy set out as his explicit project in *The Black Atlantic*, to the related but notably different project of contributing to "the making of [a] planetary humanism" that serves as the stated goal of the work culminating in *Postcolonial Melancholia*.[2]

This move, I would argue, is coterminous with Gilroy's increasingly close and complex engagement with the work of Frantz Fanon. Fanon was not a key figure in the genealogy of the black Atlantic that Gilroy set out in his earlier work; indeed, Fanon is most conspicuous by his absence from *The Black Atlantic*. Gilroy provides a quite straightforward explanation for this omission, together with that of C. L. R. James, in his preface to the book:

> there is nothing definitive here. . . . There are also many obvious omissions. I have said virtually nothing about the lives, theories, and political activities of Frantz Fanon and C. L. R. James, the two best-known black Atlantic thinkers. Their lives fit readily into the pattern of movement, transformation, and relocation that I have described. But they are already well-known if not as widely read as they should be, and other people have begun the labor of introducing their writings into contemporary critical theory.[3]

And yet, Fanon's absence from *The Black Atlantic* feels more complicated. For one thing, it is slightly different from the relative absence of James, who, while not a focal point of the text nevertheless does turn up at crucial points, including in a long endnote in the closing pages of the book. Fanon, by contrast, does not even show up in the book's index; one searches for him in the space between "Faneuil Hall" and "Fascism" in vain. But this absence begins to feel, as one makes one's way through Gilroy's argument, more like the benign neglect granted to an interlocutor whose ubiquitous presence is being taken for granted.

In other words, while Fanon is largely absent from the text, at the same time, *The Black Atlantic* is a recognizably Fanonian book. Fanon's only real appearance in the text, after the initial nod provided in the preface, is in endnotes that suggest the author's deep immersion in Fanon's writings. For example, only a few pages in, when Gilroy first introduces one of the book's key aims—the need to examine "European traditions of thinking about culture, and . . . the place which these cultural perspectives provide for the images of their racialized others as objects of knowledge, power, and cultural criticism"—an endnote informs us that the concept of "racialization" invoked here is derived from Fanon's "On National Culture."[4] Something similar occurs in a number of places in Gilroy's early work, for example in his 1987 book *'There Ain't No Black in the Union Jack'* and in his influential 1990 essay "One Nation Under a Groove." In each case, Fanon is cited to explain another concept that is a key to much of Gilroy's subsequent work: the shift "from vulgar to cultural racism."[5] From this view, what we are seeing is not so much an omission of Fanon from Gilroy's early work as a Fanonian framing of this work that is encompassing without being explicitly acknowledged. This accords with a statement made by Gilroy in an interview, in which he described his intellectual development when he was a student at Sussex University: "I was quite unhappy. . . . In my second term I was really thinking I might leave and went to see [Donald Wood, a historian of the Caribbean] . . . and he told me that I should go away and read *The Black Jacobins* and *Wretched of the Earth* which I did and that set me on my way."[6]

So this provides us with another way of understanding the seeming absence of Fanon from *The Black Atlantic*: having provided the initial impetus that set the project on its way, Fanon could remain a part of the overall framework of the text without becoming one of its central subjects. As I have already suggested, this strategy changes by the time of the publication of *Against Race*; here, as in Gilroy's subsequent work, Fanon's presence is explicitly central throughout. As I argue here, the changing place of Fanon in Gilroy's body of work simultaneously reflects and influences the development of his thinking about humanism. If the preface to *The Black Atlantic* almost immediately excused Fanon from the text (while, as I have argued, still keeping him as part of the book's implicit framework), the introduction to *Against Race* immediately shows the centrality of Fanon's work to Gilroy's more recent theorizations. Indeed, the book's epigraph is a long quote from *Black Skin, White Masks*:

> At first thought it may seem strange that the anti-Semite's outlook should be related to that of the Negrophobe. It was my philosophy professor, a native of the Antilles, who recalled the fact to me one day: "Whenever you hear anyone abuse the Jews, pay attention, because he is talking about you." And I found that he was universally right—by which I mean that I was answerable in my body and my heart for what was done to my brother. Later I realized that he meant, quite simply, an anti-Semite is inevitably anti-Negro.[7]

I later undertake a close reading of this quote, and of the significance of Gilroy's (and Fanon's) linking of racism and anti-Semitism. For the moment, what strikes the reader is this initial reference to Fanon, followed immediately by Gilroy's nod to (and gentle dismissal of) W. E. B. Du Bois, is a ground-clearing gesture that sets out the terms of his new project:

> The modern times that W. E. B. Du Bois once identified as the century of the color line have now passed. Racial hierarchy is still with us. Approaching this conundrum, this book addresses some of the continuing tensions associated with the constitution of political communities in racialized form . . . and is concerned, in particular, with the operations of power, which, thanks to ideas about "race," have become entangled with those vain and mistaken attempts to delineate and subdivide humankind.[8]

This represents a recognizably different kind of work than the "*re*-constructive intellectual labor" of *The Black Atlantic*—not a departure from that book's emphasis upon rethinking the legacy of modernism through the experience of slavery, certainly, but rather the logical next step in Gilroy's larger intellectual and political project.

Fanon enters Gilroy's argument explicitly at the moment when he begins to describe what he sees as the "crisis of raciology" and the resulting strategies that could potentially lead to a seizing of this crisis as a "cue to free ourselves from the bonds of all raciology in a novel and ambitious abolitionist project."[9] Gilroy goes on to argue explicitly that this process of racialization leads to the dehumanization of all those marked by it—not just those marked as "inferior" through the process of racial hierarchy but also those accorded the privileges of racial mastery. This is the moment when Fanon is first invoked explicitly in the text: "Black and white are bonded together by the mechanisms of 'race' that estrange them from each other and amputate their common humanity. Frantz Fanon . . . whose work frames these concerns, observed this dismal cycle through its effects on the lives of men: 'the Negro enslaved by his inferiority, the white man enslaved by his superiority alike behave in accordance with a neurotic orientation.'"[10] Elsewhere in *Black Skin, White Masks*, Fanon is more explicit in his delineation of the cause and nature of this "neurotic orientation":

> The white man is locked in his whiteness.
> The black man in his blackness.
> We shall endeavor to determine the tendencies of this double narcissism and the motivations behind it.[11]

By introducing the notion of "double narcissism" into his analysis, Fanon is of course signaling the need for a psychoanalytic interpretation of racism. But he immediately goes on to argue that while his approach is primarily a psychological one, "it remains, nevertheless, evident that for us the true disalienation of the black man implies a brutal awareness of social and economic realities." Fanon insists that "the inferiority complex" caused by racism is in fact the result of a double process—first, economic, and then, the subsequent "internalization or rather epidermalization of this inferiority"—and he proposes, as the only viable approach to analyzing and dispersing this inferiority complex, the approach that he calls "sociogeny."[12]

I take note of the multiple approach of *Black Skin, White Masks* in part because it has provided an inspiration, acknowledged or not, to much work that has followed, including Gilroy's own work. Fanon's "stretching" of psychological approaches in *The Wretched of the Earth* is in many ways analogous to his famous statement about the role of Marxist analysis in addressing colonialism and his insistence that racial difference demands a new and different approach than that provided by orthodox Marxist analysis:

> Looking at the immediacies of the colonial context, it is clear that what divides this world is first and foremost what species, what race one belongs to. In the colonies the economic infrastructure is also a superstructure. The cause is effect: You are rich because you are white, you are white because you are rich. This is why a Marxist analysis should always be slightly stretched when it comes to addressing the colonial issue.[13]

Gilroy cites this "stretching" of Marxist analysis approvingly in *Postcolonial Melancholia*, noting that "it still offends attractively against economic deterministic accounts of 'race' and racism." In a slightly different vein, Gilroy adds: "The innovative emphasis Fanon placed on the social aspect of racial mentalities originally warranted his humanist and existentialist ventures and marked his departure from the psychologism of his own training."[14]

This second comment betrays some of the hesitations that Gilroy evidences even as he invokes Fanon as a necessary part of his own project. For example, immediately upon bringing Fanon (alongside Martin Luther King) into the argument of *Against Race* by stressing his contribution to a critical strategy premised upon the founding of a "radically nonracial humanism," Gilroy qualifies this statement by suggesting that this new humanism "must be placed upon more stable foundations than those provided by King's open-minded and consistent Christianity or Fanon's phenomenologist, existential, and psychoanalytic interests."[15] He provides a similarly backhanded compliment to Fanon's early work, and in particular its grounding in existentialist thought, as part of his argument in *Postcolonial Melancholia*: "Pursuit of a partisan history of the postcolonial present can do far worse than be guided by the irreverent spirit evident in Fanon's youthful flirtations with an existentialist understanding of human agency as well as his appetite for a 'new humanism.'"[16]

This combined endorsement and hesitation can provide us with our cue to move back into Fanon's complex and agonized engagement with humanism. Such an investigation can provide a useful framework for a critical understanding of Gilroy's own strategy of planetary humanism. This is the work that I do in the remainder of this chapter. To move from Gilroy to Fanon is to make the sort of temporal shift that Gilroy himself champions in *Against Race*, a move "back to the future," since I argue that far from representing a youthful outburst, *Black Skin, White Masks* already contains a fully formed working out of Fanon's recasting of humanism against its own colonial and racialist origins. When we reread Gilroy through Fanon, we find ourselves in a better position to appreciate the specific political strategy articulated through the notion of planetary humanism—a strategy whose goal is to provide a positive content for antiracist thinking and action.

In this sense, I would argue that this shared strategy of Gilroy and Fanon is animated by more than a bit of the spirit found in Michel Foucault's late engagements with Enlightenment thought, particularly the project he described as "the critical ontology of ourselves," which

> has to be considered not, certainly, as a theory, a doctrine, nor even as a permanent body of knowledge that is accumulating; it has to be conceived as an attitude, an ethos, a philosophical life in which the critique of what we are is at one and the same time the historical analysis of the limits that are imposed on us and an experiment with the possibility of going beyond them.[17]

(Gilroy, who is by and large critical of poststructuralist theory, quotes this passage from Foucault approvingly in *The Black Atlantic*). What the strategic humanisms of Gilroy and Fanon share with Foucault's project is an orientation toward a future that has not yet come (thus the continuous need to write and rewrite "the history of the present").[18] In the case of Gilroy and Fanon, the orientation is specifically toward a radically nonracial future, together with an awareness that this future will only come through the sort of antiracist struggle that their own notions of humanism are intended to frame and enable. Gilroy's "radically nonracial humanism," in other words, must not be seen as a case of wishful thinking or of having gone soft on the legacy of the Enlightenment, as some of his critics would have it. Rather, it represents a strategy for pointing us toward a nonracial future, not by simply declaring us to be "beyond race" but precisely by showing the need for antiracist thinking (and, more and more resoundingly in his recent work, antiracist action) that can get us to that "place"—sooner rather than later.

As I have already noted, Fanon's presence in *Against Race* is made immediately palpable even before Gilroy's actual text begins. The quote that serves as the epigraph to the book introduces a link that will play a major role in Gilroy's overall argument: the explicit link between anti-Semitism and racism, which Gilroy extends into a discussion of the close link between racism and fascism. This is a key element of the book as a whole, as Gilroy suggests in his introduction when he asks "what place the history and memory of past conflicts with fascism [should] have in forging the minimal ethical principles on which a meaningful multiculturalism might be based" and goes on to note: "Answering that question takes us into an initial confrontation with the idea of 'race' and the raciological theories to which it has given rise."[19] This move, in other words, sets the stage for Gilroy's call for a form of antiracist thinking and action that would place the very idea of "race" and raciology into the past. As he notes in his conclusion, part of the work involved in building this new form of antiracism involves the need "self-consciously to become more future-oriented."[20] In this sense, the study of fascism can provide important lessons, especially through attention to "the ways twentieth-century fascist movements organized their temporal sensibilities."[21] An antiracism that takes its cue in part from antifascism would thus involve "making raciology appear anachronistic—placing it squarely in the past" through "careful judgment as to what histories of our heterocultural present and our cosmopolitan future should entail."[22]

Part of this latter work, as Gilroy sets it out in the book's opening pages, involves a rewriting of the "heroic narrative" of the war against fascism, from which the role and even the presence of nonwhite participants has been largely written out. Gilroy sets out the hope that his book might contribute to the work necessary to "write a different history of this period, one in which [these participants] were allowed to dwell in the same frame as official anti-Nazi heroism."[23] In this sense, Fanon represents an exemplary figure for Gilroy's argument in several important ways. First of all, he was himself one of these nonwhite participants in War World II. At the age of eighteen, he made a dangerous crossing from Martinique to join the Free French forces. He was actively engaged in fighting in France, was wounded in battle, and received the *Croix de Guerre* for bravery. This experience was formative in a number of ways. For one thing, his journey to the war included a crossing from the Antilles to North Africa—he landed in Casablanca and trained in Algeria (the image of Fanon making his first entry to Algeria in a French military uniform is a shocking one)—and thus it led to his initial exposure to French colonial rule in North Africa. His arrival in France initiated his first, paradigmatic experience of metropolitan racism: it is no coincidence that in the traumatic incident of racial identification and reification that lies at the center of the chapter of *Black Skin, White Masks* entitled "The Lived Experience of the Black Man," the object of the racist gaze (a figure who may or may not be Fanon himself) is a black man in uniform. Fanon's rapid disillusionment with the spirit that led him to fight for the French is apparent in a letter to his family, dated April 12, 1945, in which he laments his decision to leave Fort-de-France "to defend an obsolete ideal" and the foolishness of wanting to fight for whites in France for whom occupation by German soldiers was preferable to liberation at the hands of black soldiers in French uniforms.[24]

As part of a larger rethinking of the World War II–era struggle against fascism, it is worth noting that Joseph Henri, the *lycée* teacher who gave Fanon the memorable advice described in *Black Skin, White Masks* and cited by Gilroy as his epigraph—"When you hear anyone abuse the Jews, pay attention, because he is talking about you"—also gave Fanon another piece of advice about joining the French forces: "What is happening in Europe is no concern of ours. When white men kill each other, it is a blessing for us blacks."[25] Gilroy's counterhistory of the struggle against fascism by and large avoids encounters with this particular response from the colonized world, in which the main features of a war between European imperial powers would be a potential weakening of Europe's collective hold over the colonies. Gilroy is more interested in marshaling an embittered, and thus differently informed and motivated, reengagement with the legacy of humanism that could emerge from the reimagining of this history. It is here that Fanon, whom Gilroy describes as a "prototypical black-European," serves as such an important model.[26] Turning from Fanon's experience as a participant in the war to the body of writing that he subsequently produced, beginning with *Black Skin, White Masks*, it is possible to suggest that Fanon never completely abandoned some of the ideals that he had denounced as "obsolete" in his letter from the front—in particular the notion he had set out in an earlier letter home, which insisted that "freedom is indivisible."[27] Joseph Henri's formulation regarding "what is happening in Europe" is based on a racial particularism that, in spite of its desire to oppose the appeal of French nationalism (motivated by Henri's life-long commitment to pacifism, another important belief he wished to pass on to his students), nevertheless effectively reinscribes a form of racialization. This is a move that Fanon (like Gilroy after him) will consistently reject. The Fanon that Gilroy values most highly in *Against Race* is the one who insists that "the institution of an anticolonial and nonracial universalism" can only come about through a battle with the very notion of "race" as some timeless and unchanging essence, as his stinging words regarding racial ontology make clear: "There is nothing ontological about segregation. Enough of this scandal."[28]

In examining Fanon's conception of a "new humanism" that would come out of the struggle against racism and colonialism (as well as fascism), Gilroy introduces a Fanon, in *Against Race*, who was "both beneficiary and victim of European progress in its blood-stained imperial mode." From this position, working simultaneously "inside and against the larger cultural and intellectual structures that had shaped his consciousness," Fanon "demanded national liberation for colonial peoples but linked that project of revolutionary reconstruction to the deliberate production of a new conception of humanity."[29] As Gilroy notes, the accusation leveled by Fanon throughout his work "is not merely that European imperial powers wrongfully deprived colonial subjects of their humanity, but that Europe has perpetrated the still greater crime of despoiling humanity of its elemental unity as a species."[30] Fanon's disillusioned reading of European fascism follows Aimé Césaire in insisting that the carnage visited upon Europe by the Nazi regime must be seen as the logical conclusion of the policy of violence and dehumanization systematically pursued by all the European powers in the colonies, a violence explicitly underwritten by Enlightenment humanism:

> they hide the truth from themselves . . . that it is Nazism, yes, but before they were its victims, they were its accomplices; that they tolerated that Nazism before it was inflicted upon them, that they absolved it, shut their eyes to it, legitimized it, because, until then, it had been applied only to non-European peoples; that they have cultivated that Nazism, that they are responsible for it . . .[31]

This is Gilroy's point in insisting on the difference between a Fanonian-inspired universalism and a mere reprise of traditional humanist ideology:

"What is most important about this stance is [Fanon's] insistence that this precious universalism can only be bought at the price of a reckoning with colonial modernity."[32]

The particular temporality involved in this reckoning, which involves both a rethinking of the "past" of modernity through a direct engagement with racism and colonialism as well as a reconceptualizing of the history of the present through an antiracism inspired by the (ongoing) struggle against fascism, can be found in Fanon's echoing of one of Césaire's postwar speeches:

> When I switch on my radio and hear that black men are being lynched in America, I say that they have lied to us: Hitler isn't dead. When I switch on my radio and hear that Jews are being insulted, persecuted, and massacred, I say that they have lied to us: Hitler isn't dead. And finally when I switch on my radio and hear that in Africa forced labor has been introduced and legalized, I say that truly they have lied to us: Hitler isn't dead.[33]

There are, however, risks in contemporary attempts to apply this strategy of reappropriating the legacy of the struggle against antifascism in the same direct way as did Césaire. After all, similar sorts of direct parallels to Hitler have been used recently by right-wing forces in the United States, whether for the purpose of seeking legitimation for the illegal invasion and occupation of Iraq (through the "Saddam = Hitler" equation) or to stir up opposition to health care reform (through the current fashion of portraying President Barack Obama as Hitler). In this context, it is worth recalling Gilroy's youthful semiotic confusion when faced with ultranationalist fascist groups in Britain, "the teddy boys who terrified me as a child and their successors, the skinheads who hounded me through my teenage years"; he recalls asking his father: "Weren't fascists the same as Nazis . . . ? How could *they* be English people? How could *English* people be Fascists? Was their exciting lightning-flash the same sort of thing as the hated but fascinating swastika?"[34] We would do well to bring some of this spirit of clear-eyed inquiry to the present horrifying phenomena of digitally altered photographs that merge the faces of Obama and Hitler, or the sight of Obama's smiling face photoshopped over a figure in full Nazi regalia, images that can be found by the dozens through a simple internet search. In spite of these frightening precedents, Gilroy's strategy in *Against Race* works to keep alive Césaire's outraged call to make the continuing presence of fascism part of our history of the present (and future). We might do the same sort of work when faced with the contemporary link between fascism and Islamophobia in Europe and North America—for example, the recent fascist attacks on a partially completed mosque in Harrow, led by groups such as the English Defence League and a group calling itself Stop the Islamisation of Europe[35]— as well as the presence of white supremacist and other fascist groups as part of the rising tide of anti-immigrant rhetoric (and violence) in the United States.

Given this politically motivated reengagement with the fascist past, it is striking that Gilroy ends *Against Race* by taking a step back from the past—or, to put it more accurately, as he does in the book's final sentence, a step toward "bring[ing] even more powerful visions of planetary humanity from the future into the present and reconnect[ing] them with democratic and cosmopolitan traditions that have been all but expunged from today's black political imaginary."[36] Of course, there is hardly an abandonment of the past here but rather a call for a "temporal adjustment" that would accompany a turn away from the emphasis on "African antiquity" stressed by black nationalist and Afrocentric thought and toward "our planet's future"—especially, as Gilroy takes pains to note, "if we recognize the possibility that the contested colonial and imperial past has not entirely released its grip upon us."[37]

In making this final move into the future, Gilroy enlists another version of Fanon, the "youthful" Fanon found in the concluding pages of *Black Skin, White Masks*. There, in what Gilroy characterizes as an "indiscreetly anti-Marxist spirit" that reflects "the first flush of his youthful enthusiasm for existentialism," Fanon expressed an anger that Gilroy sees as aimed at the same two targets he has been struggling against for the length of his book: "against colonial white supremacy and what we now recognize as its black nationalist shadows."[38] Gilroy sees Fanon as "writing as though he were struggling to reassure himself as much as to direct the thoughts of the readers who had managed to complete his book's exacting course," and he proceeds to quote from Fanon's conclusion to *Black Skin, White Masks*: "I am not a prisoner of history. I should not seek there for the meaning of my destiny. . . . I do not have the right to allow myself to be mired in what the past has determined. . . . The body of history does not determine a single one of my actions."[39] Gilroy reads this as Fanon's

> imaginative supercession of history . . . the self-conscious initiation of a cycle of freedom for black populations still dwelling in the aftershock of slavery, their founding trauma. For his peers—modern blacks who were in but never comfortably of the color-coded West—claiming a more authentic Being than the racialized order

> of modernity had necessitated accepting but also turning away from the past.[40]

I would maintain that Gilroy is strategically playing down some important aspects of Fanon's thought here. But Gilroy's larger point holds: for Fanon, "the capacity to address the future, both as politically abstract and as personally concrete, was a precondition for recovery from the alienating and corrupting antisociality of 'race.'"[41] And this capacity does in fact necessitate a refusal—not a refusal of the past per se but of certain aspects of the past that can be too easily dragged into the present and future. This is why Fanon rewrites his own declaration that man is an affirmation—"Man is a 'yes' resonating from cosmic harmonies," as he puts it in the opening pages of *Black Skin, White Masks*[42]—through a subsequent insistence in the book's conclusion that "man is also a *negation.* No to man's contempt. No to the indignity of man. To the exploitation of man. To the massacre of what is most human in man: freedom."[43] It is along these same lines, a line that leads to Gilroy's refusal of the calls of identity politics and black nationalism in response to racism, that Fanon also insists that "Man's behavior is not only reactional."[44] It is this refusal that initiates Fanon's final, explicit refusal of racialized ontology in all its forms, which in turn allows for the conditions of an engagement with the past that will allow for an obliteration of racism's "double narcissism" and a move toward a fully antiracist future: "The black man is not. No more than the white man. Both have to move away from the inhuman voices of their respective ancestors so that a genuine communication can be born. . . . It is through self-consciousness and renunciation, through a permanent tension of his freedom, that man can create the ideal conditions of existence for a human world."[45]

It is this same negating move, containing within it the necessity of creating something new, which leads Gilroy, in the final pages of his book, toward the postwar writings of Theodor Adorno. In particular, Gilroy addresses Adorno's reflections, in his essay "The Stars Down to Earth," on the need to refuse easy shortcut solutions—what he refers to as the comforts provided by "pseudo-erudition" of the sort found in astrology—in the face of a present that seems to offer only a series of different unacceptable choices (for Gilroy, these unacceptable options would include the choice between continued racial abjection, on the one hand, versus the commodified glorification of the black bodies of star athletes and entertainers provided by American capitalism as an "alternative" to racism).[46] In a sense, *Against Race* comes full circle at this point, since Adorno's ultimate argument is that the forms of semi-erudition encouraged by astrology and other popular "futurologies" are identical to the tactics used by fascist governments to underwrite their racist ideologies: "astrology, just as other irrational creeds like racism, provides a short cut by bringing the complex to a handy formula."[47] The only defense against the allure of semi-erudite shortcuts is the fostering of a true critical understanding of the present, which can in turn lead to the larger realization that the present (and future) can be acted upon, not simply endured or witnessed passively. Those who have not entirely grasped Gilroy's articulation of planetary humanism in *Against Race* may have missed this element of negation, the refusing of certain aspects of the present so as to allow the arrival of dissident strands from the past and future into the evolving history of the present. The position articulated by Fanon in the final pages of *Black Skin, White Masks* provides Gilroy with a key critical tool to set out this strategy of negating the unacceptable conditions of the present in the service of bringing about a new vision of what would come after "race."

However, it is striking that while the overall framework of *Against Race* is so clearly influenced by Fanon, there is nevertheless a key aspect of Fanon's work rejected by Gilroy in the book: Fanon's description of the "Manichaeism" of the colonized world—or, rather, Gilroy's perception of Fanon's own Manichaeism. This rejection can be found most clearly in Gilroy's reading of *The Wretched of the Earth*. While he cites approvingly the well-known formulation expressed in the final lines of Fanon's final work—"For Europe, for ourselves and for humanity, comrades, we must make a new start, develop a new way of thinking, and endeavor to create a new man"[48]—Gilroy immediately adds that Fanon comes to this formulation "via a binary code almost as pernicious as the Manichean [*sic*] dualism that he sought to supplant."[49] While he describes the Fanon of *Black Skin, White Masks* as rejecting a "reactional" attitude toward racism, Gilroy finds in the later Fanon of *The Wretched of the* Earth a strictly reactional approach to the violence of colonialism: "Recall that his overly stern liberationist perspective was an organic product of wars against Nazism and colonialism. It sprang from militarized social life in the colonial city."[50] Gilroy maintains that this strand of Fanon's work needs to be rejected in the process of building a new vision of antiracism today:

> In our period Fanon, whose work yields so many precious insights, becomes less than helpful precisely because his thinking remains bound to a dualistic logic we must now abjure in asking what the analysis of culture and the development of cultural politics (and policy) might contribute to the new humanism he called for thirty

> years ago. It is not now, or rather not only, a matter of the Third World's initiating a new, less triumphalist humanism that can be its own special gift to civilization, but a matter of building upon the narratives and poetics of cultural intermixture already alive inside Europe's postcolonial popular cultures in order to see how those polar positions have already been redundant.[51]

As compared to the Fanon of *Black Skin, White Masks*, in other words, in *Against Race*, Gilroy sees the Fanon of *The Wretched of the Earth* as offering less help in working toward "adopt[ing] a more future-oriented stance"; this Fanon, it seems, must be left in the past.

It is certainly not my intention in this essay to simply defend Fanon against any and all critiques. Gilroy is right to find this strand of "overly stern" militarized thinking in certain parts of Fanon's work, in particular the essays collected in *L'An V de la révolution algérienne* (translated as *A Dying Colonialism*), written from the midst of the Algerian Revolution.[52] I suggest, however, that Gilroy falls into a too-simple reading of Fanon's late work in *Against Race*, and that this has an important effect upon his articulation of the notion of planetary humanism (as I suggest in the next section, this perspective shifts radically when Gilroy revisits Fanon in *Postcolonial Melancholia*, with a concomitant effect upon his articulation of a humanist strategy for antiracist thinking and action). In dividing Fanon into an early, "indiscreetly anti-Marxist" Fanon and a late, "overly stern" militant Fanon, Gilroy partakes in a common method of addressing Fanon's wide-ranging (especially considering his tragically short life) body of work. I have argued elsewhere against this division into "early" and "late" Fanon; instead, I propose a reading of his complete body of work as an ongoing, overlapping attempt to write a history of the present, increasingly, in the course of his life and work, from inside the Algerian Revolution.[53]

But even in terms of a reading of *The Wretched of the Earth* itself, more attention to Fanon's shifting, dialogic form of argumentation than Gilroy provides in his reading in *Against Race* is necessary, especially if the aim is to engage with the call for a "new humanism" with which the book concludes. In his reading in *Against Race*, Gilroy moves directly from the Manichaean vision set out by Fanon in the first chapter of *The Wretched of the Earth*, "On Violence," to the very last words of the book. In the intervening chapters of *The Wretched of the Earth*, however, a number of things transpire, all of which force us to reconsider our understanding of the opening. Reading "On Violence" by itself, it is indeed possible to perceive Fanon as arguing for the ineradicable Manichaeism of the colonial situation, one that can only be overturned (but never uprooted, subverted, or replaced) through anticolonial violence. However, the remainder of the book is a patient reconsideration of this suggestion. The insistent Manichaean attitude that Gilroy attributes to the book as a whole is, in other words, just the first step in an ongoing (and not necessarily linear or dialectical) argument. Indeed, about halfway through the book, Fanon calls this Manichaeism into question through his observation that national liberation movements soon learn, through bitter experience, that "some blacks can be whiter than the whites," and, similarly, that there are Europeans who go over to the "native" side. In this context, Fanon suggests, the anticolonial Manichaeism that had previously provided an anticolonial strategy breaks down, and he represents the complexity of this situation with one of his many moments of irony: "and yet everything used to be so simple before: the bad people were on one side, and the good on the other."[54] Of course, Fanon's point is that such a moment has never in fact existed. Manichaeism provides an important explanatory tool for understanding the colonial situation, but once decolonization is set in motion, a different understanding, and a new set of strategies, is clearly required.

Just as important, at least for a consideration of the "new humanism" Fanon calls for in his conclusion, is the fact that far from providing a "triumphalist" vision of spontaneous anticolonial violence that overturns the violence of colonial rule and leads inexorably to the new vision of Third World–led humanism invoked by Gilroy, Fanon's initial prediction is that everything will at first go quite wrong. In fact, the book's third chapter, "The Trials and Tribulations of National Consciousness," has proved particularly prescient in its predictions about the emergent middle class that came to rule over the newly independent nations of Africa. This section of the book is written in a tense that suggests that, far from leading toward a triumphant emergence, postcolonial history will end badly. The language of the chapter insists, not that the new middle class *may* ruin everything, but that they *will* ruin everything. Even at this point in his argument, Fanon is trying, to use Gilroy's words, to bring a vision from the future into the present, since at the time he writes the book in 1961, the outcome of the Algerian Revolution, like that of other ongoing anticolonial struggles, was far from clear. Before reaching his final exhortation, Fanon proposes a series of concrete projects that need to be passed through in order to reach a true state of decolonization: a struggle against the neocolonialism that will be imposed by the nationalist elite, the illegitimate inheritors of the postcolonial state; the forging of a national culture with internationalist strivings; and the coming to terms with the traumas inflicted and suffered by both colonizer and colonized as an inevitable consequence of the violence of the anticolonial struggle. The penultimate chapter, "Colonial War and Mental Disorders," which consists of Fanon's case notes from his psychiatric treatment of both Algerians and of French soldiers, police officers, and *colons*—that is, the tortured and the torturers, the perpetrators of colonial violence and of anticolonial counterviolence—is the best evidence of his radically non-Manichaean vision of the work necessary to build a truly postcolonial future.

So when Fanon finally reaches his conclusion, and his call for a new humanism, we must realize that this is a humanism that comes from the future, one that comes not only after colonialism but also after the aftermath of colonialism, out of the struggle (still ongoing to this day) against the neocolonial condition that Fanon predicted. From all the possible strands of the present and future, Fanon pulls out a single one. His postcolonial humanist vision involves not only the rejection of Europe, "this Europe which never stops talking of man yet massacres him at every one of its street corners, at every corner of the world,"[55] but also the rejection of simply rejecting Europe, and of thus remaining inside the terms of a Manichaean dualism—in other words, of being, in the words of the younger Fanon, strictly "reactional." Fanon's vision involves a shift in temporality identical to the one Gilroy calls for in his strategy of planetary humanism—that is, a simultaneous refusal of past time and the development of a new and different tempo for the present and future:

> No, it is not a question of back to nature. It is the very basic question of not dragging man in directions which mutilate him, of not imposing on his brain tempos that rapidly obliterate and unhinge it. The notion of catching up must not be used as a pretext to brutalize man, to tear him from himself and his inner consciousness, to break him, to kill him. No, we do not want to catch up with anyone. But what we want is to walk in the company of man, every man, night and day, for all times.[56]

There is in this formulation the same conjuring with time, space, and hierarchy that Gilroy finds so useful in Richard Wright's formulation: "Am I ahead or behind the West? My personal judgment is that I'm ahead. And I do not say that boastfully; such a judgment is implied by the very nature of the Western values that I hold dear."[57] But there is also the persistent, almost playful negation of a negation found in another of Wright's formulations not quoted by Gilroy: "Being a Negro living in a white Western Christian society, I've never been allowed to blend, in a natural and healthy manner, with the culture and civilization of the West. . . . Yet, I'm not non-Western."[58] Far from representing a celebration of Manichaeism, Fanon's new humanism, when understood as it emerges from the full complexity of his argument in *The Wretched of the Earth*, is not Western and not non-Western; it "look[s] elsewhere besides Europe" and comes from a different past and a different future, from "another level" altogether.[59] This vision has a great deal to offer to Gilroy's contemporary strategy of planetary humanism and to antiracist politics more generally.

Gilroy, in his most recent rereading of Fanon in *Postcolonial Melancholia*, agrees with this conclusion. Indeed, Fanon is introduced here, in the brilliant chapter "Race and the Right to Be Human," as the initiator of a twenty-first-century project that could be a successor to the twentieth-century struggle for civil rights that has been at the center of black political thought. This new strategy for a new century "might now be conceptualized," Gilroy suggests, "as a deliberate development of the translocal interpretations of 'race,' racism, culture, belonging, and identity that were first laid out in the complex and forbidding 'new humanism' of Frantz Fanon, where black political thought was challenged to advance an interpretation of past and present sufferings with reference to the future."[60] Here again, as in *Against Race*, Gilroy invokes "the irreverent spirit evident in Fanon's youthful flirtations with an existentialist understanding of human agency as well as his appetite for a 'new humanism,'" and goes on to suggest that "the willingness to imagine or invent political cultures capable of ending racism now demands a variety of creative work similar to Fanon's own."[61]

However, his subsequent reading of "early" Fanon in *Postcolonial Melancholia* reveals some important shifts in emphasis and in attitude, especially regarding Fanon's engagements with Marxism and existentialism. For example, while Gilroy states, in a formulation similar to those found in *Against Race*, that "the youthful Fanon trumpeted his decisionistic escape from the constraints of inherited circumstance in the closing sections of *Black Skin, White Masks*," he goes on to argue not that this indicates an "indiscreetly anti-Marxist spirit," but rather that Fanon "was operating in a framework of analysis informed by substantial elements of historical materialism" and that this "affiliation was articulated together with the distinctive 'constructionist' problematic that flowed from his intimacies with the work of Sartre and Beauvoir."[62] In addition to endowing Fanon's engagement with existentialist thought with a stronger social and political quality, this new reading leads

Gilroy toward a different understanding of Fanon's engagement with temporality and of the contribution this might make to contemporary dissident intellectual work. Remarking on the particular mix of existentialism and historical materialism found in *Black Skin, White Masks* (together, of course, with a psychological approach), Gilroy suggests:

> This combination grows in importance when we grasp its refusals of scholastic protocol. Fanon used it to strip not only the Negro but also the idea of "race" itself of the ontological claims that removed them from history and delivered them instead to the unnatural realm of what he called "timeless truths" and "ultimate radiances." This radical approach refers us back to the race-making processes he had identified in the opening pages of the same work as "sociogeny," a rather valuable and oddly neglected concept. His attachment to what Sylvia Wynter has called "the sociogenic principle" encompasses but also moves beyond a radical historicizing of racism that requires alertness to its changing forms and functions.[63]

This new reading in turn leads Gilroy to a reformulation of Fanon's engagement with (or, rather, dismissal of) the ontology of races and thus toward a different understanding of Fanon's potential contributions to a strategy of planetary humanism: "For Fanon, the ontology of races becomes historical, and the universal and the particular can enter a new relationship from which the possibility of novel forms of humanity can derive."[64] In this sense, there is a link between Fanon's project and that carried out by Du Bois in *The Souls of Black Folk* where, according to Gilroy, "Du Bois' repeated specifications of the twentieth century as the century of the color line makes vivid sense in the setting provided by his progressive impulses. Rather than arguing that we were forever to be trapped in racism's hall of mirrors, he was elevating Jim Crow to a problem of world-historic proportions."[65] However, Gilroy finds in Du Bois the remnants of a Hegelian impulse through which the "double consciousness" of the American Negro "would eventually be sublated into a 'better truer self.'"[66] By contrast, Fanon's engagement with the dualisms of racial ontology takes the form of a complete rejection of the very premises of this ontology, as set out in his 1955 essay "West Indians and Africans": "The truth is that there is nothing a priori to warrant the assumption that any such thing as a black People exists. . . . when someone talks to me about 'black people,' I try to understand what is meant. Then, unfortunately, I understand that there is in this a source of conflicts. Then I try to destroy this source."[67]

Here, unlike his analysis in *Against Race*, Gilroy concludes that Fanon ultimately rejects Manichaean thinking about race. Wherever Fanon finds it in the world of colonial rule, this Manichaean opposition results in catastrophe, and "wherever this arrangement has been established, patterns of intermixture and cosmopolitan combination were erased."[68] Furthermore, this is not a Hegelian schema; there is no possibility of a sublation of the two Manichaean terms "black" and "white" through a dialectical solution, and indeed, as long as the colonial context holds, there is no hope of any intercommunication whatsoever. Thus, a "repudiation of those dualistic pairings—black/white, settler/native, colonizer/colonized—has become an urgent political and moral task."[69] The undoing of these dualisms, Gilroy suggests, "supplies a productive starting point for the work Fanon described as 'dis-alienation,' by which he meant the unmaking of racialized bodies and their restoration to proper human modes of being in the world," a task, Gilroy concludes, that can be best carried out "via a concept of *relation*."[70] Two sentences from the introduction to *Black Skin, White Masks* encapsulate this Fanonian project of disalienation and suggest its grounding in social and historical as well as psychic realities: "We believe that the juxtaposition of the black and white races has resulted in a massive psycho-existential complex. By analyzing it we aim to destroy it."[71] There is a brilliant, compact irony here, as the word "juxtaposition" stands in for the centuries-long history of slavery, colonialism, racism, and dehumanization that has marked the relation between the black and white "races." Gilroy, following Fanon, insists that the historical nature of this juxtaposition means that there is nothing ontological or "timeless" about the identities that are formed by this history or about the continuing conflict between them. A shift in the relations caused by this "juxtaposition" is thus the necessary first step toward the total elimination of "race."

In *Postcolonial Melancholia*, as in *Against Race*, Gilroy locates Fanon's most extended analysis of the Manichaeism of colonial racism in the pages of *The Wretched of the Earth*. But his rereading of this text allows for a much more encompassing understanding of Fanon's argument than his earlier reading, with important results for his engagement with Fanonian humanism. For one thing, Gilroy gives a further account of the paradoxically ambivalent nature of the Manichaean situation of the colonies: "the ruthless binary logic of colonial government placed black and white, settler and native in mutually antagonistic relation. They were separated spatially, but conceptually their common racialization ensured that they were bound to each other so tightly that each was unthinkable without the proximity and hostility of the other."[72] This notion is found most clearly in Fanon's formulation of how the process of colonization is actually responsible for creating the identities of "colonized" and "colonizer": "It is the colonist who *fabricated* and *continues to fabricate* the colonized subject. The colonist derives his validity, i.e. his wealth, from the colonial system."[73] Equally important, as Gilroy notes, is Fanon's contention that "the spatial configuration of brutal colonial government was *not* a question of politics. The political as Europe knew it simply did not exist there. Instead, the emergence of race-coded duality marked the suspension of political relations and fostered their replacement by a rather different set of what we could call parapolitical technologies and procedures."[74] The two sectors of the colonial world, the native sector and the European sector, "confront each other, but not in the service of a higher unity," Fanon argued. "Governed by a pure Aristotelian logic, they follow the dictates of mutual exclusion: There is no conciliation possible, one of them is superfluous."[75] Thus, as Gilroy concludes, "the emphasis that Fanon placed upon Manichaeism shows how the relationship between black and white, settler and native, colonizer and colonized, denies any possibility of a comforting dialectical resolution."[76]

But Gilroy then takes the next step into Fanon's argument. Unlike his reading in *Against Race*, which jumps from Fanon's Manichaean description of the colonial world directly to his call for a new humanism, here Gilroy recognizes that while on the one hand, "Fanon argued that those great racialized 'encampments' were permeated with neurosis and a 'dual narcissism,'" he goes on to note the further twist in Fanon's argument: "This, perversely, was also his route to a hesitant universalism and, perhaps eventually, to the evasive new humanism that he wrote so fondly, so urgently, and so inspirationally about."[77] What Gilroy finds, at the end of this process, is quite different from what he described in *Against Race* as "the Third World's initiating a new, less triumphalist humanism that can be its own special gift to civilization."[78] By contrast, what he discovers in his reading of Fanon in *Postcolonial Melancholia* is a radically new (and difficult) humanist strategy brought from the future:

> In Fanon's optimistic scheme, this second, transitional formation yields eventually to a wider consciousness that can break with the alienated logic of epidermalization and open up oppositional, and for the first time fully human consciousness to a wider range of ethical and political sensibilities. This outcome, which, as I have said, is not the third term in a dialectical movement, is also spattered with blood. It provides a reminder that the association of blackness and whiteness is not just a site of ontological obstacles to the emergence of disalienated human consciousness among the oppressed and

> victimized (which was Fanon's primary concern). He also recognizes that dominance can carry its own wounds, even if they are veiled in colonial privilege and postcolonial melancholia.[79]

Gilroy goes so far as to mark this opening as the beginning of "the revolutionary stage that marks the end of 'race.'"[80]

One striking aspect of Gilroy's latest reading of Fanon is that he sees him as an exemplary figure, not just in the recasting of a new form of humanism but also in fighting against a contemporary tendency toward "scholastic reflection." Gilroy diagnoses in this scholarly orientation a turn away from antiracist politics, which has largely, he argues, been replaced by "polite" academic analyses of race. In place of this polite scholarly work, Gilroy puts forth a model of intellectual labor with a strong orientation toward practical solidarity. Gilroy is well aware that like many of the other strategic concepts he embraces in his recent work—antiracism, humanism, universalism, cosmopolitanism—"solidarity" is a highly contested term. As he notes in a section of *Postcolonial Melancholia* entitled "Solidarity Becomes Suspect": "These days, much of what passes for radical and critical thought rests on the notion that the very aspiration toward translocal solidarity, community, and interconnection is tainted. This is because it is a symptom of imperial arrogance and the mainspring of a violent ethnocentrism."[81] Gilroy's conclusions about the current political and intellectual landscape leave us with a seemingly depressing choice "between the hypersimilarity of clone identity (operating on several scales: race, nation, or ethnic group) or a different position, which abandons those forms of seriality in favor of a radically individualistic view of humanity that makes any collective identity arbitrary, transitional, and, most important, politically irrelevant."[82] The most influential version of the latter of these two unacceptable choices would be the "placeless consumer culture" that Gilroy confronts throughout his work;[83] the former position is best expressed in the new form of liberal common sense that maintains it is "easier to feel solidarity with those who broadly share your values and way of life," with apparently little concern that in such a homogenous context, the very notion of "solidarity" becomes all but meaningless.[84]

While Gilroy takes these various arguments against translocal solidarity seriously, he ultimately, and not surprisingly, refuses the terms of this supposed choice. He does so by once again moving simultaneously into the past and the future. In part, this involves the reconstructive labor of reinvigorating the impulses of socialist and feminist movements that "understood political solidarity to require translocal connections" and "turned away from the patriotism of national states because they had found larger loyalties."[85] He also proposes a rereading and reevaluation of the life and work of George Orwell, finding there forms of "cosmopolitan affiliations . . . articulated in strict harmony with Orwell's parochial attachments to England's distinctive environment."[86] His reading of Orwell gives Gilroy the opportunity to prove that he does not mean to leave traditional notions of solidarity untouched, especially in the face of the failures of what he calls "actually existing internationalism."[87] Indeed, he insists that Orwell's cosmic outlook (and, by extension, Gilroy's own) should not be understood as a "narrow brand of internationalism."[88] In fact, Gilroy expresses his particular variation on solidarity through the introduction of the term "translocal," which implies the possibility of attachments to locations and communities either larger than, or smaller than, those provided by the nation-state: it is from this perspective that Orwell's "parochialism," for example, is given a positive valence. Gilroy thereby rejects the more conventional term "transnational solidarity"; like his vision of antiracism, whose goal is not only to oppose racism but to leave the very idea of "race" in the past, Gilroy's model of solidarity not only opposes nationalism but refuses to even countenance the nation-state as a possible site from which the strategy of solidarity might be operated.

Dorothy Roberts, in her review of *Postcolonial Melancholia*, argues that in setting out his claims for translocal solidarity and the related principle that he calls "conviviality," Gilroy largely "discounts black solidarity as a morally viable path to antiracist democracy":

> The most telling evidence of Gilroy's dismissal of blacks' strategic role in antiracist struggle is the complete absence of people of color from the discussion of multicultural conviviality that occupies the book's second half. Gilroy relies heavily on the universalist leanings of W. E. B. Du Bois and Fanon in building his argument for planetary humanism and calls for a revival of "those elements of black political culture that are, like Du Bois, tolerant, humane, pluralistic, and cosmopolitan in outlook." Yet his illustrations of convivial metropolitan culture and transnational solidarity upon which he pins his hopes all involve white people.[89]

This is part of Roberts's defense of particular aspects of black nationalist thought (although her defense is hardly an unambivalent one). It is interesting in this context that Roberts herself uses the term "transnational," rather than "translocal," to describe the model of solidarity that she proposes as preferable to that set out by Gilroy: "A movement grounded in new forms of black solidarity that discard racial (and sexist) thinking, adopt a universal outlook, and solicit transnational coalitions is a more imaginative project with greater chance of defeating racism."[90] Gilroy's recent, caustic dismissal of such claims—specifically, of Roberts's questioning of "why the Enlightenment concept of humanism is capable of redemption from its colonial European pedigree whereas nationalism is not"—provides a good sense of his complete impatience with any and all nationalist models: "Nobody ever got killed in the name of cosmopolitanism."[91]

While Gilroy's pithy statement here makes for a satisfying rejoinder to Roberts, things may be a bit more complex: it all depends, for example, on how one defines "cosmopolitanism" and, for that matter, how one traces its relationship to what has been called, sometimes interchangeably, sometimes not, "internationalism." In an odd way, Gilroy's statement echoes (perhaps unconsciously) Benedict Anderson's point, in *Imagined Communities*, about the specific form of affective relationship produced by nationalism, including the willingness to die for the sake of the nation; by way of contrast, Anderson asks, "Who will willingly die for Comecon or the EEC [the European Economic Community, precursor to the present European Union]?"[92] In response, Bruce Robbins notes that such a response contains the danger of "dispos[ing] of the Abraham Lincoln Brigade, Amnesty International, and Médecins sans Frontières, allowing the internationalist or cosmopolitan to become a sub- or inhuman subject unwilling to die for anything—floating, without material base or emotional attachment to others, insubstantial."[93] Indeed, some of the participants in the forms of translocal solidarity that Gilroy celebrates in *Postcolonial Melancholia* have in fact died in the name of what might be called "cosmopolitanism," whether or not they would have named it as such. This is to say that in the future work inspired by Gilroy's, it may be necessary to better specify the various forms of affiliation demanded by nationalism, versus the new and different forms of freely given cosmopolitan affiliations and commitments that might come into existence through the strategy of planetary humanism.[94]

What happens when we introduce Fanon into this particular dispute about the grounding of political solidarity between nationalism and cosmopolitanism? Roberts is not wrong to note that Fanon, like Du Bois, is a more significant figure in the first half of *Postcolonial Melancholia* than in the second half of the book; while I hardly agree that he simply disappears once Gilroy begins to unfold his arguments about solidarity, Fanon is not specifically cited to help illustrate the particular strategy of translocal solidarity in the same way Orwell is. And it is certainly true that Fanon has often been called upon to bolster arguments for various forms of anti-imperialist, third-world nationalism. This is the Fanon for whom the development of "national culture" and "national consciousness" is a necessary step in the fight against the Manichaean violence of colonialism. Although he does not directly cite Fanon, a similar claim also lies behind the accusation of Don Robotham, who, in arguing that Gilroy "offers to replace nationalism with 'planetary humanism,'" accuses him of thereby "seek[ing] a unilateral political disarmament by the black community."[95]

Fanon's own support for national liberation movements, in his writing as in his life, is of course undeniable, and it represents a crucial current that runs through *The Wretched of the Earth*. However, there is always a complexity at work in these engagements: as with his arguments regarding colonial Manichaeism and anticolonial responses to it, Fanon's full argument regarding nationalism leads to his final position on humanism, a position that must be seen as ultimately nonnationalist without simply falling into a more traditional internationalism. As he insists at the end of the chapter "On National Culture," "National consciousness, which is not nationalism, is alone capable of giving us an international dimension."[96] Just as important, moreover, contemporary strategic thinking about translocal solidarity necessitates a full reckoning with Fanon's own ambivalent and complex place in the Algerian Revolution, as a French colonial subject from Martinique who first came to Algeria on an appointment from the French government. Fanon was thus an outsider fighting alongside his Algerian comrades against the French. Furthermore, he also found himself at a distance from many of the other outsiders in the revolution—that is, Europeans who had switched sides—in that he was perceived as being neither French nor Algerian—in being, in short, a black man and French colonial subject fighting in Algeria. This is hardly the expression of a spontaneous anticolonial nationalist fervor; rather, it represents a conscious act of translocal solidarity. Édouard Glissant, one of the few theorists to consider Fanon's participation in the Algerian Revolution in this light, makes this point by placing Fanon's commitment to Algeria in a specifically Caribbean context:

> ambiguity, discontinuity, traces, and remembering, creolization, with its unpredictable results, are not signs of weakness. They contribute to this unprecedented conception of identity that I have been discussing. . . . It is not a coincidence that so many people in the West Indies dedicated themselves to the Other: for example, the

> Jamaican Marcus Garvey in the United States, or the Trinidadian Padmore in Ghana, or the Martinican Fanon in Algeria. Open and strong identity is also a strong solidarity.[97]

Fanon's commitment to Algeria, in other words, offers a model of explicitly translocal solidarity that demands further examination in the contemporary context.

Indeed, Fanon's model of solidarity provides an interesting parallel to those whom Gilroy invokes as his most concrete contemporary example: "the growing band of people who opt to bear active witness to distant suffering and even to place their lives at risk in many parts of the world as human shields." In upholding the work of these international solidarity activists, Gilroy argues that "their practical answer to imperialism, racism, and the narcissism of minor differences mobilizes the invaluable solidarity of the slightly different" and, in the process, "represent[s] the undoing of identity politics."[98] This invocation by Gilroy provokes one of Roberts's sharpest critiques: "The most stunning example of privileging (white) cosmopolitanism over nationalist solidarity is Gilroy's celebration of European and American members of an international movement in the Gaza Strip."[99] Against Gilroy's claim that these activists are agents of "a translocal commitment to the alleviation of suffering and to the practical transfiguration of democracy which is incompatible with racism and ethnic absolutism," Roberts argues that the "significance" of their actions "can only be evaluated in relation to the Palestinians' nationalist struggle and not solely the white activists' 'impulses toward experience, suffering, injustice and truth.'"[100] There is a great deal at stake in this disagreement, not least the accusations raised by critics such as Roberts, and expressed in polemical terms by Robotham, that Gilroy's cosmopolitan strategy of planetary humanism is simply "a reformulation by a black scholar of the 'color-blind' position" held to by a more traditional humanism.[101] That Gilroy's and Roberts's disagreement over the strategy of solidarity is played out in the context of arguably the most contentious conflict of the contemporary world—the situation conventionally described as "the Israeli-Palestinian conflict"—adds, needless to say, another layer of significance. So in moving toward my conclusion, I attempt to bring Gilroy's planetary humanist strategy to bear on the question of solidarity in Israel-Palestine, an issue that has become increasingly central in Gilroy's work.[102] It is not only the case, as Roberts suggests, that Gilroy puts forth the international Palestine solidarity movement as a paradigmatic example of translocal solidarity in *Postcolonial Melancholia*. He also dedicates the book to the memory of Rachel Corrie and

Thomas Hurndall, solidarity activists who both died at the hands of Israeli forces in occupied Gaza in 2003. Just as Fanon is invoked at the outset of *Against Race* and provides an overarching framework for that text, I would argue that we must see Corrie and Hurndall as the guiding spirits of *Postcolonial Melancholia*.

The rethinking of the situation in Israel-Palestine as a site for global antiracist struggle, as I would argue that Gilroy does in his latest work, both comes out of and interestingly complicates his years-long examination of the place of Zionism as a concept within black Atlantic discourse. It also links interestingly to Gilroy's and Fanon's shared concern to address the overlapping relationship between anti-Semitism and racism in traditional Western versions of "humanism." In coming to the end of his argument in *The Black Atlantic*—and, I would argue, in beginning to set out the thinking and strategy that inform the development of his strategy of planetary humanism in his later work—Gilroy insists on the necessity of understanding and appreciating the links between the birth of modern Zionism and the development of modern black political thought. These connections range from the introduction of the term "diaspora" into the vocabulary of black studies and the practice of Pan-Africanist politics from its centuries-old place in Jewish thought, to the influence of the Zionist movement upon the aspirations and rhetoric of modern black nationalist thought.[103] Gilroy points insistently to the productive inspiration provided by the Zionist tradition for generations of blacks struggling against slavery and its legacy; from the perspective of political strategy, he questions the contemporary Pan-Africanist turn away from the powerful identification with the Exodus narrative of slavery and forced dispersal into the diaspora, and the concomitant tendency "to identify far more readily with the glamorous pharaohs than with the abject plight of those they held in bondage."[104]

In a particularly moving passage, Gilroy notes that this productive dialogue between two traditions with links to slavery and diaspora has a specifically personal nature for him:

> In the preparation of this book I have been repeatedly drawn to the work of Jewish thinkers in order to find both inspiration and resources with which to map the ambivalent experiences of blacks inside and outside modernity. I want to acknowledge these debts openly in the hope that in some small way the link they reveal might contribute to a better political relationship between Jews and blacks at some distant future point.[105]

The political strategy expressed in the final sentence of this quote also guides Gilroy's critical strategy of reading Toni Morrison's *Beloved* alongside the legacy of the Holocaust so as to inquire into the possibilities of an approach that would "set the Holocaust of European Jews in a provocative relationship with the modern history of racial slavery and terror in the western hemisphere." Gilroy concludes this discussion by suggesting that setting these two histories closer together could provide "precious resources from which we might learn something valuable about the way that modernity operates . . . and perhaps most importantly about the ideologies of humanism with which these brutal histories can be shown to have been complicit."[106] In moving, as I have argued he does, from a sympathetic but still quite critical examination of "the ideologies of humanism" in *The Black Atlantic* to the active championing of a new strategy of planetary humanism in his later work, this particular moment—specifically the effort to critically link the legacies of the struggle against anti-Semitism with those of the struggle against racism—represents an important first step toward a newly transformed and transformative humanist strategy. Indeed, Gilroy makes a similar point in his recent piece "Multiculture and the Negative Dialectics of Conviviality," where he notes the influence of the writings of Holocaust survivors Primo Levi and Jean Améry, alongside "various other observers of and commentators on the pathologies of European civilization," to help him produce work that "has aimed to answer the corrosive allure of absolute sameness and purity just as they did, with a historical and moral commitment to the political, ethical and educational potential of near-universal human *shame*."[107]

In this sense, it is not surprising that *Against Race* begins by picking up this link between anti-Semitism and racism, by way of Fanon, and outlining a strategy that could connect the struggles against both. In this sense, Gilroy is drawing on the precedent of anticolonial thinkers like Fanon, Césaire, Beauvoir, and Sartre, who understood the history of Nazism and fascism as "European colonialism brought home to Europe."[108] If the anti-Semitism carried out in Europe (and not only by fascist parties) can be linked to the racist degradations carried out in the colonies—and if, to move into Gilroy's contemporary argument, we can link both these histories to continuing forms of racism, xenophobia, and Islamophobia in Europe and North America—then we have the delineation of a global antiracist strategy that can be operated in the name of planetary humanism. This is why Fanon's insistent refusal of Octave Mannoni's argument that colonial racism was essentially unique in its nature remains crucial for current thinking about antiracism. Against Mannoni, Fanon insisted upon the indivisibility of racism (and thus, necessarily, of an antiracist response), whether in its metropolitan or colonial forms; his rebuttal makes a specific link between colonial racism and European anti-Semitism:

> Colonial racism is no different from other racisms.
>
> Anti-Semitism cuts me to the quick; I get upset; a frightful rage makes me anemic; they are denying me the right to be a man. I cannot disassociate myself from the fate reserved for my brother. Every one of my acts commits me as a man. Every instance of my reticence, every instance of my cowardice, manifests the man.[109]

As Brian Cheyette points out, here, "in exemplary fashion," Fanon "is articulating a sense of justice which is universalized beyond racial difference." To this end, Fanon cites Maryse Choisy's description of the guilt experienced by those who remained neutral during the Nazi occupation of France and subsequently "felt responsible for all those dead and all the Buchenwalds."[110] This is the antiracist strategy that Gilroy discerns, not just in the postwar writings of those like Fanon and Césaire who wrote from within the experience of colonial racism but also in the work of Sartre and Hannah Arendt, work "aimed at comprehending the fragmentation of humankind into racial groups and preventing the recurrence of genocide."[111] This work, which is the anti-racist component of the strategy of planetary humanism, continues to call to us and takes on particular importance in our contemporary moment when, as Gilroy takes pains to point out, we have witnessed a "revival of imperialism," this time in a form that presents itself as "benign, progressive, and liberal"—and, naturally, cleansed of the racism that defined the earlier era of European imperialism.[112] This revival of imperialism is most evident in the Bush-Blair doctrine of "democratization" by force, which comes complete with its own human rights rhetoric and whose deadly effects continue to be felt by the occupied peoples of Iraq and Afghanistan. There is therefore a continued need for an insistence, in the name of antiracist thinking and politics, that the "new" imperialism is indistinguishable from the "old" version, not just in its bloody effects but also in terms of an explicit racialist thinking that designates certain groups as "infrahuman" (to use Gilroy's term) and thus as potential objects of conquest and occupation. Fanon's demand that we feel "responsible for all those dead" continues to reverberate in our own time.

This is one reason why the situation in Palestine represents such a complex and controversial problem for the conceptualization of a global antiracist theory and politics. After all, by its own account, the state of Israel was established precisely as a response to the genocidal "fragmentation of humankind into racial groups" carried out in the European Holocaust. Even those who may not be particularly sympathetic to specific policies carried out by successive Israeli governments—in particular, those relating to the illegal occupation of the West Bank and Gaza since 1967—tend to accept the thesis that the culmination of the modern Zionist project in the establishment of the state of Israel should be understood as a direct response to the European Holocaust on the part of the world community. In this sense, the establishment of the state of Israel has been seen as a specifically antiracist project. By and large, this position has continued to affect the thinking of those who wish to link the battle against anti-Semitism with antiracism: Sartre himself, for example, was a vocal supporter of Israel during the Six-Day War in 1967 (a war that led, of course, to the beginning of the Israeli occupation of the West Bank and Gaza), which in turn led Fanon's widow, Josie Fanon, to demand the removal of Sartre's foreword from future editions of *The Wretched of the Earth* out of protest for his position.[113] This could stand as a paradigmatic example of the seeming conundrum facing progressive antiracist politics: how to support a nation-building project that has been understood as aimed at providing reparations to the victims of genocidal anti-Semitism, on the one hand, while at the same time also supporting the rights of Palestinians, who, since 1948, have suffered forced displacement, refugee status, unequal citizenship rights (for those Palestinians living in Israel), and, since 1967, military occupation, as a result of the establishment and subsequent actions of the state of Israel.

In this context, it is worth noting Gilroy's formula for describing the establishment of the state of Israel in Palestine in 1948: "a novel historical experiment in both nation building and colonization as reparation."[114] Gilroy links this project to two other roughly contemporary projects that mark the postwar moment: the partition of India in 1947 and the establishment of an apartheid state in South Africa in 1948. As he points out, "All of these events are linked directly to the history and decomposition of the British Empire. All involved the deployment of separatist political technologies, and all of them speak to the currency and limits of racialized governance with great power because the shadow cast over politics and government by the Third Reich was so profound."[115] In this sense, Gilroy's point in placing the establishment of the state of Israel alongside two other projects with more explicit colonial and racialized dynamics reminds us of the long colonial history of Palestine: without the backing of the colonial powers (especially Britain and, subsequently, the United States), the Zionist project could never have culminated in a state-building project.[116] Furthermore, there is a direct and consistent line in Gilroy's thinking, from a linking of the aspirations and influences of the modern Zionist and black nationalist movements to a consistent opposition to the specifically nationalist projects set out by both these movements (with more territorial success, obviously, in the case of Zionism). While the aspirations that underwrite these movements elicit Gilroy's sympathy, in that they represent responses in the battle against racism and anti-Semitism, his opposition to the nationalist form that these movements take, and the resultant militarist ideology that they adopt, is an explicit part of his larger strategy of a cosmopolitan, planetary humanism. In both cases, what is being contested is the attempt to recoup antiracist thought and action under the name of nationalism.

While Gilroy does not specifically address the attempt by the state of Israel to become the official repository and representative of the global postwar response to anti-Semitism, his critique of the attempt of black nationalist movements to monopolize the legacy of antiracism provides us with a template for a critique of similar attempts by the Israeli government. This argument was explicitly, and eloquently, set out by Andrew Benjamin during the Israeli offensive against Lebanon in 2006. Benjamin writes not only in protest of Israeli state policies but also "as a Jew and as a synagogue member [and] . . . as one whose academic work continues to move through questions of Jewish identity and the legacy of the Holocaust."[117] He notes "the perverse logic" through which responses to the policies and practices of the state of Israel have sometimes been used to explain and justify anti-Semitic attacks on Jewish communities outside Israel, such as attacks on synagogues, Jewish cultural centers, and Jewish cemeteries. This, he argues, "attests to the victory of those who have linked and continue to link being a Jew to Israel and thus for those who conflate Judaism and Zionism." One consequence, as he notes, is that anti-Semitic actions can be rationalized as protests against Israeli state practices. As Benjamin puts it, "These attacks are the result of the politics of a nation state," and in this specific sense, "Israel, in its present manifestation, sustains anti-Semitism."

But, as Benjamin goes on to point out, there is another consequence of this linkage between Judaism and Zionism: "a critique of Zionism or a disagreement over the policies of Israel are taken at best as a criticism of Jews and, at worst, as anti-Semitic." Benjamin notes the foundational argument of Israel's supporters, that "the Holocaust has made the state of Israel a necessity: a state was needed so that such events [would] not happen again," and he goes on to add: "State creation always displaces a people. And the results of that founding displacement should always be acknowledged, understood and in the end resolved." Benjamin here tacitly reminds us of the largely unacknowledged, and often genocidal, practices of settler colonialism in many parts of the world, including Australia, the location from which he writes, as well as the United States. "However," he continues, "what endures for many as an outrage is Israel hijacking the Holocaust for its political ends: the Holocaust is used to sustain a specific geo-political situation." In view of the specific political context out of which Benjamin writes, he insists, "questions need to be asked. What right does a national government have to speak on behalf of those who died? What sanctions the deploying of that legacy in order to justify the bombing of Lebanon?" He concludes: "Understanding the Holocaust, tracing its impact upon how we think today, is a project that endures. Moreover, it is a project that resists easy summation. The idea that it can figure as an element of state policy is both an intellectual and ethical scandal. This needs to be said."

We might add, with Fanon, "Enough of this scandal." One crucial aspect of Benjamin's critique is that it offers a reminder of the long and ongoing debate among Jewish thinkers—many of them intensely dedicated to battling anti-Semitism and racism—around the question of whether or not to support the Zionist project.[118] It also allows us to examine in a frank and open manner the restrictions placed upon academic discussions related to Palestine-Israel and the modes by which intellectual debate has often been stifled or silenced.[119] In keeping with his disdain for merely "polite" scholarship, this is the contentious context into which Gilroy's recent work plunges us; it is a context that those who have been involved with Palestine solidarity work have come to know intimately. One crucial response to the accusation that criticisms of policies pursued by the Israeli government or support for the aspirations of Palestinian communities amounts to a form of anti-Semitism has been to insist on the antiracist nature of the international Palestine solidarity movement. As Sherene Seikaly writes in an article posted on the website of the American organization Jews Against the Occupation:

> we are struck once again by the extent to which we are asked to disprove our anti-Semitism before we can even begin to be understood as legitimate by the mainstream discourse. This is despite the explicit diversity, the stands against the targeting of innocent civilians (Palestinian and Israeli), and the well-developed foundations of anti-racism that we draw on from various social movements. In effect, these accusations attempt to morally delegitimize our work and silence our criticism of Zionism and Israeli policy. At the same time, while we

> defend ourselves, we are left pondering: why is it that at no point are individuals and institutions who uncritically support Israeli occupation publicly asked to demonstrate their own anti-racism?[120]

What is at stake, in other words, is the place of Palestine-Israel within a global antiracist politics.

This is one reason why Gilroy's intervention in *Postcolonial Melancholia* is so crucial and so potentially productive: by citing the international Palestine solidarity movement as his paradigmatic example of a contemporary form of translocal solidarity, he places this movement squarely within "the history of suffering, rebellion, and dissidence" that has produced antiracist thinking and action and that has come down to us in the present not "through the temperate landscape of liberal pieties" but rather "via disreputable abolitionism and translocal, multicultural, and anti-imperial activism that was allied with the insurrectionary practice of those who, though legally held in bondage, were subject to the larger immoralities of a race-friendly system of domination."[121] This provides an important rejoinder to those who would question the antiracist credentials of the "disreputable" Palestine solidarity movement. It is also one reason for defending Gilroy's cosmopolitan perspective against those who, like Roberts, would reduce these forms of translocal solidarity to straightforward acts of "solidarity with their [i.e., Palestinians'] struggle for national liberation"[122]—as though there existed such a unitary thing as a "Palestinian struggle for national liberation." Such a position merely replicates the accusations of the movement's critics, that those committed to a vision of justice in Israel-Palestine can be dismissed as simply "pro-Palestine" (and therefore "anti-Israel") partisans rather than seeing them as part of a larger, more complex and more cosmopolitan global antiracist movement with a full potential that is yet to be realized.

Here it is worth noting one specific line from an email written by Rachel Corrie to her parents shortly before her death, a letter that Gilroy quotes at length as part of his discussion: "Just feel sick to my stomach a lot from being doted on all the time, very sweetly, by people who are facing doom."[123] There is a striking parallel to the words used by Fanon to describe his physical reaction, his nausea and sense of being rendered "anemic," upon witnessing the dehumanizing effects of anti-Semitism. Similarly, both give voice to the pain occasioned by a fully ethical reaction to this dehumanization: "Anti-Semitism cuts me to the quick," Fanon writes, "It really hurts me, again, like it hurt me in the past, to witness how awful we allow the world to be." Corrie responds, and her subsequent actions taken in solidarity with occupied Palestinians in

Gaza are in tune with Fanon's conclusion: "I cannot disassociate myself from the fate reserved for my brother."[124] The link here is not merely a rhetorical one; the shared form of solidarity, over geographical space as well as across the borders of identity, is occasioned by bearing witness to the specifically racialized suffering of the other and the subsequent realization of a direct sense of responsibility for this suffering, and, more important, for its alleviation. This is not to say that the racialized suffering of Palestinians—as the Palestinian poet Mourid Barghouti has pointed out, official Israeli military and governmental discourse about Palestinians includes such familiar dehumanizing tropes as comparisons to vermin, parasites, cockroaches, and cancerous viruses[125]—is somehow identical to the suffering of Jews who were made the objects of a genocidal anti-Semitism. It is simply to assert, as a crucial underpinning for a cosmopolitan strategy of planetary humanism, that as witnesses to both forms of suffering—not to mention countless other examples of such racialized, dehumanizing attacks—we bear responsibility for them and are in turn affected by them (bodily, in the cases of Fanon and Corrie). What we do once we find ourselves summoned by this sense of responsibility is a question of whether a future after "race" will be on the agenda or not.

This question, I would say by way of conclusion, may be the test of whether Fanon's and Gilroy's shared strategy of a planetary humanism can indeed mark itself as different from the forms of humanism that have gone before. Fanon, in the conclusion to *The Wretched of the Earth*, calls upon a set of comrades composed of those described in the book's title: the dispossessed, the damned, the wretched, the colonized, the racialized "others." Sartre, in his preface to the book, addressed specifically to the book's European readers, cannily suggests that Fanon's words can nevertheless be understood to have the potential to constitute an even more encompassing planetary audience:

> What does Fanon care if you read or don't read his book? It is for his brothers he denounces our old box of mischief. . . . In that case, you say, let's throw this book out of the window. Why bother to read it since it is not meant for us? . . . because Fanon analyzes you for his brothers and demolishes for them the mechanism of our alienations. Take advantage of it to discover your true self as an object. Our victims know us by their wounds and shackles: that is what makes their testimony irrefutable. They only need to know what we have done to them to realize what we have done to ourselves. . . . I, a European, am stealing my enemy's book and turning it into a way of healing Europe. Make the most of it.[126]

In *Against Race*, Gilroy is critical of the "dualism" expressed by Fanon in his call for a new humanism at the end of *The Wretched of the Earth* and of what he sees as Fanon's assumption that the Third World would initiate "a new, less triumphalist humanism that can be its own special gift to civilization."[127] Revisiting these questions in *Postcolonial Melancholia*, Gilroy eloquently expresses the possibility of a truly planetary movement that can become the inheritor of that legacy bequeathed by the antiracist and anticolonial movements in which Fanon participated and for which he has been such an important inspiration:

> At this point, colonial and postcolonial folks can acquire a distinctive mission. Our modern history as disenchanted descendants of people who were themselves commodified for sale on an international market or deemed expendable within the larger racial logic of Europe-centered historical processes gives us ready access to a fund of knowledge that is useful in a number of areas. These insights are not ours alone but will belong to anybody who is prepared to use them. This history of suffering, rebellion, and dissidence is not our intellectual property, and we are not defenders of cultural and experiential copyright. Any lessons that can be derived from the histories we have made can furnish resources for the future of this planet. Those lessons do not, of course, aim to redeem past suffering or make it worthwhile. Their very failure to be productive in this way helps to specify that they should be available to anybody who dares, in good faith, to try and set them to work in pursuit of justice.[128]

Like Fanon, Gilroy calls upon a set of "comrades" ("colonial and postcolonial folks") as the initial audience for his annunciation of a new humanist strategy. But also like Fanon, his larger strategy opens up into a call for a complete disalienation of all the participants in colonialism and racism—victims and perpetrators alike—and a call to all of us who are the descendants of this history. This new form of humanist strategy does not rest, as does a humanism built upon traditional liberal universalism, on the prior assumption that "we" all share a common humanity that transcends specific contexts. Instead, it gambles on the possibility that this shared humanity, which resists the constraints of national, racial, or other forms of identity, will emerge precisely in the struggle against "the alienated sociality that absorbs the cries of those who suffer by making them sound less human."[129]

Notes

1. David Macey, who includes this quote in his magisterial biography of Fanon, notes that "Enough of this scandal" (*Assez de ce scandale*) is a quotation from Aimé Césaire's *Notebook of a Return to My Native Land.* David Macey, *Frantz Fanon: A Biography* (New York: Picador, 2002), 534 n.11.
2. Paul Gilroy, *The Black Atlantic: Modernity and Double Consciousness* (Cambridge: Harvard University Press, 1993), 45. Paul Gilroy, *Postcolonial Melancholia* (New York: Columbia University Press, 2005), 150.
3. Gilroy, *The Black Atlantic*, xi.
4. Gilroy, *The Black Atlantic*, 5, 225 n.3.
5. Paul Gilroy, *Small Acts: Thoughts on the Politics of Black Cultures* (London: Serpent's Tail, 1993), 24. Paul Gilroy, *'There Ain't No Black in the Union Jack': The Cultural Politics of Race and Nation* (Chicago: University of Chicago Press, 1991), 40.
6. Max Farrar, "Paul Gilroy in Conversation," darkmatter: postcolonial futures. 7 May 2007. 3.
7. Frantz Fanon, *Black Skin White Masks*, trans. Charles Lam Markmann (New York: Grove Press, 1967), 101, quoted in *Against Race*, 1. Here, and in other places where I cite Gilroy's own citations of Fanon, I follow him in using Charles Lam Markmann's translation of *Black Skin, White Masks*. Elsewhere, I will be citing Richard Philcox's superior 2008 translation of the book (New York: Grove), which was, of course, unavailable to Gilroy at the time he was writing *Against Race* and *Postcolonial Melancholia*.
8. Paul Gilroy, *Against Race: Imagining Political Culture Beyond the Color Line* (Cambridge: Harvard University Press, 2001), 1.
9. Ibid., 15.
10. Ibid., 15; the quote is from *Black Skin, White Masks*, 42.
11. Fanon, *Black Skin, White Masks*, xii–xiv.
12. Ibid., xiv–xv.
13. Fanon, *The Wretched of the Earth*, trans. Richard Philcox (New York: Grove, 2004), 5.
14. Gilroy, *Postcolonial Melancholia*, 53.
15. Gilroy, *Against Race*, 15–16.
16. Gilroy, *Postcolonial Melancholia*, 40.
17. Michel Foucault, "What Is Enlightenment?" trans. Catherine Porter, in *The Foucault Reader*, ed. Paul Rabinow (New York: Vintage, 1984), 50.

18. I have made this connection between Foucault and Fanon at much greater length elsewhere. See Anthony C. Alessandrini, "The Humanism Effect: Fanon, Foucault, and Ethics without Subjects," *Foucault Studies* 7 (2009): 64–80. See also Anthony C. Alessandrini, "Introduction: Fanon Studies, Cultural Studies, Cultural Politics," in *Frantz Fanon: Critical Perspectives*, ed. Anthony C. Alessandrini (New York: Routledge, 1999), 1–17.
19. Gilroy, *Against Race*, 5–6.
20. Ibid., 336.
21. Ibid., 332.
22. Ibid., 335.
23. Ibid., 5. See also Robert J. C. Young, *White Mythologies: Writing History and the West* (New York: Routledge, 1990) and Robert J. C. Young, "Return to Moosburg: Sharing War Memories with Paul Gilroy," *Textual Practice* 17 (2003): 7–19.
24. Macey, *Frantz Fanon*, 103–04.
25. Quoted in ibid., 88.
26. Gilroy, *Against Race*, 336.
27. Macey, *Frantz Fanon*, 88.
28. Fanon, *Black Skin, White Masks*, 163.
29. Gilroy, *Against Race*, 70.
30. Ibid., 71.
31. Aimé Césaire, *Discourse on Colonialism*, trans. Joan Pinkham (New York: Monthly Review Press, 1972), 36. Quoted in *Black Skin, White Masks*, 71.
32. Gilroy, *Against Race*, 71.
33. Quoted in Fanon, *Black Skin, White Masks*, 70.
34. Gilroy, *Against Race*, 3–4, emphases in original.
35. Aiden Jones, "Rightwing and Anti-Fascist Protesters Riot in London," *The Guardian*, 11 September 2009, 1. See also Paul Gilroy, "A Land of Tea Drinking, Hokey Cokey and Rivers of Blood," *The Guardian*, 18 April 2008.
36. Gilroy, *Against Race*, 356.
37. Ibid., 335.
38. Ibid., 336.
39. Fanon, *Black Skin, White Masks*, 204–05, as quoted in Gilroy, *Against Race*, 336.
40. Gilroy, *Against Race*, 336.
41. Ibid.
42. Fanon, *Black Skin, White Masks, xii*.

43. Ibid., 197, emphasis in original.
44. Ibid., 197.
45. Ibid., 206.
46. Gilroy, *Against Race*, 347 and 355.
47. Theodor Adorno, *The Stars Down to Earth and Other Essays on the Irrational in Culture*, ed. Stephen Crook (New York: Routledge, 1994), 45. See also Anthony C. Alessandrini, "Reading the Future," *Cultural Studies* 17 (2003): 211–29.
48. Fanon, *The Wretched of the Earth*, 239.
49. Gilroy, *Against Race*, 248.
50. Ibid.
51. Ibid., 253.
52. Frantz Fanon, *A Dying Colonialism*, trans. Haakon Chevalier (New York: Grove, 1967).
53. Alessandrini, "The Humanism Effect," 71–74.
54. Fanon, *The Wretched of the Earth*, 93–94.
55. Ibid., 235.
56. Ibid., 238.
57. Richard Wright, *White Man, Listen!* (Westport, CT: Greenwood, 1978), 87, quoted in *Against Race*, 340.
58. Ibid., 79.
59. Fanon, *The Wretched of the Earth*, 239.
60. Gilroy, *Postcolonial Melancholia*, 40.
61. Ibid.
62. Ibid., 41.
63. Gilroy, *Postcolonial Melancholia*, 41. This is one of the few places where Gilroy cites the work of Wynter. Although space does not permit a further discussion of this point, her own struggle with and reconceptualization of humanism could be put into fruitful dialogue with Gilroy's strategy of planetary humanism. For more on Wynter's strategic humanism, see her texts, "The Ceremony Must Be Found: After Humanism," *boundary 2* 12–13 (1984): 19–70; "On Disenchanting Discourse: 'Minority' Literary Criticism and Beyond," *Cultural Critique* 7 (1987): 207–44; and "Unsettling the Coloniality of Being/Power/Truth/Freedom Towards the Human, After Man, Its Overrepresentation—An Argument," *CR: The New Centennial Review* 3 (2003): 257–337. See also David Scott, "The Re-Enchantment of Humanism: An Interview with Sylvia Wynter," *Small Axe* 8 (2000): 119–207.
64. Gilroy, *Postcolonial Melancholia*.

65. Ibid., 34–35.
66. Ibid., 35.
67. Frantz Fanon, *Toward the African Revolution*, trans. Haakon Chevalier (New York: Grove, 1988), 18, quoted in Gilroy, *Postcolonial Melancholia*, 41. For a rather different (and not altogether convincing) attempt to bring together Du Bois and Fanon, specifically around the concept of "double consciousness," see T. O. Moore, "A Fanonian Perspective on Double Consciousness," *Journal of Black Studies* 35 (2005): 751–62.
68. Gilroy, *Postcolonial Melancholia*, 42.
69. Ibid.
70. Ibid., emphasis in original.
71. Fanon, *Black Skin, White Masks*, xvi.
72. Gilroy, *Postcolonial Melancholia*, 51.
73. Fanon, *The Wretched of the Earth*, 2, emphasis in original.
74. Gilroy, *Postcolonial Melancholia*, 50, emphasis in original.
75. Fanon, *The Wretched of the Earth*, 4.
76. Gilroy, *Postcolonial Melancholia*, 52.
77. Ibid., 51.
78. Gilroy, *Against Race*, 253.
79. Gilroy, *Postcolonial Melancholia*, 52.
80. Ibid.
81. Ibid., 63.
82. Ibid., 63–64.
83. Gilroy, *Against Race*, 346.
84. Alan Wolfe and Jytte Klausen, "Other People," *Prospect* (December 2000): 30. Quoted in Gilroy, *Postcolonial Melancholia*, 146.
85. Gilroy, *Postcolonial Melancholia*, 5.
86. Ibid., 76–77.
87. Ibid., 5.
88. Ibid., 77.
89. Dorothy Roberts, "A World without Race: Does Black Nationalism Have to Go Too?" *Boston Review* (January/February 2006): 34.
90. Ibid., 35.
91. Paul Gilroy, "Multiculture and the Negative Dialectics of Conviviality," chapter 4 in this volume.
92. Benedict Anderson, *Imagined Communities: Reflections on the Origins and Spread of Nationalism* (New York: Verso, 1983), 55.
93. Bruce Robbins, *Feeling Global: Internationalism in Distress* (New York: New York University Press, 1999), 69.

94. For more on the question of distinguishing between various forms of cosmopolitanism, see Bruce Robbins, "Actually Existing Cosmopolitanism," in *Cosmopolitics: Thinking and Feeling Beyond the Nation*, ed. Pheng Cheah and Bruce Robbins (Minneapolis: University of Minnesota Press, 1998); and "Cosmopolitanism: New and Newer," *boundary 2* 34 (2007): 47–60. For one recent version of Gilroy's take on this question, see Paul Gilroy, "A New Cosmopolitanism," *Interventions: International Journal of Postcolonial Studies* 7 (2005): 287–92; and Tommie Shelby, "Cosmopolitanism, Blackness, and Utopia: A Conversation with Paul Gilroy," *Transition* 98 (2008).
95. Dan Robotham, "Cosmopolitanism and Planetary Humanism: The Strategic Universalism of Paul Gilroy," *South Atlantic Quarterly* 104 (2005): 575.
96. Fanon, *The Wretched of the Earth*, 179.
97. Édouard Glissant, "Creolization in the Making of the Americas," *Caribbean Quarterly* 54 (2008): 87.
98. Gilroy, *Postcolonial Melancholia*, 79.
99. Roberts, "A World without Race," 35.
100. Ibid., 35, and Gilroy, *Postcolonial Melancholia*, 79.
101. Robotham, "Cosmopolitanism and Planetary Humanism," 575.
102. A recent—and quite striking—example can be found when, soon after the election of Barack Obama, Gilroy was asked, together with a number of other international intellectuals, to comment on one thing he hoped for from the new Obama administration, one thing he feared, and one piece of advice for the new president. Gilroy responded, "Hope: That Obama will tell the Israeli government to release Marwan Barghouti. Fear: That the Israeli government will not listen. Advice: Read up on the history of the British empire's overthrow and collapse so that he can understand why releasing Barghouti might be helpful." ("Barack Obama: Hope, Fear . . . Advice," openDemocracy. 21 January 2009. http://www.opendemocracy.net/article/barack-obama-hope-fear-and-advice#3.) Gilroy is hardly the only intellectual to call for the release of Barghouti, a Palestinian parliamentarian who has been imprisoned by the Israeli government since 2002, and to see this as a necessary step toward achieving justice in Israel-Palestine. See Jo-Ann Mort, "Why a Jailed Dissident Is Palestine's Best Hope," *Foreign Policy* (14 August 2009). But making it part of the primary message he would wish to deliver to Obama, and linking the occupation of Palestine to the actions of the British Empire, indicate both his close attention to the situation

in Palestine precisely as a continuing form of colonialism and of apartheid practices, and also the centrality of this situation to his own political thinking.

103. Gilroy, *The Black Atlantic*, 205.
104. Ibid., 207.
105. Ibid., 205–06.
106. Ibid., 217.
107. Gilroy, "Multiculture and the Negative Dialectics of Conviviality," chapter 4 in this volume, emphasis in original.
108. Young, *White Mythologies*, 8. See also Genevieve Lloyd, "Masters, Slaves and Others," in *Radical Philosophy* 34 (Summer 1983): 2–9.
109. Fanon, *Black Skin, White Masks*, 69.
110. Bryan Cheyette, "Frantz Fanon and Jean-Paul Sartre: Blacks and Jews," *Wasafiri* 44 (2005): 7–8. See Fanon, *Black Skin, White Masks*, 70. The circles of influence become particularly fluid here, since Fanon's *Black Skin, White Masks*, which is so crucially influenced by writings on anti-Semitism, in turn became a major influence upon Jean Améry in his attempts to write about the genocidal effects of European anti-Semitism and the aftermath of the Holocaust. As Améry noted in an essay in 1969, upon first encountering Fanon's work, he was immediately struck by the fact that "'The Lived Experience of the Black Man,' as Fanon had portrayed it, corresponded in many respects to my own formative and indelible experience as a Jewish inmate of a concentration camp." See Jean Améry, "The Birth of Man from the Spirit of Violence: Frantz Fanon the Revolutionary," trans. Adrian Daub, *Wasafiri* 44 (2005): 13.
111. Gilroy, *Postcolonial Melancholia*, 15–16.
112. Ibid., 82.
113. Vikki Bell, "The Violence and Appeal of Raciologies: Colonialism, Camps and Cosmopolitan Utopias," *Theory, Culture & Society* 19 (2002): 252.
114. Gilroy, *Postcolonial Melancholia*, 15.
115. Ibid.
116. One of the best recent accounts of this history is given by Ilan Pappe, in his book *A History of Modern Palestine: One Land, Two Peoples* (New York: Cambridge University Press, 2004); see especially the chapter "The Mandatory State: Colonialism, Nationalism, and Cohabitation" (72–122). Other authoritative accounts include Charles D. Smith, *Palestine and the Arab-Israeli Conflict: A History with Documents*, 5th ed. (New York: Bedford/St. Martin's, 2004); and Rashid Khalidi, *The Iron*

Cage: The Story of the Palestinian Struggle for Statehood (Boston: Beacon, 2007). For a briefer, but nevertheless thorough, overview, see the online primer published by the Middle East Research and Information Project, "Palestine, Israel, and the Arab-Israeli Conflict: A Primer," accessed 10 October 2009, http://www.merip.org/palestine-israel_primer/toc-pal-isr-primer.html.

117. Andrew Benjamin, "Israel Does Not Act or Speak for Every Jew," *Sydney Morning Herald* (4 August 2006): A20.
118. For an overview of some of these debates, together with contemporary responses, see Tony Kushner and Alisa Solomon, eds., *Wrestling with Zion: Progressive Jewish-American Responses to the Israeli-Palestinian Conflict* (New York: Grove, 2003).
119. David Theo Goldberg and Saree Makdisi, "The Trial of Israel's Campus Critics," *Tikkun* (September/October 2009).
120. Sherene Seikaly, "Palestine, Justice, and Anti-Racism," Jews Against the Occupation, accessed 13 September 2009, http://www.jatonyc.org/sherene.htm.
121. Gilroy, *Postcolonial Melancholia*, 56–57.
122. Roberts, "A World without Race," 35.
123. Quoted in Gilroy, *Postcolonial Melancholia*, 82.
124. Fanon, *Black Skin, White Masks*, 69.
125. Mourid Barghouti, "Verbicide," *New Internationalist* (August 2003).
126. Jean-Paul Sartre, preface to Frantz Fanon, *The Wretched of the Earth*, trans. Richard Philcox (New York: Grove, 2004), xlvii–xlix.
127. Gilroy, *Against Race*, 253.
128. Gilroy, *Postcolonial Melancholia*, 56.
129. Ibid., 57.

Part II

Retrieving the Human

Two Scholars in Dialogue

4

Multiculture and the Negative Dialectics of Conviviality

PAUL GILROY

Purely scholastic writing is not interested in racial discourses, divisions, and hierarchies. To speak of race and racism is, apparently, to be unserious. It is particularly odd that what those formations might reveal in the context of debates over multiculture and human rights has not often been thought worth investigating. Instead, the history of the race idea gets allocated to ever more esoteric academic specialisms. If the history of *racism* appears at all, it is principally the history of its many victims—something that is usually invoked as an act of Europe-centered, holocaust piety.

These lapses comprise a missed opportunity. It has been compounded by the rise of *literary* postcolonial studies. That enterprise has contributed to a situation in which racialized government, law, and politics don't get much attention. The current governmental clamor for a revival of imperial and colonial relations and the transformation of sovereignty means that such inattention should not continue.

The reluctance to link the history of racism to considerations of human rights and postcolonial politics is symptomatic, but it can also be hard to interpret. Very few writers have been prepared to break the complicity that produces that almost-silence, to approach the metaphysical potency of racism and to become engaged by what the history of its expression shows about the constitution and the agency of sovereign power, the contraction of justice, and the functional articulation of rationality with irrationality.

It would seem that the desire to understand the relationship of race and racism to politics and power was an unorthodox impulse long before the industrialization of genocidal killing made it into an urgent matter. The rare figures who have taken that path are an odd collection. Humanist and antihumanist, they range across the spectrum of formal politics.[1]

There is an additional unevenness here as well. The thinkers who did become interested in the history of racializing bodies, skulls, bones, and blood did not often show the same enthusiasm for thinking through relationships between racism and nationalism and the national state, or for exploring the development of legal and governmental orders to which the principle of racial hierarchy was intrinsic.

Academic fashions have been strongly affected by the fear of being called politically correct. The climate of infowar changes the tempo of scholarly life. Even the most promising fields of inquiry can be taken over by complacent, timid, and drab work: the study of the body can, for example, be reduced to a generic enterprise. The ability to maintain focus on which bodies are at stake and the conditions in which they are assembled as the objects of attention can be lost. It becomes difficult to address the diverse ways in which the operations of racial discourse make those bodies meaningful—always *in relation* to each other. Similar conceptual and political problems arise when official and institutional patriotism requires that racism and nationalism must drift apart. Then, the racialization of war and law is retained only as an overspecialized topic relevant to a few exceptional places (e.g., South Africa and Israel) characterized by racialized polities and forms of citizenship that, in turn, institutionalize the patterns of exclusionary inclusion that race hierarchy facilitates and renders acceptable.

The reluctance to consider racism as anything more or less than ideology in general, or to see racial difference as anything other than a straightforward effect of nature is, to my mind, an extension of an old pattern in which mechanistic assumptions about progress, nationality, and survival were overdetermined by and made congruent with various forms of racial theory, usually as an accompaniment to conquest and expropriation.

Recent political advocacy for the reintroduction of colonial rule by Robert Cooper, Niall Ferguson, and various others has academic correlates and consequences. Among other things, their intervention demands a rewriting of the history of colonial domination. This represents something like the undoing of postcolonial approaches to the humanities. If that proposition seems exaggerated, it has been clear for many years that the humanistic enterprise in education cannot be the same on the other side of even the most narrowly scholastic studies of genocidal atrocity, rationally applied terror, and other, less spectacular manifestations of belligerent racial thinking. These revisionist voices wish to do away with the changes that followed having to face up to the ordinary, unheroic testimony of ordinary human witnesses to "Western" colonial crimes and contact with the rational irrationalities of the racial orders that reduced hopeful, suffering people first to infrahumanity and then to ashes and memories. Adorno captured this with characteristic acuity in his famous essay "Education After Auschwitz": "Every debate about the ideals of Education is trivial and inconsequential compared to this single ideal: never again Auschwitz. It was the barbarism all education strives against."[2]

As far as human science is concerned, Adorno's work, along with Norbert Elias's monumental studies of the civilizing process and Michel Foucault's explorations of power and the body, might be cited as evidence that can reveal the stimulation that derived, unexpectedly, from the need to bear witness to mass death and confront the continuing menace represented by Hitlerism, by its imitators, and indeed by its colonial precursors. That ethical work generated new forms of knowledge from its exposure to the atrocities of the Third Reich. It created the sociology of the body and altered approaches to power, bureaucracy, and secrecy, but, apart from rare moments like those few tantalizing, memorable sentences at the end of the first volume of the *History of Sexuality*, this variety of work, premised upon opening out the "never again" injunction and moving it away from any narrow ethnic interpretation, was always oblique about its relationship to those twentieth-century horrors. None of those inadvertent students of palingenetic ultranationalism was able or willing to place their discoveries inside the broader historical framework of colonial statecraft that they seem, increasingly, to demand.

That task fell first to Voegelin and Arendt. It has in some aspects been continued in the less historically inclined work of Giorgio Agamben.

As part of a difficult and exhilarating argument that the concentration camp represents institutionally and historically, what he calls the "nomos of the political space in which we are still living," Agamben has criticized approaches to understanding spaces of exception and their social relations, that strive to deduce their "essence" from accounts of what happened there. He suggests, instead, that it will be more productive to invert that line of enquiry and ask instead: "What is a camp, what is its juridico-political structure, that such events could take place there?" Describing the camp as order without localization, he argues that it has displaced the city from its traditionally central place in political philosophy and, in doing so, provided the key to a wholly novel and deeply disturbing transformation of relationships between sovereignty, territory, and political culture: of the articulation of law and life. The origins of these practices lie in conquest and they are refined in the practice of colonial government.

Today, the constellation Agamben has identified asks *us* to consider the difference between the colonial archive's role as a historical resource and its contribution to understanding how colonial and postcolonial crimes should be remembered and understood as part of debates over torture, colonial warfare, and human rights. Are those crimes to be part of the history of our present? And, if so, how are we going to grasp their historicality? I suggest that we need a reengagement with race hierarchy and racism as well as a new familiarity with the histories of empire in order to accomplish that task satisfactorily.

In considering the colonial precedents for some contemporary practices, I borrow the phrase "useful violence" from Primo Levi. He employed it in *The Drowned and the Saved* at the very end of his examination of the gratuitous, excessive violence characteristic of the concentrationary system. Inspired by his work, by the philosophical writings of his fellow Auschwitz inmate and interlocutor, Jean Améry, and various other observers of and commentators on the pathologies of European civilization, my work has aimed to answer the corrosive allure of absolute sameness and purity just as they did, with a historical and moral commitment to the political, ethical, and educational potential of near-universal human *shame*. I hope to show that this can also be significant in the political opportunities opened up by talk of human rights.

Améry was an eloquent proponent of what he termed "radical humanism." Through discovering his Jewishness under the impact of somebody's fist but more especially as a result of having been tortured, he acquired a great interest in the politics of dignity that could answer the governmental actions that brought racial hierarchy alive and made it legitimate. Perhaps for that very reason, he found through his postwar reading of Fanon that "the lived experience of the black man . . . corresponded in many respects to [his] own formative and indelible experience as a Jewish inmate of a concentration camp."[3]

With Améry and Fanon, Levi shared a distinctive, midcentury commitment to extracting humanistic and liberatory perspectives from the extremity he had survived in the *Lager*. Analytical insights toward that end flow freely in his writing, especially in *The Drowned and the Saved*. It is a book that can most profitably be approached as an examination of the *reductio ad absurdum* of key motifs in the history of bureaucratic and military rationalities that help us define the specific attributes of modern governmentality. These qualities are seen with special clarity in government's encounters with those vulnerable people who, outside the protection of rights but nevertheless firmly under the rule of law, can be tortured and killed with impunity. The famous essay on "useless violence" lies at the center of his exploration of civilization's inner tensions and the implication of decivilizing racial divisions that are not to be dialectically resolved into a reconfigured narrative of progress.

Levi offers a luminous treatment of the spectacular brutality that, according to standards of rational reflection, appears at first to be without purpose. He concludes with the notion that what he calls "the outrage motive" intruded into and compromised the more familiar mechanisms of the profit motive, which were not altogether absent from the social world of his camp where slave labor was a routine supplement to the procedures of the adjacent death factory. Analysis of this outrage delivers us to a critical and historical engagement with racial metaphysics. The subordination of profit to outrage was a sign that the power of racism and the order of race hierarchy were active.

Building on that insight, I want to pursue the proposition that racism has a distinctive and substantive significance and, further, that focusing on the point where the colonial archive articulates with the West's "internal" dynamics helps to make it recognizable in the postcolonial present. This observation may, I suppose, be thought contentious, perhaps even vulgar, but I hope it is not trivial. The forces of national liberation were marshaled by many who, like Fanon, Kimathi, and Senghor, had imbibed a distinctive political morality through their military deployments in Europe's war against fascism. Their subsequent attempts to adapt that ethical system so that it would legitimize anticolonial resistance and, in some cases, explain the need for armed struggle all involved arguments of this type. Today their arguments cut deeply into the problems of how *we* are to understand states of exception, how *we* analyze the causality of genocide, and how *we* set about preventing the possibility of its recurrence, as well as how *we* answer crypto-racist and civilizationist common sense of the Samuel Huntington/Bernard Lewis varieties, which have dressed up the old doctrine of doomed races for the era of infowar.

This agenda has the additional merit of directing our attention toward two other fundamental issues. They can be conceptualized as counterpoints to Zygmunt Bauman's analysis of postmodern morality as well as to a larger program of critical work that can be conducted under the sign of human rights. This project can be abbreviated as a double concern: with the loss and the recovery of human dignity. There is, first, the dignity that was stripped away by the biopolitical processes that systematically produce infrahumanity—for the explicit benefit of the killers, torturers, and abusers. And then, there is the dignity that might, intermittently at least, be salvaged by acts of narration, of storytelling, even if, as Walter Benjamin puts it, they "borrow their authority from death."

Let me emphasize that, in Levi's exposition and enactment of this difficult problem, what appears to be a brutality without purpose eventually discloses its secret significance. That apparent uselessness does have a value, and he suggests that it can only be seen when we consider the position of its perpetrators who require it in order to complete their tasks with the minimum of emotional and psychological disturbance.

In a memorable conclusion that divorces that particular history from any proscriptive uniqueness and shifts it into an inspiring world-historical mode, Levi raises the possibility that there exists another form of violence that he hopes will be useful in the longer run. Perhaps with his imminent suicide in mind, he names this variant as the self-inflicted suffering involved in inducing himself and others like him, first, "to speak of the fate of the most helpless" in their attempt to reconstruct and comprehend the alien logic of their murders and torturers, and then to move beyond that necessary but insufficient goal into a different stance in which witnessing as psychopathology unfolds into witnessing as ethics.

At that point, talk as trauma is succeeded by talk as pedagogy and exchange. That conception of utility is something daring and unexpected, upon which a more elaborate conception of what I propose indelicately to call antiracist pedagogy in the service not only of human rights but of a new humanism can, even now, be built.

It should not be necessary to add that the benefits of this proposed ethical exercise can only increase if it is appreciated that the opportunity has been summoned—conjured into being—in explicit opposition to the racialization of the world: an outcome that usually invites the accusation of political correctness but that, in this neck of the woods, is probably more likely to be read as part of some deadly pact with the neoliberal advocates of color blindness.

The old notions of racial and absolute ethnic difference that characterized nineteenth-century empires appear to be quietly active within the calculus that currently assigns differential value to lives lost according to their locations and supposed origins and considers that some abject human bodies are more easily and appropriately tortured, humiliated, imprisoned, shackled, starved, and destroyed than others. These distinctions have become very important in the conduct of "the war on terror." In other words, the infowar has revived a recognizably colonial economy in which infrahumanity, measured against the benchmark of civilizationist standards, evaporates rights and postpones recognition indefinitely.

The generic enemies of that interminable war, the detainees, the rendered, and all the other shadowy "third things"[4] that racial rationality has lodged between animal and human, all these forms of infrahuman life are best administered as waste:[5] under flexible governance produced by special emergency rules and exceptional or martial procedures in which the law is suspended in its own name. My point is that race hierarchy is not inferred in this process: it remains integral to it.

The wretched, biopolitical condition common to all those groups underscores the fact that they are not reciprocally endowed with the vital, authentic humanity enjoyed and monopolized by their rulers, captors, conquerors, judges, executioners, and other racial betters.[6] However, that should not persuade us to abandon the language of the human as a sham or a fantasy. The struggle against racism demands and licenses a reengagement with it.

As I said, Arendt, Foucault, Agamben, and a few others have dissented from the habitual professional disinterest in these matters. They have also drawn from and engaged in dialogue with the theoretical reflections offered up by the movements of the enslaved and colonized as part of their battles for independence, autonomy, and liberation. Their nascent countertradition has shown us aspects of how race hierarchy entered into a process that institutionalizes sovereign powers and warrants the belligerent conduct of their competitive statecraft, the management of their colonies, and eventually, the forms of biopolitical government that were being developed in the core metropolitan areas where different jungles, savages, and degenerate types were being discovered. (Today, those colonial precedents may still have much to teach us about the future of the racial nomos.)

Turning away from the political ontologies of race, class, and nation, these thinkers appealed to variations of "constructionism" that, when applied to race, had origins in the intersection of existentialism and phenomenology.

When racial and ethnic identities were assembled in absolutist forms in order to secure the interests of oppressed and exploited minorities, this approach was not influential. However, it did thrive where the normative character of hierarchical heterosexual reproduction could be presented as a political and historical accomplishment that overthrew the commonsense assumption that nature could somehow speak, unmediated for itself.

Timidity set in and the moral and political tempo of studying racism was slowed ironically by the success of struggles against apartheid and by the demise of the social movements created by black Americans in pursuit of substantive citizenship. The fading of those great struggles left a disturbing sense that the most radical practitioners of *historical* ontology were becoming wary of working on race and racism. Ian Hacking, for instance, has recently declared himself committed to the obligation to defend race on the grounds of its statistical utility.[7]

Others working loosely in the spirit of his "*dynamic* nominalism" opted for calmer waters: usually, as I have said, where the creation of gendered subjects and sexual differences could be explored without trespassing on the political sensibilities of racial and ethnic minorities who did not appreciate their particularity being deconstructed and made to appear absurd; and, to see this more critically, where the elaboration of easy antihumanist positions was unlikely to be disrupted by any inconvenient clamor from the vulnerable groups whose political rights have become entangled with demands for recognition as human beings in an unjust world that denies them even that dubious protection.

However contentious it may be, the easy, popular response to the minorities' assertions of sovereignty over their experiences of victimage is the idea that we should become resigned to racial orders because they are uniquely natural kinds: a permanent, significant, and immutable aspect of human social and political life. Attempts to denature race, to become estranged from its obvious common sense, to focus on its *dynamic* constructedness and its implication within particular institutional settings are, in the corona of identity politics anyway, judged harshly and often thought to belong more naturally and spontaneously to the Right. That is certainly true in North America where, perhaps because it is a coldly calculated and premeditated stance rather than a spontaneous expression of the natural preference for the company of one's own kind, the liberal sin of color blindness is currently thought to be a bigger offense than white supremacism.

The approach that Foucault pioneered, more I think as a result of his political commitments than his critique of epistemology, though they are of course connected, would not accept that the appearance of a political language of race and its growing relationship to the administration and reproduction of governmental powers were incidental developments: just coincidences in which the languages of natural difference and real kinds was momentarily addressed to the pragmatic challenges of colonial rule or the shifting tempo of class conflict. Instead, he suggests, the historical currency of race thinking, and its tight grip on a world of empires, can tell us something fundamental and useful about the quality of biopolitical life, about the objects of government and the nature of subjection. Something like a historical ontology of races could then be used to illuminate all the contradictions—legal, ethical, military—of a civilizing mission that had to mystify its own systematic brutality in order to be effective.

We can agree with Arendt that race talk and racial solidarity prosper where politics, political institutions, and "the political" are diminished or compromised. However, there is a sense in which her bold and inspirational linkage of Europe's colonial rule with its genocidal ultranationalism can be misleading. Though she is deeply interested in the relationship of the race idea to imperialism, Arendt's view of racism is more problematic. It remains comfortably and tidily ideological rather than metaphysical, and, as Margaret Canovan puts it, racism for Arendt "was the spontaneous and comprehensible response of civilised men confronted with savages."[8] The consequences of this tension are strongly evident at the end of the famous chapter on the decline of the nation-state and the end of the rights of man that is so pivotal in the development of human rights scholarship. Arendt emphasizes that rights come from national states and that the vulnerability of statelessness is compounded by rhetorical appeals to humanity. She moves rapidly on from those insights to elaborate upon another problem that resides in the fact that "the world found nothing sacred in the abstract nakedness of being human."[9] Identifying this observation explicitly with the experience of survivors of the Nazi death factories, Arendt argues that "the abstract nakedness of being human was their greatest danger." A repeated preference for the national over the natural dictated that, when people appeared outside the protection of their political community, a discomforting sense of their fragile humanity may even have been an inducement to violence against them. She continues: "[It] seems that a man who is nothing but a man has lost the very qualities which make it possible for other people to treat him as a fellow man."[10]

I want to suggest that Arendt misrecognizes the "abstractly naked" human as a natural or essential human. Instead, that vulnerable figure might be described much more accurately as a *racialized* human: a particular, infrahuman creation rather than a specimen of the catastrophically empty humanity that she wishes to repudiate. Her error corresponds to a refusal to engage racism directly and critically.

The possibility that this abstract nakedness is not so much a cipher of insubstantial humanity but a sign that racial hierarchy is in operation arises directly from the work of survivors themselves. It bears repetition that Améry recognizes his experiences through reading Fanon. Levi, who interprets exercises in brutal racial formation as having been conducted for the benefit of their perpetrators, suggests that racism's capacity to reconcile rationality and irrationality is captured in that dominance of the outrage motive over the profit motive. The infrahuman victims are compelled to perform the subordination that race theory requires and anticipates but which their bodies do not spontaneously disclose.

Levinas, who offered a very different but dazzlingly insightful diagnosis of these questions in the years before the Third Reich, posed the same fundamental problem in a 1934 article for the journal *Esprit*:

> How is universality compatible with racism? The answer—to be found in the logic of what first inspires racism—involves a basic modification of the very idea of universality. . . . But here we return to well-known truths. We have tried to link them to a fundamental principle. Perhaps we have succeeded in showing that racism is not just opposed to such and such a particular point in Christian and liberal culture. It is not a particular dogma concerning democracy, parliamentary government, dictatorial regime, or religious politics that is in question. It is the very humanity of man. (71)

Agamben's important recent interventions exhibit some of the same failings as Arendt's account. His philosophical ambitions mean that he discovers nothing specific in the power of *racial* discourse or in the way that *racialized* forms of law contribute to the problem of exclusionary inclusion. Oddly, he shares with complacent human rights theorists of the Ignatieff school a sense of the triviality and insignificance of mere racism, which is nothing at all when compared to the juridical metaphysics of alterity in Roman law or Manichaean political theology of the Schmitt variety.

The specific dynamics involved in colonial war and law don't come into those metaphysical and juridical stories from which racism must be kept out at all costs. This is a grave oversight because, as Sven Lindqvist has argued, an issue like the legitimacy of preemptive violence is directly linked into the parapolitical and judicial rules of racialized government that Schmitt himself understands to be connected to the development of European public law, particularly in relation to the colonization of the Americas.[11]

Perhaps, like Arendt, Agamben has missed something. His distinctions between zoë and bios, physis and polis pass over the intermediate figures that arise where the rational irrationalities of race and blood are set to work. Even if we accept that toward the end of this grim road lies bare life in the figure of the "Musselman," we are entitled to ask about the historical and geopolitical stops along the way, the points of conflict, intersection, and confluence that looped colonial procedures back into the core of European social life with such dreadful results. How does the ultimate destination represented by that bare life relate to the other forms of political ontology that have specified who may be slain with impunity in the name of racial hygiene and whose life counts for nothing? Where, for example, is the andrapoda, the noncitizen, the slave represented in the figure of Aristotle's man-footed beast? Where are the alien denizens who even now function as the constitutive outside of *your* shrinking citizenship? Where are the colonial functionaries and Malthusian rulers who engineered and manipulated famines as a way of waging war or recruited the desert itself into their calculations as to the rational and natural mechanisms of genocide?

At the start of his rich chapter on the camp as the "Nomos" of the modern, Agamben does acknowledge the historical association of the concentration camp with the prosecution of colonial warfare. He notes that the camp was not born from ordinary or criminal law but comes instead from the strategy of "protective custody" and the state of exception. The initial colonial staging of this parapolitical technology does not detain him. As soon as that fatal connection is noted, it is set aside and his larger philosophical and juridical argument resumes with a discussion of the state of exception as a bridge—he calls it a constitutive nexus—into the Third Reich from the ordinary judicial processes of the governments that had preceded it.

I have no major quarrels with the way that argument unfolds, though I am not convinced that the National Socialist concept of race did not involve "the identification of a certain biological body." His haste in passing over the specificities of the question of racism, its political ontologies, its legal ordering under the sign of the national state and its larger epistemological shape interests me because it seems to be symptomatic of more than a philosopher's refusal of history. Colonial statecraft, colonial government, and the legitimate deployment of forms of law and power that would be unacceptable in other locations all drop out of his important reflections.

Arendt and Agamben are linked by their apparent distaste for analyzing racism but also by their complex and critical relations to the idea of the human. This combination of positions facilitates a special hostility to the project of human rights that, as I have said, can be dismissed for its inability to face the political and strategic processes from which all rights derive and the related refusal to address the analytical shortcomings that arise from the dependence of human rights on an expansion of the rule of law—which, incidentally, can be shown to be fully compatible with colonial crimes.[12]

Histories of colonial power and genealogies of racism can help to explain both of these problems and to break the impasse into which the analysis of human rights has fallen. That is why antiracism remains important. It does not argue naïvely for a world without hierarchy but practically, for a world free of *that particular* hierarchy that has accomplished untold wrongs. (That is my reply to Dorothy Roberts's critique that I borrow cosmopolitanism from the wellsprings of Enlightenment but leave nationalism alone. Nobody ever got killed in the name of cosmopolitanism).[13]

I have tried to emphasize that racial terror administered by governments has repeatedly assumed paralegal as well as legal forms. This raises the additional role of racism in supplying the means of their articulation. Racial discourse might be thought of as contributing to a system for making meaning that feeds the tendency to create exceptional spaces and populate them with vulnerable, infrahuman beings.

The colonial battlefields gave birth to the plantation, which points in turn to the legal regimes of protective custody that generated and generalized the camp as a routinely exceptional space. If the life of racism is taken substantively into account, those exceptional spaces become explicable and racial discourses become an essential and dynamic element in their legitimation. The resulting nomos—the spatial ordering of law and power—corresponds to hierarchically ordered forms of moral personality and legal subjectivity and, of course, to particular kinds of violence.

The governmental dynamics of settler colonialism were distinctive. In example after example, racial hierarchy and the domination of a large number of people by a much smaller number with a greater measure of force set up particular patterns. Law became partial, fractured, and flexible. Violence on the other hand was spectacular, excessive, and yet imagined to be functional. A radical insecurity common to the colonial settler, the slaveholder and the militarily superior extractive agent inclined them all toward the deployment of terror as a means of political administration. Their violent dramaturgies of power were routinized and ritualized to mark out the spaces in which normal rules were suspended or inapplicable.

Mick Taussig's study of the colonial administration of the Putumayo during the rubber boom provides one especially memorable example of procedures that typified the operation of corporate power in what he terms the colonial "space of death."[14] This was an essentially privatized military topos that, as the well-known example of the Congo Free State also reveals, existed in an ambivalent relationship to the national state system and its official statecraft. Recent interest in the history of Belgian colonialism shows how important these formations still are to understanding imperialism in its relation to private power on one side and on the other to avowedly humanitarian state-making practice. The problems that these states of exception posed for citizenship and political rights had been recognized long before they assumed twentieth-century form, and Arendt made them relevant to political theory, casting around to uncover the causality of industrialized genocide in Europe.

The struggle to appropriate the language and political morality of the rights of man was a long one that had overlapped with the struggle against slavery but also went beyond it. This battle can be thought of initially as having to rework the assumptions that had led to articulating the unthinkable prospect of black citizenship and black humanity in the form of those famous rhetorical questions: "Am I not a Man and a brother?" "Am I not a woman and a sister?" A century and a half later, Rosa Parks would describe her own motivation toward insubordination in the same familiar terms: "I had decided that I would have to know once and for all what rights I had as a human being and a citizen, even in Montgomery, Alabama."

In the archives of the black Atlantic, David Walker's critique of the humanitarian language and tacit racialization of the US Constitution in his 1830 *Appeal to the Coloured Citizens of the World, but in Particular, and Very Expressly, to Those of the United States of America* supplies a useful symbolic starting point for this critical perspective.[15] Erecting secular demands over the foundation of his Pauline Christianity, Walker made the problem of black humanity and the related issue of rights—political and human—intrinsic to the issue of *world* citizenship long before Du Bois picked up that rather Germanic theme. The tactical reduction of this universalist argument to the local issue of joining the United States can be seen in the work of Frederick Douglass—particularly in his extraordinary speech on the meaning of the Fourth of July to the slave.[16] The same issues were notably rearticulated in the run-up to Du Bois's famous formulations at the end of the nineteenth century by Ida B. Wells in her lucid, sociological discussion of the paradoxical force of Lynch Law and its relationship to a penal system that had continued the practice of slavery long after its formal abolition:

> [. . .] "Lynch Law" has . . . been the name given to the summary infliction of punishment by private and unauthorized citizens. This law continues in force to-day in some of the oldest states of the Union, where the courts of justice have long been established, whose laws

> are usually executed by white Americans. It flourishes most largely in the states which foster the convict lease system, and is brought to bear mainly against the Negro.

Reconstructed with care, this African American tradition of comment and opposition has the power not just to alter the official genealogy of human rights but to rework it entirely around the trope of racial difference. Allied with parallel insights drawn from other parts of the colonial world, it shapes a counterhistory and prefigures the contemporary conundrum of rights and their tactical deployment, which has divided the academic field and reduced it to an unproductive quarrel between complacent jurists who think that the world can be transformed by a better set of rules and gleefully deconstructive skeptics who may know the limits of rights talk but are always disinterested in racism and its metaphysical capacities.

These African American thinkers were all alive to what we now call a deconstructive approach. They identified problems with rights rhetoric. They grasped the empirical limits of rights-oriented institutional life and the struggle over citizenship. But, a vivid sense of the power of racism meant that the luxury of any casual antihumanism would not be countenanced. They wished to keep the human in human rights alive and to differentiate their universalistic aspirations from the race-coded exclusionary humanism that made whiteness into a prerequisite for recognition. By keeping the critique of race and racism dynamic and by demanding nothing less than the opening of world citizenship to infrahuman beings like the Negro, their critical assessments of the complicity of rights-talk with unfreedom and routine brutality induced them to try and speak in humanity's name. Perhaps this was the new humanism of which Fanon spoke.

Now this contributes to a critique of what Mahmood Mamdani calls "rights-talk" and disrupts the idea that the global politics of human rights is best understood as evolving tidily through three discrete phases: 1) The French Revolution of the eighteenth century; 2) the Russian Revolution of 1917; and 3) the Universal Declaration revolution in 1948. A challenge to that overly simple scheme helps to show how the history of colonial government is useful in understanding how rights come to be asserted by torturers and how histories of raciology and colonial rule might illuminate persistent problems in the way that racism makes rights irrelevant and therefore useless.

Grasping the distinctiveness of the racial nomos, this dissident understanding of the ways in which race worked to compromise and corrupt politics could also, counterintuitively, show that the entities we know as races derived from the very racial discourse that appeared to be their scientific product.

The special accomplishments of racial discourse can thus be explored: its elisions, locutions, and performatives then become historical problems to be understood rather than simple but enigmatic emanations pulsing out from the decisive world of biology to shape the course of history, the rhythm of culture, and the conduct of social life.

In particular, we can consider the role of race and ethnic absolutism in securing the modes of inclusive exclusion that characterize what we might call the age of rendition—a period that, with its combination of public and private powers, mercenaries, pirates, contractors, and securitocrats, harks back to the eighteenth century.

The challenge before us is to maintain and perhaps to refine critical work in an unstable field, a field that retains heavy investments in the explanatory capacity of race as an abstraction even when the nature of that abstraction has moved away from nineteenth-century biologics and toward a different kind of political anatomy reconfigured on a molecular scale and oriented toward genes. The attachment to race and its habitual scholastic partner—the refusal of critical humanism—conceal and mystify this change. Their combination maintains potent metaphysical principles and racialized patterns of political reasoning in governmental and scientific institutions and at the very center of everyday life. Fanon, who reminds us constantly that the infrahuman Negro "symbolises the biological," is the best known of several thinkers who have shown that this mystification is not simply an effect of visible difference.

Epidermalization was the result, rather than the origin, of the "sociogeny" he described producing the racial order and then substituting it for the evasive liberatory possibility he described as "the real dialectic between body and world," a different, I am tempted to say postracial rather than antiracist possibility that humanized the Negro, drawing him or her into the "slow composition" of the "self as body in the middle of a spatial and temporal world . . . a definitive structuring of the self and the world."[17]

Racialized subjects were created by being induced to see racial difference from specific angles and under particular light. They were disposed to appreciate difference within certain technical and technological settings that were articulated together with the political, cultural, and economic institutions to which race lent the full force of its obviousness.

The complex formations that result still contribute a great deal of common sense to popular understanding of the logic of type and the nature of difference in general. And yet, the reproduction of racial orders is not a *uniquely automatic* fact of social and political life, and if we are to take Foucault's example seriously, and perhaps amend it by giving greater attention to the issue of political agency, we may arrive at a position in which transforming the discourse through which our nature becomes intelligible can be instrumental in altering the outcomes that mandate racial observance.

If that possibility sounds unacceptably idealist in this neck of the woods, let me conclude by adding that oppositional, antiracist work cannot of course proceed without all the usual attention to formally political and economic matters. That commitment does not dispose of the problem that resides in whether we are to accept the integrity and validity of race as a concept and how we are to manage the contending claims made upon raciality by racism's victims as well as its practitioners: enthusiastic and unwitting, indifferent and dogmatic. The ability to conscript the future into the service of racial equality remains pending in this choice and so does the political success of initiatives based upon the idea of human rights.

Notes

1. The figures include Du Bois, Gandhi, Voegelin, Arendt, Levinas, Sartre, Fanon, Foucault, and Agamben.
2. Theodor Adorno, *Critical Models: Interventions and Catchwords* (New York: Columbia University Press, 2005), 191.
3. Jean Améry, "The Birth of Man from the Spirit of Violence: Frantz Fanon the Revolutionary," trans. Adrian Daub, *Wasafiri* 44 (Spring 2005): 13–18.
4. What Du Bois calls (in the *Souls of Black Folk*) a "tertium quid."
5. Zygmunt Bauman, *Wasted Lives: Modernity and Its Outcasts* (Oxford: Polity, 2004).
6. Giorgio Agamben's theory of bare life is an interesting way of identifying this problem, even if it is articulated in an idiosyncratic poetics.
7. See Ian Hacking, *Historical Ontology* (Cambridge: Harvard University Press, 2002).
8. Margaret Canovan, *Hannah Arendt: A Reinterpretation of Her Political Thought* (Cambridge: Press Syndicate of the University of Cambridge, 1992), 37. Canovan is quoting Arendt in "The Political Meaning of Racial Anti-Semitism" (1946). See Hannah Arendt, *Origins of Totalitarianism* (London: Allen and Unwin, 1967), 436.

9. Arendt, *Origins of Totalitarianism*, 299.
10. Ibid., 300.
11. See, for instance, the work of Enrique Dussel in *Beyond Philosophy: Ethics, History, Marxism, and Liberation Theology*, ed. Eduardo Mendieta (Oxford: Rowman & Littlefield, 2003). See also Sven Lindqvist's *Exterminate All the Brutes: One Man's Odyssey into the Heart of Darkness and the Origins of European Genocide* (New York: Norton, 1996).
12. See Nasser Hussain, *The Jurisprudence of Emergency: Colonialism and the Rule of Law* (Ann Arbor: University of Michigan Press, 2003).
13. For a reply to this comment, see Anthony Alessandrini's essay, chapter 3 in this volume.
14. See Michael Taussig's "Culture of Terror—Space of Death: Roger Casement's Putumayo Report and the Explanation of Torture," *Comparative Studies in Society and History* 26, 3 (July 1984): 467–97.
15. See http://docsouth.unc.edu/nc/walker/menu.html.
16. "Fellow citizens, above your national, tumultuous joy, I hear the mournful wail of millions! Whose chains, heavy and grievous yesterday, are, today, rendered more intolerable by the jubilee shouts that reach them. If I do forget, if I do not faithfully remember those bleeding children of sorry this day, 'may my right hand cleave to the roof of my mouth'! To forget them, to pass lightly over their wrongs, and to chime in with the popular theme would be treason most scandalous and shocking, and would make me a reproach before God and the world. My subject, then, fellow citizens, is American slavery. I shall see this day and its popular characteristics from the slave's point of view. Standing there identified with the American bondman, making his wrongs mine. I do not hesitate to declare with all my soul that the character and conduct of this nation never looked blacker to me than on this Fourth of July! Whether we turn to the declarations of the past or to the professions of the present, the conduct of the nation seems equally hideous and revolting. America is false to the past, false to the present, and solemnly binds herself to be false to the future. Standing with God and the crushed and bleeding slave on this occasion, I will, in the name of humanity which is outraged, in the name of liberty which is fettered, in the name of the Constitution and the Bible which are disregarded and trampled upon, dare to call in question and to denounce, with all the emphasis I can command, everything that serves to perpetuate slavery—the great sin and shame of America!"
17. Frantz Fanon, *Black Skin, White Masks*, trans. Charles Lam Markmann (London: Pluto, 1986; orig. French ed. 1952), 111.

5

For a Dialogue with Paul Gilroy

JONATHAN BOYARIN

Paul Gilroy's essay on "Multiculture and the Negative Dialectics of Conviviality" may be read as a manifesto for a critical, actively antiracist humanism. In it, Gilroy lays out a broad claim for the reassertion of claims to rights in the name of a humanity that is *shared* but not *bare.* He seeks to articulate a notion of that humanity as freed from the reified hierarchies of a racism forged in the adventure of colonialism abroad and genocide in the European cosmopole but as still constituted within human history rather than merely posited in terms derived from Aristotelian analytics.

The project is extraordinarily ambitious and is by all means one to be cheered and fostered, not least for the courage that necessarily underlies the scope of its vision—a reexamination of the relation between the exclusionary mentalities and practices of Nazism, their colonial prologues or analogues, and the encompassing framework of racialization and dehumanization. Exploring this nexus in a way that fosters understanding is only possible when one is able to recognize and continue to speak in the midst of the tension between, on the one hand, giving the experiences of Nazism and the anti-Jewish genocide their historical due[1] and, on the other, not fetishizing Nazism or, indeed, the Nazi genocide as "wholly other."[2] Gilroy has done so here; I hope, but cannot quite trust, that I respond in like spirit, drawing on some of Gilroy's published writings as well as the conference address. It may be said at the outset (and, as here, most of my response will indeed address very particular points in Gilroy's address) that one fruit of careful balancing between this historical specificity and enormity of the consequences of European twentieth-century anti-Semitism on one hand, and its place within a more general history of European-based but worldwide racializations on the other, is to redirect the question of whether opposition to Zionism necessarily "is" or "is not" anti-Semitic toward more fruitful areas of critique. Thus, as Gilroy notes, "the racialization of law and war is retained only as an overspecialized topic relevant to a few exceptional places [South Africa, Israel] . . ." I read Gilroy here not (of course) as equating South Africa to Israel, nor yet dismissing the critique of the racialized logic of law and war in those places, but still insisting that there is something peculiar and distorting (whether or not inspired by anti-Semitism) for restricting the critique to these two situations. (As one counterexample to which Gilroy's insight directs us, consider the claim that the South African apartheid "passbook" system was actually inspired by the territorial surveillance of First Nations people in Canada.)

Perhaps like any manifesto, however, Gilroy's implicitly holds certain truths to be self-evident. In my response to Gilroy's "Multiculture," I point to several moments in the essay where such givens appear to limit the rhetorical force of his argument in its current iteration and where further interrogation (by Gilroy and/or by others) still in the spirit of an antiracist, critical humanism might advance the discussion.

At least three such key moments may be readily identified. One can be discerned in Gilroy's reference to "the history of racializing bodies, skulls, bones, and blood," a reference that begs the entire question whether there really was a time "before racism." Without disputing the specificity of scientific racism or its especial pertinence to rationales of colonial domination and active dehumanization, something more must be said, even in summary fashion, about the forms and rationales of domination that preceded colonialism (and, perhaps, even about the ways that European colonial domination drew upon precolonial domination in the colonized world). To be sure, I agree that the new discourse of scientific racism marked an epochal shift in the Western discourse on "race." Scholars of late antiquity through the European Middle Ages have been for some decades now tracing discourses of racial difference in those periods.[3] While one may still make a serious claim that these earlier discourses should not be called "racism," there is no longer a scholarly consensus on that point.

This interrogation leads in turn to a second key moment: Gilroy's paraphrase of Agamben's assertion concerning the replacement of the polis by the camp in political philosophy. There is a profound ambiguity here, perhaps in Agamben but certainly in Gilroy. Is the replacement said to take place solely in philosophical discourse, or (as seems more in keeping with Gilroy's text) is the shift said to take place in the realm of the overall logic of governance? If the latter, then this assertion contains the assumption that, prior to colonialism and genocide, the exercise of power was *generally* governed through something like an Athenian polis. Surely Gilroy does not mean to suggest that colonialism comes to corrupt such a prelapsarian, generalized European "political" democracy, but again, this slippage seems to betray unstated assumptions about the kind of ontological break represented by colonialism and its attendant racist practices.

The third key moment, perhaps less directly articulated with the former two, is an extension of Gilroy's observation that Agamben's "distinctions between zoë and bios, physis and polis pass over the intermediate figures that arise where the rational irrationalities of race and blood are set to work." Gilroy is correct to interrogate these dichotomies that reiterate classic European (post-)Christian notions of the clear difference between animal and human, between natural and civilized, and he is right to point our attention toward "third," intermediate categorizations.[4] However, Gilroy has not addressed here a further critique of Agamben, which is that any discourse on "bare life" (that is, unsymbolized, unmediated life) is already rhetoricized; there is no direct access to "bare life" any more than there is direct access to "the body."[5] As a corollary, distinctions among humans are not limited to "race" and "blood." What, for example (perhaps, but not necessarily, more than example), shall we do with this odd category of "religion," which is arguably at least as modern, if not more modern, more culturally specific in its scope, than the concept of race, at least if taken as an extension of premodern rhetorics of genealogical identity? (To be sure, the notion that religion might be a more restricted and contingent divider of persons than race upsets conventional assumptions, so this assertion might be better understood as a provocation on my part in an attempt to unsettle some of the "things" that remain self-evident.) Once again, and as Gilroy certainly understands well (this is, I think, the thrust of his address to the extent it addresses the scholarly work implied in antiracist humanism) if the *specificity*—historical, not ontological—of racism in relation to colonialism and genocide is to be asserted, it must be actively traced as well. To allude again to Zionism, this seemingly innocuous assertion might help us (antiracists all, to be sure, but in sometimes sharp disagreement over the relation between Jewishness and racism in our own day) understand better some of the passions aroused by the (mostly past?) "Zionism is racism" debate, inasmuch as it can be taken to *reduce* Zionism to its arguably racist aspects or (even worse) to mythologize Zionism as the essence and source of racism in the world today. Without that leveling and dehistoricizing "is," "Zionism racism" might, I suppose, be taken just as well to mean "Zionism is a response to racism" as "Zionism is the same as racism." Specifying the links between racist practices and discourses, between (and moving in both directions) past and present, between (again, in both directions) "Europe" and the rest of the world, Jews and other Europeans, Jews and other survivors of colonial and metropolitan racism, again points to possible ways to move beyond the shouting match of "is / is not." More broadly, the relation of Zionism and other solutions for Jewish survival and continuity in the post-Emancipation period to other forms of difference—let us say, for shorthand, all logics of endogamy (though we need to be at least cautious about reinscribing marriage rules as the fundamental motor of reasserting both group difference and group identity)[6] here, now, and for the future must be interrogated as well, so that we can be clearer about a possible shared vision of the legitimacy of difference in a convivial world to come.

To suggest by contrast that for Gilroy, Jewishness is an operative term here is no stretch: Consider the epigraph right at page 1 of *Against Race* (published as *Between Camps* in the United Kingdom), a quote that eloquently captures the dilemma of alternative articulations of identity that we are talking about here, as we waiver irresolute and anxious between talk of resistant "particular collectives" on one hand and suffering, putatively "unessentialized" humanity on the other. The quote is from Fanon:

> It was my philosophy professor, a native of the Antilles, who recalled the fact to me one day: "Whenever you hear anyone abuse the Jews, pay attention, because he is talking about you." And I found that he was universally right—by which I meant that I was answerable in my body and my heart for what was done to my brother. Later I realized that he meant, quite simply, an anti-Semite is inevitably anti-Negro.[7]

We might pause in passing to note how eloquently Fanon articulates *at once*—or at any rate, sequentially—a concern for the specific well-being of "Negroes," and a call for universal "brotherhood."

In her contribution to the conference that preceded this volume, Laura Chrisman highlights Gilroy's ethical focus on the suffering of "abject" human beings in an adumbrated critique that reminds me of William Connolly's trenchant if friendly comments, in his 2000 volume *Why I Am Not a Secularist*, on John Caputo's call for a bluntly detheorized "'obligation to reduce and alleviate suffering.'"[8] Caputo's claim is cast in very corporeal language, evoking exuberantly "'[f]lesh. . . . [that] tears, bleeds, swells, bends, burns, starves, grows old, exhausted, numb, ulcerous . . .'"[9] The passages in Gilroy that Chrisman evokes here do seem consistent with this ethos. Thus, there is indeed, as Chrisman says, in Gilroy's *After Empire* (published as *Postcolonial Melancholia* in the United States) a profound valuation of "the fragile, emergent substance of vital planetary humanism."[10] In his recent essay on Bob Marley, Gilroy comes close to addressing the problem of how to value such species-consciousness without an implicit and inevitable Christian underlay and implicitly distances the idea of "vital planetary humanism" from what he calls "dubious feelings of [consumerist] charity."[11] Connolly's response to Caputo, at any rate, is to reassert the emancipatory value of claims for audibility that are not prepolitical but precisely "political," in that they effect an intervention and, when at least partly successful, force petrified and sterilized cultures of normalcy into movement. But in any case it is clear that such individualized, decollectivized gestures are not all Gilroy values, since he also promotes the virtue of "conviviality," which is inherently more social and, in Connolly's terms, "political" than a bare ethos of attending to the abject suffering other would imply.

Chrisman refers approvingly to Arendt's project "that accords equality to fascism and colonialism as oppressive, separate if intertwined forces of the twentieth century."[12] Indeed, Gilroy cites precisely Arendt on this point, in the epigraph to chapter 2 of *After Empire*; and we may also look profitably again at other references to Arendt and to Césaire on this point throughout that book. This may be the best time to say that it was precisely Gilroy's clear articulation of that link in *The Black Atlantic* that especially moved me in reading that earlier work, and even if Gilroy states that he wants to focus on "blacks [as] witness to Europe's failings . . . inside Europe," I do not see how that amounts to a diminution of the importance of imperialism in his work.[13] On the contrary: he calls, in his inaugural address at the London School of Economics, for a revival of that institution's earlier focus on "understanding the economic, political and oral impact of imperialism inside this country and beyond it"[14] and denounces the popular obsession with "Britain's heroic triumph against the Third Reich" as "block[ing] out both imperial and colonial history."[15]

Gilroy refers in that essay to the "transform[ation of] a pattern of diaspora culture from a simple, one-way dispersal starting at a fixed point of origin, into a multi-nodal, webbed or relational network that is constituted through multiple points of intersection."[16] I take the opportunity here to reiterate that this must not be read as a shift from the old, neurotic, Judaic diaspora to a somehow more liberatory "new diaspora" formation, as I trust Gilroy does not intend here but as has been expressed in older British cultural studies;[17] nor is it clear that this should be read as describing an evolutionary or "modern" development in the actual dynamics of diasporas, as opposed to our understandings and evaluations of them. It strikes me that, while a distinction between "melancholic" and "convivial" structurings of diasporic collectivity and culture can plausibly be made (including by those in diaspora), doing so should be made most cautiously, first, so as not to restore neat distinctions, made as if from some place outside and above them, between sane and unsanitary cultures, and second, because it may be all too easy for us to delude ourselves into thinking that we have transcended some ultimate recourse toward an unquestioned faith in an ultimately ameliorative or progressive trend in human affairs by, for example, celebrating the emergence of what Connolly calls "the politics of becoming," or Gilroy, the convivial.[18]

Along similar lines, I confess I'm put off by the word "cosmopolitanism."[18] It still smacks to me of an unexamined individualism and devaluation of group identity, nor is it clear that Bob Marley's choice to remain in diaspora was, as Gilroy has suggested, "more difficult" than resettling in Africa would have been. (For me, developing a non-Zionist strong Jewish identity has been I suppose more of an adventure, but I can't say that my life in the United States has been harder than a life in Israel would have been.)

And one more question addressed to Gilroy's earlier writings, before turning in some more detail (but still in fragmentary fashion) to his manifesto on critical antiracism: It is not clear to me what "accepting the salience of the social and political processes that the United States knows and sees as a natural phenomenon called 'race' does absolutely nothing to address the multiple mystifications wrought by racism either in US political culture or elsewhere"[20] means. Is this not (and here indeed I invite a further dialogue with Gilroy and others) an incomplete statement? Not all parties—and indeed, among them not the most powerful parties—even accept this "salience," let alone going further (and this I think is the critical thrust intended by this sentence) to acknowledge the salience *and* challenge the naturalization of "race." As it stands, this incomplete sentence of critique risks ignoring the politics, for example, of the US Supreme Court, where Justice Scalia, in *Adarand Constructors v. Colorado*, said in the early 1990s that "[i]n the eyes of the Court, there is only one race here—and it is American."

To invoke the Supreme Court of the United States as it is currently composed is a sobering reminder that our "camp," and of course I use the term advisedly, has been losing for some time now. Paul Gilroy may be one of the best we have at articulating our current challenges and tasks, but that does not make them much less daunting. One begins to suspect that Gilroy's largest project now is to rearticulate the notion that solidarity and diversity *can indeed coexist*.[21] The effort is difficult not least because it requires repeated iterations of the distinction between denaturalization of social categories on one hand and the bootless attempt to obviate their social power on the other. If the rearticulation is necessarily imperfect, the effort cannot be refused.

And so to a series of further modest comments on "the negative dialectics of conviviality." Gilroy, then, notes the frequency of "[references to racism as] something that is usually invoked as an act of Europe-centered, holocaust piety." Pulled out of context, this phrase could be taken as almost dismissive, akin to the ambiguity of Fanon's reference to the Nazi genocide against Jews as a "family quarrel";[22] that is not what Gilroy intends at all of course but rather a sharp reminder of how the "universalization" of the Holocaust can be and has been used as a way to reassert an ever-more-tenuous Eurocentrism (which bears links to the dauntingly tortured ways that Zionism remains both an attempt to escape Eurocentrism and an extension of it). Indeed, Gilroy is always at pains to *relate* rather than separate; as he points out, "the operations of racial discourse make [. . .] bodies meaningful—always *in relation* to each other." That is to be sure a reminder that if Paul Gilroy is thinking of the Jews *with* other differences, that is not done in order to make nice to me (taking myself, for this moment, as an exemplary Jew). He practices a refusal of paternalism that, to be sure, is more commonly and vigorously (if always inadequately) checked for when the associations are being made "in the other direction," from the Jewish to the epidermally racialized; but that vigilance against paternalism directed *toward* the figure of the Jew is all the more welcome and convivial for that.

Invoking Arendt, Gilroy cites "the racial orders that reduced hopeful, suffering people first to infrahumanity and then to ashes and memories." This rhetoric risks folding back into a sentimental memorialization of historical victimization, and hence it must be worried, picked at, opened up. Why these three "levels" or categories and not others? Why stress the processes of dehumanizing the many rather than the process of superhumanizing the few, since racism (and certainly Nazi ideology) seem to indulge in both of these forms of mystification? And what purchase is gained by invoking, in commonsense fashion, the baseline "humanity" of these "suffering, hopeful people" as a norm against which the camp regime is in some fashion exceptional? The near-ordinary pathos (how numbed we are by our decades of Holocaust talk!)

of Gilroy's sentence as it stands risks deafening us, for example, to the outstanding challenge of Hannah Arendt's complex assertion that much as the guilt of the Nazi perpetrators was beyond calculation and comprehension, so too (*lehavdil*, to separate that which cannot be compared) was the "innocence" of the victims "deformed and beyond the reach of human justice."[23]

Gilroy calls for "a different stance in which witnessing as psychopathology unfolds into witnessing as ethics." I note that witnessing has never been just one or the other of these: take the exemplary act of witness that was the suicide of Szmul Zygielbojm, representative of the Jewish Workers' Bund to the Polish Government in Exile, on May 12, 1943, to dramatize the catastrophic situation of Polish Jewry.[24] If there has ever been a case of ethical suicide, this was it. Nor will witnessing ever be free of all psychopathology. To suggest otherwise does not only risk implying that we can heal ourselves through discourse. More than that, attempting to neatly separate sick and healthy witness to trauma risks the further illusion that there is a neat separation between witnessing for oneself (psychopathological?) and for others (ethical)? It seems to me rather that there is always a range of foci or addresses, between witnessing for oneself (individual, collective) and witnessing for the other. In much the same way, there is a range between acquiring a group-name identity in a way that does not neatly distinguish between that name and whatever might be "human" (a phenomenon found not only among those isolated groups for themselves means "the people" but also, for example, in the many situations among traditional East European Jews where *yid* could mean simply "person") and becoming aware of a group name applied to oneself in a way that sets one, and one's group, apart from humanity.[25] Those who acquire their group name in a less alienated way are perhaps likely to witness more ethically, less psychopathologically, but it is not clear they are to be especially commended for their relative good fortune. "At that point, talk as trauma is succeeded by talk as pedagogy and exchange." What's contained in this passive "is succeeded" (or, put differently, in making the "talk" rather than the "talkers" do the action)? Is it new talkers who engage in pedagogy and exchange? What happens to those for whom talk remains trauma? What, for another outstanding example, of Levi's suicide *after* the time when its example might have saved the threatened lives of others?

My tone is a bit sharp here, but Gilroy poses tough questions more clearly perhaps than anyone before him has done. None of this—and it cannot be written in bold enough print—gainsays the clear welcome and challenge to witness "ethically." It is the particular responsibility of those of us who are paid to witness (to research, to record, to teach) the resources and the wounds of the past. I do well understand that "the opportunity has been summoned—conjured into being—in explicit opposition to the racialization of the world." And I welcome it as Gilroy does.

More than that: unlike Gilroy, whom I not only declare as a friend but do so for once (without embarrassment but not without trepidation vis-à-vis my fellow Jews) as a "friend of the Jews," to use an old-fashioned term, *not all those who profess to be foes of anti-Semitism are friends of the Jews.* Thus in his essay in a volume devoted to the figure of Hannah Arendt, Christopher Hitchens cites, as evidence of the anti-Semitism he sees cropping up everywhere but especially among Muslims, that those fighting against the United States–backed government of Iraq call United States soldiers there *yehud.*[26] Hitchens does not acknowledge that (assuming this claim is accurate) it might have some connection to the process by which, in the West Bank and Gaza, visibly Jewish headgear (for example) came to be associated with the term *jeysh* (army) while *Israeli* soldiers came to be called *yehud.* Consistent with this dehistoricization is the florid character of his last paragraph, suggesting that perhaps "anti-Semitism is something that has the power to manifest itself in unpredictable seasons and unexpected places, and is always to elude the work of the mind of the analyst."[27] What's striking is how this creation of an indestructible phantom, at once protean and essential, resembles precisely the classic anti-Semite's phantasm of the Jews and their worldwide conspiracy. Perhaps Hitchens means to strike precisely that note of irony. Yet to remark that such things are *still* possible in the twenty-first century is hardly the beginning of wisdom. We need (with Gilroy, and with countless others) to historicize rather than remystify.

In his rapid discussion of the origins and fate of some of the seminal discussions of the social construction of racial oppression,[28] Gilroy opens the tremendously complex question of the intersections between intellectualism, popular (or national) discourses of group identity, and material interests. More specifically, it seems to me, he alludes to the failure of social constructionist ideas to "take" in the face of national and other liberation movements in the immediate postwar decades, contrasted to a later understanding that the naturalization of differences (including those in the name of which these liberation movements struggled) was itself a motor of domination. The argument here appears almost as a debriefing strategy session. (What happened when we interjected the notion of the social construction of race? Why weren't the people ready for it? What was the moment when it seemed useful? At and after that moment, as it seems, did it contribute to the weakening of effective antiracist activism?) But it cannot, I think (nor need or should it) be entirely separated from the vexed question of how much we are to dignify the notion of *group autonomy* (or, what amounts to much the same thing, how much we will be willing to allow groups to go on reifying themselves). Overall, in the tension between what Henri Atlan identifies as the twin deaths (for personal or group identity) of "crystal" (that is, petrification of identity) and "smoke" (that is, its dissolution),[29] Gilroy leans now one way, now the other—as all of us trying very hard to be ethical witnesses must, it seems to me. More often than not, he leans a bit more closely than I would in the direction of what indeed might be the lesser danger, that of group dissolution.

Gilroy notes and criticizes Arendt's view in which "rights come from national states and . . . the vulnerability of statelessness is compounded by rhetorical appeals to humanity." My response to this: it is reflective of a rhetoric that speaks (understandably, but problematically) of Nazism as a decline or deviation from some civilizational standard, a rhetoric that likewise seems to shadow some of Gilroy's earlier discussions of Arendt and Levi. The problem comes up again in the quote from Levinas, which, because it comes without comments, appears to be directly endorsed by Gilroy but to state that racism threatens "the very humanity of man . . ." Who would dare to dissent, but what does this tell us about what humanity *is*? Gilroy points out, acutely again, that "Arendt misrecognizes the 'abstractly naked' human [of 'bare life'] as a natural or essential human. Instead, that vulnerable figure might be described much more accurately as a *racialized* human." But is the alternative really the equally abstract *individual*, possessed of nothing determined beyond the enjoyment of liberty, equality, and fraternity?

In his critique of Agamben, Gilroy asks, "Where are the colonial functionaries and Malthusian rulers who engineered and manipulated famines as a way of waging war or recruited the desert itself into their calculations as to the rational and natural mechanisms of genocide?" Lest this seem exaggerated from contemporary perspectives, consider the machinations of various capitalist (now capitalist, such as China and Russia, along with Canada, the United States, et al.) governments, jockeying for the spoils of a deiced Arctic (what might be called, in a frightening reminder of earlier colonialism, the scramble for the Arctic) in order to grab as much profit as possible before the world burns entirely to a crisp. Much as one might say there is a world-consumption motive at work as well as a profit motive in this race for the Arctic, such that in effect (to the extent we continue to speak of the consumption motive and the profit motive as separate) they feed on each other in a deadly and suicidal feedback spiral. Is *their* motive profit only? By analogy, where Gilroy cites Primo Levi's identification of a genocidal "outrage motive" to accompany the "profit motive," these too should not be taken in a philosophically realist sense as designating separate entities or sources of desire but more nominally, as different moves in our desperate attempt to describe what has happened to us.

A last comment: Gilroy writes, "The colonial battlefields gave birth to the plantation which points in turn to the legal regimes of protective custody that generated and generalized the camp as a routinely exceptional space." It seems likely to me, however, that the phrase "routinely exceptional" should already direct us further away from a Schmittian fascination with the state of exception and instead prompt us to attend to the range of regimes and corresponding names that broadly fell under the master category of *Lager* under the Nazis and through World War II: *Konzentrationslager*, but also *Arbeitslager*, *Totenlager* . . . as a way to reinforce that Gilroy rightly "points to" (so that we do indeed see more clearly and investigate more closely as historians) but does not identify as a unique cause the relation between the rationales and bureaucratic techniques of colonial plantation or other forced-labor economies and those of Europe at the middle of the twentieth century. Moreover, precisely in order to see how important what Gilroy calls "the plantation" may have been in this process of bringing racist mass administration back home, it is also important to consider the plantation *alongside*, rather than instead of, historical European processes of spatial control of Jews and other Others. Ghettoization (by no means the "medieval" norm but rather a phenomenon primarily of the early modern period in Western Europe) is only the most obvious of these, as the ghettos created for Jews by the Nazis in Warsaw, Vilna, Lodz, and countless smaller cities were likewise significant, and disastrous, "regimes of protective custody."[30]

May our vigilant witness help spare us and our fellows such evil, now and in the future. Amen.

Notes

1. As captured, for example, by Markha Valenta's stunning formulation: "[I]t is the continuing resonance of Europe's bestial impulses half a century ago that today spurs Europe's continued resistance to engaging fully the most fundamental challenges it faces." "How to Recognize a Muslim," in *Political Theologies: Public Religions in a Post-Secular World*, ed. Hent de Vries and Lawrence E. Sullivan (New York: Fordham University Press, 2006), 444–74; 464. It is important to recognize that this can be

true *and* it can also be true that the colonial plantation was a key training ground for the administration of the Nazi camp.

2. "We must think, know, represent for ourselves, formalize, judge the possible complicity among all these discourses and the worst (here the 'final solution')." Jacques Derrida, "Force of Law," in *Acts of Religion*, ed. Gil Anidjar (Routledge: New York and London, 2002), 298.
3. See my recent *The Unconverted Self: Jews, Indians, and the Identity of Christian Europe* (Chicago: University of Chicago Press, 2009).
4. See, for example, Andrew Benjamin, "Particularity and Exception: On Jews and Animals," *South Atlantic Quarterly* 107, 1 (2008): 71–87.
5. A conundrum acutely addressed by Judith Butler, *Bodies That Matter: On the Discursive Limits of "Sex"* (New York: Routledge, 1993).
6. See Jon Stratton, *Coming Out Jewish: Constructing Ambivalent Identities* (London: Routledge, 2000), for the argument that Jewish assimilation in liberal democracies consists in a semi-coerced surrender of Jewish endogamy for the larger endogamy of the racialized "white" majority population.
7. For a more ambivalent reading of this quote, see Bryan Cheyette, "Frantz Fanon and Jean-Paul Sartre: Blacks and Jews," *Wasafiri* 20 (2005): 7–12.
8. Laura Chrisman, "The Vanishing Body of Frantz Fanon." Symposium presentation in possession of author.
9. Quoted in William Connolly, *Why I Am Not a Secularist* (Minneapolis: University of Minnesota Press, 2000), 49–50.
10. Gilroy, *After Empire*, 88.
11. Paul Gilroy, "Could You Be Loved? Bob Marley, Anti-Politics and Universal Sufferation," *Critical Quarterly* 47 (2005): 226–245; 242.
12. Chrisman, "The Vanishing Body," 14.
13. Paul Gilroy, *The Black Atlantic* (Cambridge Harvard University Press, 1993), 76.
14. Paul Gilroy, "Multiculture in Times of War," inaugural address at the London School of Economics, 2006, 35.
15. Ibid., 39.
16. Gilroy, "Could You Be Loved?" 241.
17. See Stuart Hall, "Cultural Identity and Difference," in *Community, Culture, and Difference*, ed. J. Rutherford (London: Lawrence & Wishart, 1990), 222–37.
18. I *do* want to suggest nevertheless that New York City, as I experienced it from the late 1970s on, was and has been not "multicultural" but convivial. I can't speak for New Haven—or Chapel Hill, for that matter. A great

example, and consistent with Gilroy's salutary emphases in both of his recent essays on multiculturalism on the intersection between commerce and conviviality, is the Domino's New York–style pizza commercial with the lady passenger saying, "Fold it like a man!" and the immigrant, possibly Middle Eastern, driver saying, "I am folding it like a man!"

19. I refer in particular here to its evocation at page 241 of "Could You Be Loved?"
20. Paul Gilroy, "Multiculture, Double Consciousness, and the 'War on Terror,'" *Patterns of Prejudice* 39 (2005): 431–443; 442.
21. See Gilroy, "Multiculture in Times of War," 29.
22. Frantz Fanon, *Black Skin, White Masks* (London: Pluto Press, 1986), 115; Gilroy, "Multiculture in Times of War," 29.
23. Hannah Arendt, "The Image of Hell," in *Essays in Understanding, 1930–1954: Formation, Exile, and Totalitarianism*, ed. Jerome Kohn (New York: Schocken, 2005), 198.
24. http://www1.yadvashem.org/about_HOLocaust/documents/part2/doc154.html, accessed 19 March 2010.
25. We can all think of countless examples, many, alas, from personal experience. One brief but eloquent account is in Jacques Derrida's "Abraham, the Other," in *Judeities: Questions for Jacques Derrida*, ed. Bettina Bergo, Joseph Cohen, and Raphael Zagury-Orly (New York: Fordham University Press, 2007), 1–135; 10.
26. Christopher Hitchens, "Reflections on Anti-Semitism," in *Thinking in Dark Times: Hannah Arendt on Ethics and Politics*, ed. Roger Berkowitz, Jeffrey Katz, and Thomas Keenan (New York: Fordham University Press, 2010), 27.
27. Ibid.
28. "When racial and ethnic identities were assembled in absolutist forms in order to secure the interests of oppressed and exploited minorities, this approach was not influential. However, it did thrive where the normative character of hierarchical heterosexual reproduction could be presented as a political and historical accomplishment that overthrew the commonsense assumption that nature could somehow speak, unmediated for itself."
29. See Henri Atlan's *Entre le cristal et la fumée: Essai sur l'organisation de vivant* (Paris: Le Seuil, 1979).
30. Max Weinreich, "The Reality of Jewishness versus the Ghetto Myth: The Sociolinguistic Roots of Yiddish," *To Honor Roman Jakobson* (The Hague: Mouton, 1967), 2199–2212.

Part III

Debating the Human in Everyday Spaces

6

Sedentary and Mobile Poetics

Paul Gilroy and the Aesthetics of Postcolonial Theory

RANU SAMANTRAI

Those of us accustomed to the critique of race and nation that Paul Gilroy has sustained since his tellingly titled first book, *'There Ain't No Black in the Union Jack,'* might have been surprised by the story of Ingrid Nicholls featured in the preface to *Postcolonial Melancholia* (published as *After Empire: Melancholia or Convivial Culture?* in the United Kingdom). Mrs. Nicholls, you might recall, a "forty-six-year-old black, British mum was a prospective amputee."[1] About to lose a leg, she faced the unsavory choice either of being fitted with a free, pink prosthetic device or of paying 3000 GBP for a brown one. "Instead of a matching artificial leg," Gilroy drily notes, "her local Health Authority had offered her counseling." But this story did not play out as "another sad instance in which the truths of racial division and hierarchy, already known and absolutely familiar but always denied and forgotten, burst out into the light to trigger shock, disgust, and a new bout of emotional self-flagellation." Instead, the media and the public rallied to protest the "affront to [Mrs. Nicholls's] dignity." As a result of that surprising response, "A small but significant act of reparation was turned spontaneously into an informal act of antiracist pedagogy," writes Gilroy.[2] "Britain was rightly ashamed but on this occasion did not turn guiltily away from the source of its discomfort."

For Gilroy these events reveal the uniqueness of the place wherein they occur. He observes, "It is hard to imagine any other place where a double tale like this one—of racial difference being recognized and human dignity simultaneously denied—would have commanded such wide popular attention."[3] And following the helpful public and media response to Mrs. Nicholls's predicament, he confesses "the flowering of my ambivalent love of England." Indeed, the complexity of his emotional connection to England is in part the context for the volume, and the sentiment of ambivalent love shepherds our entry into the text: the lectures that comprise *Postcolonial Melancholia*

> grew in a chosen exile and were shaped by long New England winters as well as many brief, painful, and exhilarating journeys back to the homeland that I was never sure I had had. The arguments below were refined by the digital crackle of Radio 4 and Five Live heard over the Internet, by *Private Eye* and *The Observer* delivered a few days late, and by disruptive snatches of real news twisted into new meanings by being played out-of-synch with local clocks.[4]

Exiled in a distant land that perhaps did not provide a new haven, this melancholic turns back to a belatedly beloved homeland. This glimpse of his exile, though brief, is quite complete: hunkered down for long, cold winters, listening to the crackling radio, eagerly awaiting snatches of news from across the seas. The scene transports us to a time when families gathered—we might even say huddled, against those long, cold winters—around another wireless to catch the sounds of treasured voices from far away. And indeed in this exile, newspapers must travel a great distance, but their words are no less eagerly anticipated for being outdated. Even as they connect the reader to the place of real news, or the place of the important reality, papers from home serve also to remind him of his distance from the community for whom they are intended—the community that apprehends their true meaning, the community from which he is exiled.

We have here a distinction between the metropole and its hinterland. Be it province or colony, this ironically named outpost obviously fails to be a new England. As is customary in such distinctions, the place of exile is referred to as "local," a descriptor that casts the metropole, by opposition, as cosmopolitan, transcending the limitations of particular locality. The locality has its own time that, of course, lags behind the present of the metropole—which distinction also casts the metropole as occupying the future and leading the way on. Yet, in this place stuck in the past, all but cut off from civilization, love flowers and books grow. Though our melancholic appears suspended in a perpetual winter, there was a spring of flowering and a summer of growth, even here. Perhaps those images from a once useful nature should temper our distaste for this hinterland. But not so fast: if nature belongs to the hinterland, then what is left for the metropole? Culture, and more specifically, urban culture, that icon of modernity against which localities associated with nature are said to be undeveloped, backward, stuck in the past.

Formally this passage is a pastoral in miniature. In the classical pastoral, the poet leaves the city for a season, is moved by his experiences in the country, and returns home the wiser for his sojourn. The return to the city is crucial for my purposes; indeed we might read it as the point of the pastoral. For there is little fear that the poet might remain in the country or any doubt that he, being urbane, properly belongs to the city. The wisdom he gains in the country thus enriches the city; that is its purpose. Hence, service to the city is the role of the country, as is customary in metropole-hinterland relations. To value rural settings or proximity to nature under these conditions is to pay them a rather backhanded compliment. They are not worthy per se; their worth derives from their utility to the cultured life possible in the city.

I admit a certain gratification in finding the United States thus provincialized and an admiring incredulity that its diminution is accomplished relative to England. But that England should be so memorialized as home is equally surprising. "Home" is not an oft occurring word in Gilroy's lexicon, "homeland" perhaps even less so. As he notes, his ambivalent love is "a peculiar generational and historical affliction" having everything to do with his generation's accomplishments: the children of the settler generation who, dissatisfied with being treated as perpetual interlopers in the land of their birth and unwilling to accept the limiting of their options to assimilation or segregation, chose instead to demand that their nation alter its understanding of itself to acknowledge the reality of their presence.[5] From his first book (*'There Ain't No Black in the Union Jack'*) to his most recent (*Black Britain*), Gilroy has celebrated the new cultures of black Britain and has insisted on "the conspicuous gains brought about in [Britain's] civil society by an unkempt, unruly, and unplanned multiculture."[6] As the pioneers of black Britishness, his generation reoriented the terrain of national identity around itself; much of Gilroy's work has been devoted to delineating the far-reaching effects of that intervention. Those effects are most evident in the transformation of England's cities, from where Gilroy draws his examples of, as he puts it, "dwell[ing] convivially with difference."[7] Here, in the convivial pleasures possible in the contact zone of difference, is where he *dwells*, not just lives. That is to say, his dwelling, the home for which he yearns, is not England but the urban centers of that land where a hybrid multiculture thrives. To these settings Gilroy turns for evidence that our present racial and cultural arrangements are not absolute and the desire to surpass them not hopelessly utopian.[8]

Gilroy's delight in England's cities spills out in his latest book, *Black Britain*, a photographic history of the black presence in Britain in the twentieth century. The images, culled from the Getty Images archive, document primarily the experiences of postwar migrants and their children, members of Gilroy's generation. The handful set in places that are not immediately identifiable as urban depict black people on the cricket pitch,[9] airfields,[10] the *MV Empire Windrush*,[11] or simply on a nondescript patch of grass.[12] Only one clearly locates a black face in a rural setting, and that photograph is from 1937, before the advent of the "Windrush" generation.[13] What explains this nearly complete exclusion of the rural? No doubt the archive contains many more urban than nonurban images, for migrants did settle primarily in industrial centers.[14] But of the two primary generations here explored, has not even one member ventured out to the countryside?[15]

Reading the archive, Gilroy notes that in the 1930s the camera seems to move indoors when "the first images of the interior spaces are brought to light."[16] Because of that move, "there are fewer images of blacks outside." We move outside again in the subsequent decades but only to gritty urban scapes where close buildings, hoardings, and the like function to extend the enclosure of interior space. The effect of the volume's representation of the mid-1950s through mid-1980s, read perhaps against the grain of the nostalgic pleasure of its historical exploration, is of an intense containment of black people. Certainly such ghettoization occurred, but it was also contested. We are not told whether the archive includes any pictures of black faces in England's green and pleasant land. If it does not, that lack seems a representational choice worthy of comment. If it is does, but Gilroy chose not to include examples of those images, that too is a noteworthy interpretive act.

In his study of contemporary British fiction, Robert Lee writes, "In summer 1991 the magazine supplement of the *Independent on Sunday* ran a feature highlighting the absence of Black British faces in media images of the countryside. Whether in Tourist Board or British Rail posters, TV documentaries or Post Office stamps, the myth of pastoral England (with its customary aggregation of Scotland, Wales, and Ireland) as a white-populated, and at least nominally Christian, island garden, it concluded, largely continues to hold sway." Lee points to instances when the presence of nonwhite faces prompts reactions that "in part derive from some viscerally felt transgression of white rural England." "Once again," he concludes, "'agreed' England, pastoral England at any rate, seems under challenge. In this respect [. . .] has not 'colour,' like 'ethnicity' or 'race,' again historically been thought more the domain of the city than the country and, as a kind of epilogue, of the suburbs?"[17]

Little has changed in the nearly two decades since. A recent interview in *The Guardian* with Benjamin Zephaniah, the poet, includes the following exchange:

> HP: You live in a small village in Lincolnshire. I'm always confused by black people who choose to live in the English countryside. Why do it to yourself?
> BZ: Because it's great, and we're British and we can live anywhere we want to. This is our country, and if we keep living in inner cities people will stereotype us as inner-city people.
> HP: Are you trying to prove something by living there?
> BZ: No. I love jogging and the outdoor life.[18]

Perhaps the interviewer, Hannah Pool, is motivated by concern for Zephaniah's well-being, as her first question indicates. Perhaps she imagines, or knows, that life in the countryside is unpleasant for black people. But when Zephaniah does not confirm her implied opinion of his experience, her concern drops away to reveal suspicion of his motives.

In this brief exchange we see acknowledgment of Lee's agreed England, a land that effectively is divided into racial zones, with the countryside and blacks positioned as mutually exclusive and perhaps mutually hostile.[19] Moreover, the codification of the countryside as a whites-only space creates pressure on blacks to stay in their place. In the interesting phrasing of her initial question, Pool suggests that encountering rural unpleasantness is an experience that black people inflict upon themselves; hence they should avoid such experiences simply by conforming to the racial boundaries of a segregated England. Like Gilroy, she regards the city as the proper place for the black British. But her questions make it clear that the inability to disrupt the logic that links land to race results in a de facto containment of black people in urban areas. Moreover, as we shall see later, it confirms the argument from the supporters of contemporary English racism that the blame for racial antagonism must fall not on those who defend segregation in the form of racist nationalism but on those who defy it. As a result, it limits the potential for the transformation of Englishness that Gilroy sees occurring in cities.

In the English national imaginary the opposition of country and city is well established, with the country serving as the place of retreat and recovery from the flux and falsity of urban life. The city has long been a point of vulnerability for the nation, the place that allows intrusion from the outside and harbors enemies within. Its crowded streets, factories, slums, and, until recently, docklands have been feared as home to crime, disease, illicit sexuality, and other pathologies associated with displacement and defilement. The city is the place where people are out of place, where travelers, workers, immigrants, and other unsettled people mix with and contaminate each other and the nation. In contrast, the land of England has long been nationalized: from the earliest sixteenth-century maps to Shakespeare's Arden, from Kipling's Puck to Tolkien's Hobbits, land and nation have been joined in a metonymic relationship.[20] Since the mid-twentieth century the racialization of the opposition between city and country has been exacerbated by responses to the migration and settlement of people from Britain's former colonies in South Asia, the Caribbean, and Africa. Most have settled in cities: data from the 2001 census indicates that the vast majority of England's ethnic minorities are clustered around the major industrial centers, with fully 50 percent residing in metropolitan London. But that data also tells us that no place in England, no matter how remote, remains entirely white.[21]

If, at its best, the pastoral describes an exchange between margin and center, that circuit of symbolic interdependence seems to have broken down in contemporary England. Today's version prefers segregation and a defensive autonomy to counter the threat that the urban poses to the rural. This resurgence of the countryside is in part a response to contemporary conditions: recent attempts to reenchant the landscape as what Gilroy has called the "geo-body of the nation"[22] respond to the loss of family farms, the growth of agribusiness, genetically modified crops, diseases that require the wholesale slaughter of livestock, increasingly aggressive private ownership, erosion of customary public rights of way and use, ambitious motorways that blur the distinction between urban and rural, and a host of other British and European Union interventions and regulations. In short, England, which was once a feudal inheritance guarded by a landed aristocracy and briefly a common possession entrusted to a socialist state, is now a for-profit corporation administered by CEOs and bureaucrats in New York, London, and Brussels. In response, the contemporary pastoral yearns for a countryside that is both source and haven for the soul of Englishness. It harkens back to a simpler time by harnessing the resources of racial discourse to reenchant the land as home country. Rejecting the city as no longer truly English, the contemporary pastoral refuses the exchange between rural and urban in order to safeguard the purity of the former from contamination by the latter.

That the rural aesthetic is mobilized to represent the nation as a threatened geo-body is not surprising. More troubling is the possibility that those who criticize conceptions of the nation as a racial zone might not break with this segregationist logic. Preoccupied with the icon of the city as the setting for the innovations of cosmopolitan, hybrid cultures, postcolonial theorists leave undisturbed the reenchantment of the countryside as the privileged repository of Englishness. Their unacknowledged and perhaps inadvertent preference for an urban aesthetic signals their debt to modernism—to the great modern thinkers, certainly, and especially Marx, but also to the icon of the city in modernist aesthetics. Postcolonial theory is not transparent description, like a mirror held up to an autonomously existing world. It is a representational practice; that is, it names into being the object of its analysis. There is no distinction between aesthetics and politics in this practice of representation. The political is articulated, made plausible and compelling by aesthetic devices that themselves have a history. Perhaps because of its reliance on those aesthetic devices, the world that postcolonial theory represents remains within the terms of English racial discourse. Nor has that critical apparatus kept pace with aesthetic practices that do contest the closure of an exclusionary Englishness.

In short, in contemporary England a deeply entrenched and widely shared structure of feeling opposes country to city and nationalizes the land of England through race. Both nationalists and anti-nationalists seem willing to settle for a segregation that divides their nation in two: the urban, cosmopolitan England where racial and cultural innovations are fostered, and the rural, homogeneous England where the national essence is preserved.[23] England is divided into racial zones such that people of color are effectively contained in one and excluded from the other. As long as such symbolic and actual segregation continues, many English citizens will be regarded as interlopers creating problems for the otherwise homogeneous and harmonious nation. As a leading theorist of postimperial Britain, Gilroy has from the start of his scholarship taught us to understand black Britishness as an aesthetic intervention, one that uses the symbolic resources of expressive culture to effect political and economic change (*'There Ain't No Black in the Union Jack'*).[24] In the remainder of this essay, then, I consider some of the reasons for his aesthetic preferences, from the push of English racial discourse to the pull of the modern city. My argument is not that Gilroy is wrong but that his preference for the urban and fear of the rural is a blind spot in his scholarship, one that limits our understanding of contemporary racial discourse and thus hinders our ability to challenge it. Moreover, the tools for mounting such a challenge exist within that same scholarship and, if developed, could enrich our understanding of the history of the black presence in England and the magnitude of its challenge to the closure of a racially exclusive Englishness.

Postcolonial theory speaks from a long history of the valorization of the city as a site of change and of the country as a site of continuity. In England there appears to be no end of examples of the use of the countryside as site and cause of a unique and transhistorical national essence. To take one typical example, the philosopher Roger Scruton turns to the land as the literal and metaphoric ground of Englishness, the source of an enchantment that accounts for England's unique institutions, history, and, till recently, people. The "core religious experience of the English," he writes, "was of the consecrated nature of their island."[25] So powerful was this experience that even the Catholic Church was remade by the land into a domestic, appropriately modest faith.[26] Its rather ostentatious god was transformed into an "Anglican God, who in turn had been made in the image of the landscape."[27] The law of England was the law of the land, a common law because the land is a common inheritance.[28] English painting and literature were devoted to the enchantment of the land, as "in Shakespeare's Arden, in Milton's Eden, in Gray's Elegy, in the poetry of John Clare, in the novels of Fielding, in Blake's lyrical and mystical writings and—pre-eminently—in "The Prelude" by Wordsworth."[29] Later writers—Hardy, Hopkins, Lawrence, and Eliot—"turned to the landscape not in order to sentimentalise it, but in order to discover another order, a hidden order, which had been overlayed by history but which was, nevertheless, the true meaning of that history and the deep-down explanation of our being here."[30] The governmental structure of England reflects the countryside, from peers who "subordinate their family names for ever to a piece of English territory"[31] to the geographic distribution of power through local governments.[32] In short, Scruton concludes, the English were a settled people, a people who, like Charles Kingsley's water babies and Beatrix Potter's rabbits that populated the literature of his childhood, were "safe, quiet and untouchable" in their island home.[33]

For Scruton, the England that is no more was not a nation; still less was it a kingdom or an empire. Rather, it was a land, an enchanted territory and a home country. He writes about that country in the past tense because it has been disenchanted by those who deride the traditional values, characteristics, and accomplishments of the English, specifically the likes of Raymond Williams, Tom Nairn, and Perry Anderson—intellectuals who, according to

Scruton, are "seditious bigots."[34] Those who confuse England with Britain are also to blame: Scruton reminds us that the British acquired their empire "'in a fit of absence of mind'" as the unintended consequence of rather good-natured, boyish, and emphatically private, amateur adventuring and trading.[35] But, he hastens to add, although the empire and the other British Isles were added onto England, they were never integrated into it. And surely those who dwell on the dark side of British history—on slavery, the treatment of the Irish, the excesses of colonialism—are particularly to blame for this mistaken rejection of English ideals and character. They are mistaken first because they blame England for British flaws and second because they exaggerate the shortcomings in question. "[S]washbuckling adventurers" may have made their fortunes as slavers, but the condition of slavery was not recognized in "the land of the free"' it cannot therefore be considered integral to English history and character.[36]

Scruton denies any role for racism or even racialism in his account of the virtues of rootedness, going so far as to repudiate "the absurdity of racial ideas when invoked to explain national character."[37] He is proud of England's ability to accept external influences, as evidenced by a language that "absorbs words easily from other languages, and sets them hospitably within its own easy-going syntax."[38] Every wave of European migrants and conquerors—the Huguenots, the Dutch, the Germans—were received with hospitality and absorbed into Englishness.[39] Nevertheless, he notes with sorrow that there are people who did not allow themselves to be changed by the land to which they came. Though we might know them as numerous and varied, they are identified by Scruton as a single entity:

> Only one group of Her Majesty's subjects saw itself as British—namely, those immigrants from the former Empire who seized on the idea of British nationality as a means of having no real nationality at all, certainly no nationality that would conflict with ethnic or religious loyalties, forged far away and years before. There were black British or Bangladeshis, but not black or Bangladeshi English; and there were few black British who saw themselves primarily as subjects of the English Crown.[40]

This group's inherent unsuitability for habitation in England is summarized as its "*unnaturalness*"—Scruton emphasizes the word, taking advantage of its multivalence to underline the metaphysics of belonging. And this group's presence accounts for the death of Scruton's beloved England: although he writes about numerous other causes of disenchantment, only the disenchantment caused by the presence of people of color is described as "fatal":

> These new citizens were "naturalised British subjects"—in other words, not really Englishmen at all, but people who had become *British*, by a strange process which overcame the *unnaturalness* that distinguishes foreigners. The disquiet over immigration was the result, it seems to me, not of racism, but of the disruption of an old experience of home, and a loss of the enchantment which made home a place of safety and consolation. Until this fatal disenchantment, immigrants were regarded by the English as newcomers to the home, entitled to hospitality while they found their feet. (Emphasis in original.)[41]

Because of this disruption and the subsequent lies of England's detractors, the English have lost their unself-conscious confidence in their belonging to their land.[42] Consequently, "they have become an urban people, extolling their countryside as the symbol of what they no longer are. The landscape where their ancestors dwelled is one which they are merely passing through. And sensing this, and sensing that they no longer truly belong in the land which made them, they have lost their self-confidence as a people."[43] Things have deteriorated to such an extent that this once proud people now allows itself to be governed by those not of their soil, that is, by foreigners in Europe.[44] In other words, in becoming British, the English have become rootless, divorced from their natal land, and colonized—rather like the peoples they once governed and transported for their purposes. However much he declares that the English were not influenced by their empire, Scruton abhors the changes that have collapsed the distance between the rulers and the ruled, signaled by their proximity in urban areas. And no matter how assiduously he disavows the romantic nationalism that underlies the ugliness of racism and xenophobia, the eruptions above signal the persistence of those undercurrents in his text.

At this point I imagine Gilroy sighing in weary familiarity, perhaps wondering why the spectacle of a staunch member of the English right blaming the presence of people of color for England's postimperial demise should be worthy of note.[45] For such a political creature, and perhaps even unbeknown to himself, the love of the countryside is an alibi for the logic of segregation, by way of the racial zone. Ideology critique is indeed the appropriate method for analyzing the ideas of a member of the dominant majority: we lift the veil of Scruton's intended meaning and find, predictably, mechanisms of exclusion and oppression. But Gilroy would go further: it's not just that talk of the intimate connection between land, nation, and people is dangerous when deployed by an anxious racial majority. Rather, that chain of signifiers is so crucial to modern racism that it is dangerous in any hands, for it can undermine even the best antiracist intentions. The trajectory from land to race is inevitable, precisely because of the persistent logic of the racial zone.

We find this argument in Gilroy's response to Nelson Mandela's inaugural address when assuming the presidency of South Africa, the nation that until recently dedicated itself to fulfilling the logic of the racial zone. Gilroy writes that the new state president proposed a "transformed relationship between body and environment that would transcend the irrelevancies of Apartheid South Africa's redundant racial hierarchies."[46] Mandela appealed to his fellow South Africans to recognize each other as people of their common land:

> "To my compatriots, I have no hesitation in saying that each one of us is as intimately attached to the soil of this beautiful country as are the famous jacaranda trees to Pretoria and the mimosa trees of the bushveld.
>
> Each time one of us touches the soil of this land, we feel a sense of personal renewal. . . . That spiritual and physical oneness we all share with this common homeland explains the depth of pain we all carried in our hearts as we saw our country tear itself apart in a terrible conflict."[47]

Gilroy declares Mandela's goals "laudable" but remains suspicious of such "powerful claims of soil, roots, and territory." He recommends that they be set aside in favor of "the idea of movement," which, he believes, "can provide an alternative to the sedentary poetics of either soil or blood." But Mandela does not link soil and blood; he does not claim that the people of South Africa are biologically one. On the contrary, he turns to land precisely because they are not. Does Gilroy connect the two because he believes the linkage is inevitable, that because soil and blood often have been joined in nationalist discourse, therefore their articulation is permanent? He does not explain himself in this context, but we know from his previous writings that he is informed deeply by structuralism and has argued vehemently against the position that social and linguistic categories are preceded by the nature to which they refer. Indeed, it was his first book, *'There Ain't No Black in the Union Jack,'* that made it fashionable for a time to place the word "race" in quotation marks in order to emphasize its historical contingency. Nevertheless, here he seems to suggest that the articulation of soil, blood, roots, and territory is so powerful as to be, in effect, inherent.

Gilroy's preference for the aesthetics of motion, for the city over the country, is echoed by a host of writers who celebrate their sense of belonging in England's urban landscape and who use their ease in that setting to distance themselves from the provinciality of preceding generations. In Salman Rushdie's *Satanic Verses*, Salahuddin Chamchawala "gabble[s] out, like a mantra, like a spell, the six letters of his dream city, *ellowen deeowen*" but is bewildered by the grotesque mutations and tropicalization of that city by its colorful inhabitants.[48] In the film *Sammy and Rosie Get Laid*, Rafi is similarly disturbed by the changes wrought in his beloved city by the assertive, anti-assimilationist new generation. Declaring London to be "'a cesspit,'" he advises his son to return home to Pakistan.[49] But Sammy responds, "'I am home, Pop.'" As we see scenes of Sammy's life with Rosie in London his voiceover informs us, "'We love our city and we belong to it. Neither of us are English, we're Londoners you see.'"[50] In *Haven't Stopped Dancing Yet*, Shymala Perera's narrator similarly enumerates the spaces of her beloved London, from Park Lane to Brick Lane, and declares that city to be the place where all roads meet, "a giant control center" of the world.[51] "'I'd die in the countryside,'" another character confirms.[52]

The scholarly counterparts of these writers are no less enamored of the possibilities of urban life in formerly imperial nations. In her reading of *Sammy and Rosie Get Laid*, and despite her reservations regarding "the postcolonial elite," Gayatri Spivak suggests that in "the urban public culture of the migrant," national hostilities are "provisionally suspended."[53] And Homi Bhabha grows uncharacteristically lyrical when he considers the challenges to the ideology of the nation that migrants have mounted in first world cities. He writes,

> it is to the city that the migrants, the minorities, the diasporic come to change the history of the nation. If I have suggested that the people emerge in the finitude of the nation, marking the liminality of cultural identity, producing the double-edged discourse of social territories and temporalities, then in the west, and increasingly elsewhere, it is the city which provides the space in which emergent identification and new social movements of the people are played out. It is there that, in our time, the perplexity of living is most acutely experienced.[54]

Like Gilroy, Bhabha articulates his preference for the experience of perplexity by noting with disapproval the nationalist associations of the natural world:

> To end with the English weather is to invoke, at once, the most changeable and immanent signs of national difference. It encourages memories of the "deep" nation crafted in chalk and limestone; the quilted downs; the moors menaced by the wind; the quiet cathedral towns; that corner of a foreign field that is forever England. [. . .] These imaginative geographies that spanned countries and empires are changing; those imagined communities that played on the unisonant boundaries of the nation are singing with different voices. If I began with the scattering of the people across countries, I want to end with their gathering in the city. The return of the diasporic; the postcolonial.[55]

From this example of the aesthetic transformation of historical and political exigency we might conclude that we take up our positions in a given discourse, for example, nationalism or antinationalism, through the styles it makes available. The old English are country people who see in their land a faithful reflection of their collective personality and their responsibilities. By contrast, migrants and new settlers join the urban masses in celebrating the vitality of their own heterogeneity.

Bhabha notes but does not contest the chain of associations that harnesses the work of culture to that of nature. Like Gilroy, he turns away from a style that values simplicity and unity and recommends one that prefers complexity and difference. With this gesture he implies either that the chain cannot be broken or that such a task is simply not worth the trouble. Far beyond making a virtue out of necessity, Bhabha divides the possibilities of the postcolonial world into two sensibilities, accepts their spatial segregation, and makes significant claims for the political superiority of the urban. If we remain within his description we must conclude that rejecting the political implications of romantic nationalism requires abandoning its symbolic resources as irredeemably tainted. If we wish to celebrate the song sung with the different voices, we must reject the moors and downs. The diasporic and postcolonial return but not to rural settings. Their presence, contained in cities, does not spill out to disrupt the song of settled, rural England. That latter space remains the safe haven to which the beleaguered, real English can retreat.

Perhaps Bhabha and Gilroy are influenced by the early work of Stuart Hall and his colleagues at the now-defunct Birmingham Centre for Cultural

Studies, whose paradigmatic *Policing the Crisis* established the virtues of the urban sensibility for British racial politics. Hall et al. credit the urban experience for the rise of a black consciousness that made it possible to be simultaneously black and British. The containment of the postwar migrant generation in certain urban areas led to "the birth of the thriving 'native quarter' at the heart of the English city." That "colony society" provided the material base for cultural revival, first of a West Indian consciousness and then of "a powerful and regenerated 'black consciousness.'"[56] The subsequent "'colony' generation" unapologetically claimed a black cultural identity and rejected the quietism of their parents: "The first wave constructed the 'colony'; the second generation was born into the 'colony.' They are its first true progeny. They have no other home."[57] Unhampered by their predecessors' "greener memories of home," this generation is "less outfaced than their parents were by the reality of life in the metropolis: less willing to endure and survive in patience; less deferential to white society; and more aggressively confident about who they are. In this sense the 'colony' has provided a basis for the construction of positive alternative cultural identities."[58]

Note again the aestheticization that renders what might be a straightforward opposition between two historical experiences into a contrast of sensibilities and modes of existence. Memories of home are "green," so that domesticity and the natural world together signify a past that must be outgrown. The only shade associated with the city is black. It is as though all the associations of the natural world, including color, have to be swept aside to allow the emergence of a new and politically mature generation, black by choice and black because it has never known the experience of rootedness. And, for Hall et al., therein lies its political potential: freed of the constraints of belonging, either in the previous or the present country, this generation's militancy proves capable of challenging Britain's racial order in "an unorganised political rebellion."[59] "The second generation simply *is* a black generation, knows it is black and is not going to be anything else but black," they assert. "It is most unlikely, then, that this generation would ever set its feet, willingly, on the path to assimilation" (emphasis in original).[60]

From the city, to a new people with a new sensibility, to political agency and rebellion, to a challenge to the established, rooted power of the nation itself: enormous claims are made for the political potential of urban life. Postcolonial scholars make no similar claims for the possibilities of the countryside. Perhaps this is due in part to their political commitments—for some, explicitly Marxist—and intellectual training that, for all, includes Marx. All are familiar with the Marxist argument that the advent of industrial capitalism destroyed the social and economic relationships, good and bad, that held each individual in his or her place in a feudal community. Hence the title of Marshall Berman's influential treatise on the experience of modernity, *All That Is Solid Melts into Air*, taken from this famous passage of *The Communist Manifesto*:

> Constant revolutionizing of production, uninterrupted disturbance of all social relations, everlasting uncertainty and agitation, distinguish the bourgeois epoch from all earlier times. All fixed, fast-frozen relations, with their train of venerable ideas and opinions, are swept away, all new-formed ones become obsolete before they can ossify. All that is solid melts into air, all that is holy is profaned, and men at last are forced to face with sober senses the real conditions of their lives and their relations with their fellow men.[61]

Relying on Marx as the primary theorist of the modern era, Berman emphasizes "the dialectical motion of modernity" evident at the end of the passage, such that every historical juncture contains the seeds of its own destruction and of the emergence of the next historical phase.[62] Displaced from their land and their homes, the peasants that congregated in rapidly industrializing centers were transformed into masses of workers. It was in urban areas that they became a class, first in itself, but gradually, through struggle against their common conditions of oppression, a politicized class for itself.

Hall et al. follow this template to explain the "momentous" shift from quietism to militancy among the black British. To do so they have to abandon the foundational place of production and reverse the trajectory that begins with conditions of production and leads to consciousness. In black Britain, they admit, consciousness changed first, inspired by independence struggles in Africa and Black Power in the United States.[63] That international black consciousness eventually became specific to conditions in Britain, but even then the common experience in the emergent racialized class was not that of work but of "'worklessness.'"[64] In other words, it was not appreciation of its productive capacities that brought about the politicized consciousness of a class for itself but a cultural, already militant identity that expressed itself in certain economic demands. Such reversals stretch the logic of materialism to its breaking point, but one thing remains constant: the city is the setting of this momentous shift from colonial immigrant to black British. Every other condition of the Marxist template can be suspended, but the concentration of the dispossessed in urban areas with the attendant loosening of their ties elsewhere remains necessary. The political potential of the city provides the continuity required to apply the Marxist account of class to contemporary racial politics. Their setting allows Hall et al. to link the two as peculiarly modern phenomena, parallel expressions of the seismic dislocations and ceaseless motion that characterize modernity.

For Berman, as for Marx and Engels, modernity thus characterized leaves considerable tragedy in its wake, but the dialectic ensures that those who adapt to its cadence are offered a hitherto unknown political potential. Hence in *The Communist Manifesto* the displacement of peasants is also explained as the bourgeoisie "rescu[ing] a considerable part of the population from the idiocy of rural life."[65] Berman echoes these sentiments in his reading of Goethe's *Faust*, a text he regards as the paradigmatic tale of the development of the modern individual. The countryside and its settled way of life are represented here as the pre-urban world that must die to make way for the new, and Berman makes no apology for that fortunate fall. He contends, "In the two centuries between Gretchen's time and ours thousands of 'little worlds' will be emptied out, transformed into hollow shells, while their young people head for great cities, for open frontiers, for new nations, in search of freedom to think and love and grow."[66] Driven by his desire for self-development, Faust is determined that the world around him must also develop to its fullest potential. "Emigrants and refugees from a hundred Gothic villages and towns"[67] amass and become workers in his great project of harnessing the sea for human use.[68] Those who cannot adapt to the new world he is bringing into being must die. Unfortunately, that includes an old couple that will not give him their small plot of land. Notably, Faust experiences their resistance as the limits of his control over the natural world. He declares, "'I want their lindens in my grip, / Since these few trees that are denied me / Undo my worldwide ownership.'"[69] And again we hear the opposition of old and new, the traditional and the modern expressed through the opposition of manufacture and nature.

In the murder of the old couple, Berman reads the homogenizing drive of modernism, so that Faust presages Le Corbusier's plan to bulldoze the boulevards of Paris and Robert Moses's disdain for the neighborhoods of New York.[70] But before that triumph of corporate modernism, out of the tragedy of development emerges a new kind of human being, one adapted to the speed and complexity of city life. Moving to Baudelaire, Berman finds, "The archetypal modern man, as we see him here, is a pedestrian thrown into the maelstrom of modern city traffic":[71]

> The man in the modern street, thrown into this maelstrom, is driven back on his own resources—often on resources he never knew he had—and forced to stretch them desperately in order to survive. [. . .]
>
> Baudelaire shows how modern city life forces these new moves on everyone; but he shows, too, how in doing this it also paradoxically enforces new modes of freedom. A man who knows how to move in and around and through the traffic can go anywhere, down any of the endless urban corridors where traffic itself is free to go. This mobility opens up a great wealth of new experiences and activities for the urban masses.[72]

Herein lies the key to the primacy of the city street in Berman's analysis of modernity: that setting both motivates and manifests the experience of freedom, and not only for the bourgeoisie. On the boulevards of Baudelaire's Paris, the bourgeoisie cannot control its encounters with the proletariat, and the discarded stepchildren of modernity step forward as equal in their desire for the benefits of the new capitalist economy.[73] When the poor clerk in Dostoevsky's *Notes from the Underground* refuses to give way to his wealthy nemesis on the Nevsky Prospect in St. Petersburg, he becomes "a New Man"[74] who "confront[s] the ruling class and insist[s] on his equal rights."[75] His struggle, Berman writes, dramatizes "the struggle for human rights—for equality, dignity, recognition."[76] Despite their otherwise obvious dissimilarities, both Baudelaire and Dostoevsky describe what Berman regards as "primal modern scenes":[77]

> everyday encounters in the city street that are raised to first intensity [. . .], to the point where they express fundamental possibilities and pitfalls, allures and impasses of modern life. For both writers, too, the sense of political urgency becomes a primary source of energy, and the personal encounter in the street emerges as a political event; the modern city works as a medium in which personal and political life flow together and become one.[78]

These aesthetic and political consequences of modernization are echoed by black British scholars, including Hall and Gilroy, who use encounters on the street as primal scenes of British racial politics. Both theorists refer to confrontations between black youth (read male) and the police as exemplary instances of the increasing militancy of disenfranchised people who will no longer be contained in segregated spaces, will not yield their right to occupy public space and, by extension, the space of England itself. Ample instances in *Policing the Crisis* are paralleled more recently by the significance Gilroy finds in the 1993 murder on a city street of the young, black student Stephen Lawrence. In *Postcolonial Melancholia*, too, the city is characterized repeatedly as convivial, civil, hybrid, multicultural, and potentially democratic, and city streets in particular are characterized as the site of a brutal reality that gives the lie to those who would minimize the significance of racism.[79] Such depictions of the black British suggest an answer to Berman's question, "What if the multitudes of men and women who are terrorized by modern traffic could learn to confront it together?"[80]

But perhaps nowhere is that message delivered with more aesthetic pleasure, and hence more persuasively, than on the front cover of *Black Britain*. The camera here is arrested by a woman striding forward with such assurance that all else seems to blow back around her and be caught up in her draft. Everything about her and her male companion is in motion: her hair and her vibrantly striped dress—in black and white, of course—blow back, as do his trousers, as if they can hardly keep pace with her forward movement.[81] The image unfortunately is undated and unattributed but appears to have been taken on a city street in England, likely in the 1950s. The obviously well-appointed couple is in a public space. The street is wide and well trafficked by cars and pedestrians. It is a main commercial way, not the narrow lane of a segregated neighborhood. The white men standing to the side suggest, at the least, that this is a mixed-race space, but the probable date of the photograph makes me read in the white gaze something other than disinterested curiosity. The couple occupies the center of the pathway, and they do not lean together. They claim nearly all its space, as if they own it—a claim reinforced by the boldness of the woman's stride and by her attention-grabbing attire. In contrast, around them all is still. The stolid brick and stone buildings; the old flagstone sidewalk; the white men who stand gazing impassively, hands clasped behind their backs; the parked cars, solid and heavy by today's standards: all appear to be stable and permanent to the point of immobility. Providing the only movement in the image, the couple appears to be pulling the scape with them as they stride forward. And with them the winds of change come even to the stolidity of this well-established place: the photograph most likely was taken on a windy day, but it looks as though the white man in the gray suit is turning to catch a glimpse of the force that sweeps past him, ruffling his hair and lifting his jacket as it moves, pushing him from out of the center of the frame and of the story, relegating him to the status of onlooker.[82]

Cover image of *Black Britain: A Photographic History.*

This is Berman's archetypal urban street scene, one in which the marginalized step forth to claim the promises of modernity as their birthright. Displaced by the forces of urbanization, they occupy the city as its true natives in a scape that now looks as if it was built for them, as if all along it had awaited their appearance to grace and complete it. The composition would have no center, no subject, if not for them. Their appearance on the city street not only claims but displays the political potential of that space of encounter. As the black couple outpaces the automobiles that are the avatars of 1950s modernity, they put to rest any lingering suspicion that they are helplessly adrift in the maelstrom of technologically driven, rapidly changing times. On the contrary, they are so adept and graceful in their setting that they bring beauty to its rather drab ordinariness. Rather than a backward people, a people from the past, or a people without a history, this gorgeous image displays them as the juggernauts of history. The dialectic turns as these descendants of slaves briskly shoulder past history's erstwhile masters.

This image helps me identify commonalities that I find in a range of postcolonial theorists who share a model of how history works, and who all respond to a particular aestheticization of that historical model. If postcolonial theory is indebted to the urban aesthetic of modernism, that is in part because much of it seeks to explicate the political promise of recent dispersions and gatherings. To do so it borrows from analyses of previous world-changing demographic shifts. But even when not explicitly Marxist, as in the case of Homi Bhabha, the momentum of the analysis proffered derives from the dialectical tension between what has been and what could be. Moreover, that tension and its political valence are represented aesthetically as the opposition between country and city. Bhabha offers a choice between "emergent," "new," and "movement," on the one hand, and "finitude," on the other; between the vitality of "singing" and playing, and already accomplished "unisonant" "boundaries"; between the liveliness and beauty of motion and the static depth associated with burial ("the corner of the foreign field that is forever England"). In other words, we are offered a stylistic and affective choice between life and death. But the dialectic ceases with the rejection of the rural as death in favor of the urban as life. There is no looking ahead to what might come after the gathering of the diaspora in the city or beyond the aesthetic of mobility. Instead, yearning for belonging in and to a place is dismissed as nostalgic, simplistic, and probably dangerous.

Postcolonial theory presents itself as peculiarly suited to the world in which we live, a world characterized by rapid change, constant motion, and the often-bewildering emergence of multiple new ways of being. Much of it represents a rural aesthetic as hopelessly outdated, if not irrelevant, then dangerous, and its proponents as either misguided or malevolent. Like vampires among the living, those proponents keep alive an old world that should have died to make room for the new. Stuck in "the sedentary poetics of soil and blood," clinging to the gravesites that are "forever England," these representatives of death suck the vitality that belongs to the living. Such an ideology critique of the rural aesthetic raises the veil from the love of land to expose the logic of racial segregation. But because it accepts the country-city binary of English racial zoning, this critique does not give us a way to undo segregationist logic. Nor does it suggest how we might insert love of and habitation in the countryside into another chain of meaning and perhaps read the presence of nonwhite faces in the English landscape as something other than bizarre.

For land, even the land of South Africa, is not inherently meaningful. In her study of apartheid discourse, Aletta Norval observes that in the 1930s and '40s, "A set of equivalences were [*sic*] drawn between the city, Englishness, amorality, relativism, artificiality and atheism, while the *platteland* (countryside) was associated with a close communion with nature, God, a rounded humanity, simplicity and resoluteness characteristic of Afrikaner life."[83] The brutal spatial application of this chain of signifiers meant that by the 1970s and '80s, "[t]he nation was white. Coloureds, Indians and Africans had no place in it."[84] South Africa under apartheid exemplifies the sedentary, metaphysical tendencies that Gilroy disdains, but my point is that ceaseless repetition over several decades was required for the nationalization and racialization of land. The meaning thus constructed through painstaking and brutally enforced repetition can be disrupted, the elements of its chain of signifiers disarticulated. Indeed, as Gilroy himself suggests, Mandela's inaugural address can be read as one such attempt at disarticulation and rearticulation. Nevertheless, Gilroy recommends that we "consider what might be gained if the powerful claims of soil, roots, and territory could be set aside."[85] Whether he does so because he believes Mandela's project to be doomed or simply because he prefers another project, he does not say. The contrast he emphasizes between "the idea of movement" and "the sedentary poetics of either soil or blood" suggests that the choice is not only ideological but also aesthetic. It is a question of style.

Is it possible to insert the countryside into another poetics, one that does not regard land as an obdurate anchor for the categories—race and nation—that imprison the modern individual and constrain our collective emancipatory possibilities? Of course, since at least Raymond Williams and Henri Lefebvre, scholars have emphasized the contingent history of the rural and its status in circuits of exchange with the urban.[86] As any postmodern geography might attest, the land is far from the immobile and ahistorical inheritance of Scruton's yearnings.[87] But, bearing in mind Gilroy's ambivalent love, another way to ask this question might be: how would one change the emotional valence of a landscape so that it encompasses the presence and memories of multiple, even new inhabitants? When Zarina Bhimji inscribes traces of the history of slavery and colonialism on photographs of a country house, a claim is staked: the historic significance and presence of people of color is evident in the most iconic sites of nationalist history.[88] When, in Gurinder Chadha's *I'm British But . . .* the camera pans over gently rolling, green hills and we hear not a hymn but a *qawwali*, a claim is staked: it is the affiliations of its inhabitants that make the land grippingly, hauntingly meaningful.[89] And when, in Lenny Henry's television series *Chef!* Caroline Lee-Johnson leans over roses outside her home, the aptly named Tudor Cottage, and becomes for a moment the English rose, a claim is most wittily staked.[90] That claim of belonging is evident in the image of Benjamin Zephaniah jogging through his Lincolnshire village and in his retort to his interviewer's incredulity: "we're British and we can live anywhere we want to. This is our country."[91]

The challenge of transforming the meaning of England's land has already been engaged by these culture workers. Just as the post–World War II settlers and their children produced the convivial multiculture that Gilroy celebrates in cities, these culture workers foray further afield in their demand that the nation's story change to acknowledge their presence. There is no reason to suppose that their incorporation in the national story will be tantamount to assimilation, as though beyond the mobility of migration lies nothing but a settlement so sedentary that it might as well be burial. Indeed, we can do no better than turn back to Gilroy's unveilings of roots and routes (*Black Atlantic*) to remember how powerfully the black British have demonstrated that mobility and settlement are a false opposition. Following his generation and the next into the countryside, we might discover a pastoral that restores the symbolic exchange between urban and rural. Black and Asian Britishers might then be the agents who reconcile the divisions in a nation segregated by its fears and fleeing from its history.

Notes

1. Paul Gilroy, *Postcolonial Melancholia* (New York: Columbia University Press, 2004), xiii.
2. Ibid., xiv.
3. Ibid., xiii.
4. Ibid., xiv.
5. I am grateful to Jay Garcia for pointing out that this ambivalent love for England does not represent a new departure in Gilroy's work. On the

contrary, it has always been evident in his desire to be both British and black.

6. Gilroy, *Postcolonial Melancholia*, xiv.
7. Ibid., 5.
8. Ibid., 4.
9. Paul Gilroy, *Black Britain: A Photographic History* (London: Saqi in association with Getty Images, 2007), 132.
10. Ibid., 40, 49.
11. Ibid., 69.
12. Ibid., 84, 313.
13. Ibid., 37.
14. David Owen and Mark Johnson, "Ethnic Minorities in the Midlands," in *Ethnicity in the 1991 Census: v. 3, Social Geography and Ethnicity in Britain: Geographical Spread, Spatial Concentration and Internal Migration*, ed. Peter Ratcliffe, produced by the Office for National Statistics (London: H.M.S.O., 1996), 227–68; Susan J. Smith, *The Politics of "Race" and Residence: Citizenship, Segregation and White Supremacy in Britain* (Cambridge: Polity, 1989); Susan J. Smith, "Residential Segregation and the Politics of Racialization," in *Racism: The City and the State*, ed. Malcolm Cross and Michael Keith (London: Routledge, 1993), 128–43.
15. From the 1991 census Rees and Phillips report that although 51 percent reside in the top twelve, primarily urban districts, nevertheless, "People of Black-Caribbean origin are found in virtually every English district and in most of the urban districts of Wales and Scotland." Philip Rees and Deborah Phillips, "Geographical Spread: The National Picture," in *Ethnicity in the 1991 Census: v. 3, Social Geography and Ethnicity in Britain: Geographical Spread, Spatial Concentration and Internal Migration*, ed. Peter Ratcliffe, produced by the Office for National Statistics (London: H.M.S.O., 1996), 227–68; 39. In the same volume, see also Tony Champion, "Internal Migration and Ethnicity in Britain," 135–73. And the 2001 census suggests the presence of nonwhite faces in even the most remote areas. See Office of National Statistics, *Census 2001: National Report for England and Wales* (Norwich: The Stationery Office, 2004). For scholarship addressing this representational gap and its consequences, see Neil Chakraborti and John Garland, eds., *Rural Racism* (Cullompton, Devon: Willan, 2004) and Sarah Neal and Julian Agyeman, eds., *The New Countryside? Ethnicity, Nation and Exclusion in Contemporary Rural Britain* (Bristol, UK: Policy Press, 2006).

16. Gilroy, *Black Britain*, 41.
17. Robert A. Lee, "Changing the Script: Sex, Lies and Videotapes in Hanif Kureishi, David Dabydeen and Mike Phillips," in *Other Britain, Other British: Contemporary Multicultural Fiction*, ed. Robert A. Lee (London: Pluto, 1995), 69–70.
18. Benjamin Zephaniah, "Question Time," an interview with Hannah Pool. *The Guardian*, 21 May 2009, http://www.guardian.co.uk/lifeandstyle/2009/may/21/benjamin-zephaniah-interview, accessed 24 August 2009.
19. The concept of the racial zone is borrowed from Michael Banton, *Racial Theories* (Cambridge: Cambridge University Press, 1998).
20. Reading maps from 1579 to the mid-seventeenth century, Helgerson argues for the contemporaneous nationalization of the land its inhabitants: the modern English self was defined with reference to love of country, with the country itself defined as the land. See Richard Helgerson's *Forms of Nationhood: The Elizabethan Writing of England* (Chicago: University of Chicago Press, 1992) and "The Land Speaks: Cartography, Chorography, and Subversion in Renaissance England," *Representations* 16 (1986): 51–58.

    The literature documenting the association of land to Englishness over subsequent centuries is vast, but see, for instance, Elizabeth Helsinger, *Rural Scenes and National Representation: Britain, 1815–1850* (Princeton: Princeton University Press, 1997) and David Matless, *Landscape and Englishness* (London: Reaktion Books, 1998). For examples of the far less vast but growing literature on the troubling contemporary consequences of that association, see Chakraborti and Garland, *Rural Racism*, and Paul Cloke and Jo Little, eds., *Contested Countryside Cultures: Otherness, Marginalisation and Rurality* (London: Routledge, 1997).
21. *Census 2001.*
22. Paul Gilroy, *Against Race: Imagining Political Culture beyond the Color Line* (Cambridge: Harvard University Press, 2000), 58. (Published as *Between Camps: Nations, Cultures and the Allure of Race in the United Kingdom.*)
23. The identity called "black British" is an example of the innovation I have in mind: seen as a sign of a nonassimilative integration by some (e.g., Hall et al., discussed later), it is read by Scruton as evidence of the bastardization of legitimate identities. For the emergence of a peculiarly British blackness, see my *AlterNatives: Black Feminism in the Postimperial Nation* (Stanford: Stanford University Press, 2002).

24. Paul Gilroy, *'There Ain't No Black in the Union Jack': The Cultural Politics of Race and Nation* (Chicago: University of Chicago Press, 1987).
25. Roger Scruton, *England: An Elegy* (London: Chatto and Windus, 2000), 18.
26. Ibid., 18.
27. Ibid., 90.
28. Ibid., 9, 10, 119, chapter 6.
29. Ibid., 40.
30. Ibid., 41.
31. Ibid., 151.
32. Ibid., 181.
33. Ibid., 61. Scruton was fortunate to know the enchanted England in its twilight years, which, by a remarkable coincidence, correspond exactly to the years of his own childhood. See Scruton, *England*, 18.
34. Ibid., 249.
35. Ibid., 2, 16–17. Here Scruton quotes John Robert Seeley, *The Expansion of England in the Eighteenth Century* (London: 1883).
36. Scruton, *England*, 20.
37. Ibid., 76.
38. Ibid, 78.
39. Ibid., 8.
40. Ibid., 4. Note that whenever this kind of homogenization is attempted, Jewishness must be erased. If all true English are Anglican or at least Christian, and if evidence of adherence to a religion, people, or culture exceeds England's boundaries, then Jews cannot be English. Unless they too are taken to be an alien race, Jews undermine the racial division here attempted. But whereas the targeting of nonwhites seems acceptable on the grounds of culture, scholarship of this sort generally shies away from blunt anti-Semitism, preferring simply to ignore the existence of English/British Jews.
41. Ibid., 7–8.
42. Interestingly, Scruton does not often provide evidence that the detractors are wrong. His position appears to be that though they may have the facts right, nevertheless they should not think as they do. Hence he says of historians such as Hilaire Belloc, *History of England* (London: 1915) and Linda Colley, *Britons: Forging the Nation, 1707–1837* (New Haven: Yale University Press, 1992), not that their scholarship is incorrect, but only that it is philosophically flawed. Scruton, *England*, 3.

43. Scruton, *England*, 242.
44. Ibid., 251.
45. Scruton is founding editor of the *Salisbury Review* and author of, among numerous other texts, *The Meaning of Conservatism* (Manchester, UK: Pelican, 1980). Oddly, he lives in Virginia as well as in England, apparently feeling himself to be a creature of both lands and nations.
46. Gilroy, *Against Race*, 111.
47. Speech reprinted in *The Independent*, 11 May 1995, 12. Quoted in Gilroy, *Against Race*, 111.
48. Salman Rushdie, *The Satanic Verses* (New York: Viking, 1989), 37.
49. Hanif Kureishi, *Sammy and Rosie Get Laid*, in *London Kills Me: Three Screenplays and Four Essays* (New York: Penguin, 1992), 195–264; 233.
50. Ibid., 234.
51. Shymala Perera, *Haven't Stopped Dancing Yet* (London: Hodder and Stoughton, 1999), 57.
52. Ibid., 233.
53. Spivak's disdain for the associations of the natural world is apparent in the terms she uses to reject nostalgia for origins: "Because anyone who can conceive of looking for roots, should, already, you know, be growing rutabagas." In Gayatri Spivak, "Postmarked Calcutta, India: Conversation with Angela Ingram," in *The Post-Colonial Critic: Interviews, Strategies, Dialogues*, ed. Sarah Harasym (New York: Routledge, 1990), 93.
54. Homi K. Bhabha, "DissemiNation: Time, Narrative, and the Margins of the Modern Nation," *Nation and Narration* (New York: Routledge, 1990), 319–20.
55. Ibid., 319.
56. Stuart Hall, Chas Critcher, Tony Jefferson, John Clarke, and Brian Roberts, *Policing the Crisis: Mugging, the State, and Law and Order* (London: Macmillan, 1978), 351.
57. Ibid., 354.
58. Ibid.
59. Ibid., 357.
60. Ibid., 355.
61. Karl Marx, *Manifesto of the Communist Party*, in *The Marx-Engels Reader*, ed. Robert C. Tucker (New York: Norton, 1972), 469–500; 476.
62. Marshall Berman, *All That Is Solid Melts into Air: The Experience of Modernity*, 2nd edition (New York: Penguin, 1988 [Simon and Schuster 1982]), 21.
63. Hall et al., *Policing the Crisis*, 356.

64. Ibid.
65. Marx, *Manifesto of the Communist Party*, 477.
66. Berman, *All That Is Solid Melts into Air*, 59.
67. Ibid., 66.
68. Ibid., 62.
69. Goethe, *Faust*, 11239–52; quoted in Berman, *All That Is Solid Melts into Air*, 67.
70. Berman, *All That Is Solid Melts into Air*, 68.
71. Ibid., 159.
72. Ibid., 159–60.
73. Berman's example is drawn from "The Eyes of the Poor" (*Paris Spleen* #26) as discussed in Berman, *All That Is Solid Melts into Air*, 150–55.
74. Berman, *All That Is Solid Melts into Air*, 228.
75. Ibid., 227.
76. Ibid., 228.
77. Ibid., 148.
78. Ibid., 229.
79. Gilroy, *Postcolonial Melancholia*, 124. This text also contains a reading of Montesquieu's *Persian Letters* that, in its approving characterization of the modern as uprooted, itinerant, encountering otherness, and thereby bearing positive political potential, is startlingly reminiscent of Berman's use of *Faust*.
80. Gilroy, *Postcolonial Melancholia*, 163.
81. The image is reproduced on the cover in black and white, as are all the images in the volume. Mysteriously, we are not told whether any of the original photographs were in color, or by whom they were taken, or where they first appeared. In any case, for the purposes of this essay, I am examining the image on the cover of *Black Britain* and not the photograph from which that image is taken.
82. The only fully legible sign in the image, "Bombay Restaurant," also indicates something of the changes that have come to this urban setting.
83. Aletta J. Norval, *Deconstructing Apartheid Discourse* (London: Verso, 1996), 20.
84. Ibid., 216.
85. Gilroy, *Against Race*, 111.
86. See Henri Lefebvre, *The Production of Space* (Cambridge, MA: Blackwell, 1991) and Raymond Williams, *The Country and the City* (New York: Oxford University Press, 1973). Williams haunts this essay, in more ways than one. On the one hand, my presuppositions obviously are deeply

informed by his *Country and City*. On the other, he is an excellent example of how the chain of associations that links land to race forms a common sense shared by those across the political spectrum. As Gilroy points out, it is precisely Williams's preference for the "rooted" over the transient or new that reveals the limits of the Left's critique of the nation, the point of that critique's "apparent endorsement of the presuppositions of the new racism" (*'There Ain't No Black in the Union Jack,'* 50). Representing, as they do here, the opposed aesthetics of the sedentary and the mobile, Williams and Gilroy are each other's blind spot. Indeed, it is possible that taken together the two might create a substantial instability in the otherwise well-buttressed discourse of race and nation. As such the potential conversation between (rather than resolution of) their positions is very rich and far more complex than can be pursued within the confines of this essay.

87. Doreen Massey, *Space, Place, and Gender* (Minneapolis: University of Minnesota Press, 1994); W. J. T. Mitchell, ed., *Landscape and Power* (Chicago: University of Chicago Press, 1994); Jonathan Murdoch, *Post-Structuralist Geography: A Guide to Relational Space* (London: Sage, 2006).
88. Bhimji is a photographer and media artist whose 1998 series, Cleaning the Garden, includes photographs of Harewood House, an eighteenth-century stately home with gardens designed by Lancelot "Capability" Brown. The home was designed for the Lascelles family, whose fortune was made through the various trades—slave, sugar, tobacco—of the West Indies. See Simon David Smith, *Slavery, Family and Gentry Capitalism in the British Atlantic: The World of the Lascelles, 1648–1834* (Cambridge: Cambridge University Press, 2006).

    Among other things, Bhimji superimposes advertisements for the return of runaway slaves from newspapers of the day onto the image of the house and its gardens.
89. Gurinder Chadha, dir., *I'm British But . . .* , British Film Institute and Channel Four, 1989. I'm thinking of the footage of the Welsh shepherd riding through his pastures accompanied, for us, by the voice of Nusrat Fateh Ali Khan, the great singer of Sufi devotional songs. But this is one of many examples of provocative mergers of image and music in this short film.
90. I refer to "Personnel," the inaugural episode of *Chef!* See "Personnel," written by Peter Tilbury, *Chef!* created by Lenny Henry, BBC, London. 28 January 1993. A BBC television comedy, the show was broadcast in three series from January 1993 to September 1996. The comedian Lenny

Henry played the lead; Caroline Lee-Jones, also a black British actor, played his wife and business partner. Together their characters ran Le Chateau Anglais, a *haute cuisine* restaurant situated in an idyllically rural Oxfordshire.

91. In another interview Zephaniah speaks of his love for his chosen home: "I love England and have always wanted to live in a country village. [. . .] My village is wonderful place—when all the touring is over it's a great, great place to come back to." See Benjamin Zephaniah, "My Family Values," an interview with Nikki Spencer, *The Guardian*, 4 July 2009. http://www.guardian.co.uk/lifeandstyle/2009/jul/04/benjamin-zephaniah-family-values, accessed 24 August 2009.

7

Dynamic Nominalism in Alain Locke and Paul Gilroy

JAY GARCIA

For all absolutistic thinking, however idealist, has totalitarian potential.
—Alain Locke, "The Need for a New Organon in Education"

References to the African American philosopher and cultural critic Alain Locke in Paul Gilroy's work are fleeting, ephemeral things. Yet the references are nevertheless striking. In *Against Race* (published as *Between Camps* in the United Kingdom), Gilroy appends "great sage" to Locke's name. Elsewhere, Locke's writings on music emerge as those of the "Baha'i sage," a nod to Locke's Baha'i faith. Elsewhere, Locke supplies a model for criticism itself. In *The Black Atlantic*, Gilroy praises the exemplary sensitivity to "cultural development, mutation and change" that Locke revealed in *The New Negro* (1925), an anthology that presented stories and accounts of a contradictory and polyvalent modernity.[1] Locke thus models for Gilroy an intellectual practice that meets the interpretive challenges posed by cultural forms generated within the nexus of national belonging and race hierarchy. Despite the brevity of Gilroy's references, then, Locke represents a key intellectual resource for Gilroy's thinking. Further, if the African American intellectuals with whom Gilroy is most often associated include W. E. B. Du Bois, Richard Wright, and Frederick Douglass, his work as a cultural and political critic often bears a far closer and more obvious likeness to the writings of Alain Locke. While Locke fails to emerge as one of Gilroy's favored *dramatis personae*, Locke's theoretical interventions and philosophical starting points arguably inform, and resurface within, Gilroy's arguments more consistently than those of Wright, Douglass, or even Du Bois, making Locke a pronounced dialogic presence in Gilroy's cultural criticism.

Gilroy's recent cultural inquiry channels Locke's critical practice in several ways. Much as Locke's writings beginning in the early twentieth century set out to rid "race" of prepolitical valences, Gilroy's recent work presses the analysis of "race" even more dramatically than in his earlier work into the domain of the political. The result is a renewed refusal of absolutism in interpretations of racist social environments. Indeed Gilroy's theoretical positioning vis-à-vis categories bequeathed by racism and race hierarchy closely corresponds to the meticulous parsing of the many functions of the race concept that Locke undertook in lectures he delivered at Howard University in 1915–1916. The lectures anticipate Gilroy's later efforts to open, not close, the "categories with which we conduct our political lives," for Locke is everywhere insistent on the arbitrary and contingent character of "race" categories. As Gilroy renders Du Boisian double consciousness ineffective as a resource for the analysis needed to make sense of the present, his perspectives more and more adhere to the main philosophical contours of Locke's investigations of "race," which insisted upon both a "center of meaning" requiring analytical scrutiny in itself *and* an arena of dynamic fluctuation demanding interventionist cultural politics. In so doing, Gilroy's readings of postcolonial metropolitan cultures in the twenty-first century revive Locke's cultural politics, sharing with it what we can call, following Ian Hacking, a constitutive *dynamic nominalism*.

Recognizing affinities between Locke's writings from the first half of the twentieth century and Gilroy's writings from the late twentieth and early twenty-first century provides a way of understanding key strands of Gilroy's work. Yet because Locke can serve as something of an absent presence in Gilroy's work and therefore deter analysis of those affinities, I devote this essay to congruent intellectual preoccupations in the modes of inquiry that Locke and Gilroy have furthered. However, I do not propose a deterministic relationship between Gilroy's work and Locke's preceding cultural commentary but instead place the two critics on the same plane so as to enable analysis alert to similarities and differences, while obviating any one-to-one relationship between the bodies of cultural criticism developed by each writer. Reading through a paradigm of affinity reveals comparable antagonism toward not only race hierarchy but also the absolutist thinking that undergirds racist ideologies and practices. Such a paradigm demonstrates how Locke anticipates problems in cultural theory that recur in Gilroy's work. In a larger sense, concentrating on such affinities prompts a reconsideration of the place of African American intellectual culture in Gilroy's thinking, and thus of the complex, translated "American-ness" that helps to organize his antiracist critical practice and how that practice has itself been revised in the years since *The Black Atlantic* appeared.

Race, Creeds, and Absolutism

Locke was born in Philadelphia in 1885 into a family of educators who had long been members of the city's free black community. Locke taught at Howard University for four decades after a formal education that included a Harvard doctoral degree and studies at the University of Berlin. Along the way, he became the first African American Rhodes Scholar. Early on at Howard, Locke devised a course made up of lectures on "Race Contacts and Interracial Relations," an effort to rethink race hierarchy and racial ideology. The lectures were published in 1992, almost ninety years after Locke delivered them in 1915– 1916. In much the same vein as contemporaneous efforts such as those carried out by anthropologist Franz Boas, Locke undermined the validity of scientific conceptualizations of "race" but then moved to what he considered as yet underdeveloped areas of analysis, among them the historical emergence of "modern race creeds," political and practical conceptions of race, and the phenomena of what he called "race contacts," the interaction of different groups in the complex arenas of "social culture."[2] From the start, Locke renders "race," like decisions about how best to analyze its historical and social impact, intrinsically political. Given that the stakes in conceptions of "race" were not abstract exercises, Locke begins with the view that race must be regarded as a "center of meaning." To acquire a clarified understanding of this center and develop a rational conception of race, Locke writes, represents "one of the unworked opportunities of social science."[3] Since I turn to W. E. B. Du Bois later, it is worth noting briefly here that Locke's premise serves as something of a theoretical alternative to Du Bois's well-known description of the unfolding twentieth century as the century of the color-line. Where Du Bois's words emphasize race hierarchy and the challenges it has set in motion, projecting these into the foreseeable future, Locke for the most part refuses the mode of forecast and identifies an active, existing, and complex "center of meaning"—"Race is not one thing—it is many things"—as his main preoccupation. While the two formulations do not exactly contradict one another, the different inflections and possibilities they intimate in relation to the analysis of "race" provide constructive means of assessing recent arguments in Gilroy's work, which I discuss in the essay's conclusion.

Writing about Locke's most well-known work, *The New Negro*, Houston Baker, Jr. has written about the "world projected by Locke's collection" as one of a "nation comprised of self-consciously aspiring individuals who view their efforts as co-extensive with global strivings for self-determination and national cultural expression." Indeed the most compelling interpretations of Locke's *New Negro* stretch considerably beyond the claim that the book serves as an instantiation of a nationally delimited cultural pluralism. Baker also rightly emphasizes the remarkable "flight from the common racialist ground of its era" that *The New Negro* signaled.[4] Yet for all the effective reframing conducted by scholars, readings of Locke's work continue to revert to a set of deliberations on the philosophy of cultural pluralism. Without a doubt, Locke invoked cultural pluralism as a term, contributed to its development as a locus of political theorization, and understood his work as making cultural pluralism an effective orientation that provided a counterpoint to race hierarchy and racism. But cultural pluralism was never one thing, and the literature on its impact has only recently begun to distinguish its varieties. Locke's cultural pluralism, as Louis Menand has noted, differs from that of the American theorist Horace Kallen, who is credited with coining the term. If for Locke, cultural pluralism provided a platform from which to envision forms of cultural renewal in which race hierarchy and racism had no place, Kallen put forth a different version, one that quelled the push for social mobility by advancing a "kind of noninvidious segregation," as Menand writes.[5] For Locke, the groups dubbed "races" were "ethnic fictions," and he regarded his efforts in part as the revaluing of these fictions so as to make them useful for projects of social and cultural renewal that eschewed separateness and notions of cultural proprietorship.[6] To the extent that *The New Negro* drew upon a commitment to cultural pluralism, then, it put forth Locke's cultural pluralism and its antiracist, antiseparatist aims.

Ross Posnock has written that Locke's writings were marked by a certain "cultivation of paradox," which had the effect of always keeping him "out of focus." This lack of focus in turn invited misconceptions of Locke as a standard "race man" or else an "apolitical aesthete."[7] A related difficulty in assessing the range of Locke's philosophical, educational, and cultural commentary is the singular and overshadowing role that *The New Negro* has been assigned in scholarly accounts of his intellectual trajectory. For all of its conceptual and political ingenuity, Locke's anthology differs in orientation from the writings that preceded and followed the famous collection, and therefore cannot stand in for all of Locke's work. Locke's extraordinary set of lectures from 1915–1916—*Race Contacts and Interracial Relations*—are among the most rigorous reflections on race hierarchy and racial ideology in early twentieth-century American writing. Locke's forum—a hall at Howard University—and the posthumous character of his arguments have given the lectures at best a muted status in American intellectual life. Yet the long interregnum between conception and publication of the lectures does not explain the relatively slight scholarly attention they have received. Many of Locke's most significant post–*New Negro* writings have likewise garnered only occasional mention. Locke's close association with cultural pluralism, pragmatism, and, above all, the Harlem Renaissance, has rendered his writings on politics and culture into the 1940s and 1950s at best a postscript in investigations of his intellectual contributions. Yet Locke continued to produce literary and cultural criticism throughout these years, increasingly linking his analysis to emergent decolonizing projects in such works as the coedited volume *When Peoples Meet: A Study in Race and Culture Contacts*.

The rejection of absolutisms and criticism of their encroachment on political thought and everyday life stand as basic premises throughout Locke's writings. And while his anti-absolutism draws in part from the pragmatism of William James, Locke carries that influence forward in distinctive ways. He invokes it in the early 1940s, when he describes fascisms as "new secular absolutisms" that build on older racisms and philosophical dogmatisms. In Locke's view, these "modern Frankensteins" must be investigated in terms of how they bring older dogmas to life and license tyrannies that, far from being aberrant, represent complex strains within Western sociality, "the germ plasm of our culture."[8] Here, Locke's work notably prefigures themes in Gilroy's work and demonstrates an overlap in theoretical vocabulary. Gilroy's key essay "Nationalism, History and Ethnic Absolutism" put forth arguments that have remained durable and reliable features of his work. In the same philosophical register Locke employs, Gilroy voices his opposition to absolutistic thinking in general, even as he specifically presents his disapproval of the complex forms of ethnic absolutism he sees marring political culture and social life alike in the last third of the twentieth century. These ethnic absolutisms often emerge as the rhetoric of "cultural insiderism," varieties of which in turn give life to "unacceptable ideas of homogenous national culture and exclusionary national or ethnic belonging."

For all of his attention to the hazards of absolutism, in his Howard lectures Locke veers away from those who "feel that race is so odious a term that it must be eradicated from our thinking and from our vocabulary." He sees a viable course proceeding only "through a substitution of better meanings for the meanings which are now current under the term."[9] If the race category is to be "superseded," Locke writes, it will have to be "by some revised version of itself." For Locke, the retention of race carried social and political possibility as a "counter-doctrine of racial solidarity and culture." He places such a counter-doctrine in the decided service of antiracist and assimilative politics, not isolation, "nor even racial integrity." Locke sees revising the race category as the only viable path for race theorists in the early twentieth-century United States, but it is important to note that the "race" Locke wishes to retain is a markedly limited one, one that cannot fuel powerful creeds. In Locke's remaking, "race" endures as "social races," a category that "from the point of view of anthropology are ethnic fictions" but that nevertheless help to name a "sense of kind, that sense of kith and kin which undoubtedly is somewhat of an advantage to any ethnic group that can maintain [it]."[10] The social races Locke has in mind are what "modern man talks about" when he talks about "race," a naming process that he does not consider intrinsically objectionable. Locke comments that social races "maintain in name only [the] fetish of biological [purity]" but are in fact the "product of countless interminglings [and] infinite crossings of types." Social race need not mutate into a destructive force in Locke's conception, for as nothing more or less than "consciousness of kind," social race only becomes a problem when actively redirected and made to serve the "maintenance of unhealthy and rather unjust distinctions in human society."[11] Absent such redirection, Locke appears to suggest, ubiquity renders social race innocuous and ordinary.

In his claim that "race" can be redirected and made to serve different ends, Locke predicts a basic supposition in Gilroy's *'There Ain't No Black in the Union Jack.'* "Multiple meanings have grouped around the central symbol of racial alterity—the colour black—and it is difficult to anticipate the outcome of the political struggle between the different tendencies they represent—ethnic absolutism on the one hand and a utopian, democratic populism, on the other," Gilroy writes.[12] In his meticulous reading of the varieties of antiracism in British political culture, Gilroy not only advances historical approaches to racial thinking, he also brings "race" squarely into the symbolic and discursive terrain that Locke calls what "modern man talks about." Locke was well aware that his concept of social race did not by itself contradict, let alone jettison, other conceptions that fed and hardened race hierarchy. Yet even these seemingly politically insuperable conceptions had to be understood in terms of their discursive constitution and internal ambiguities. Thus, when he discusses legal restrictions and race hierarchy, Locke stresses the difficulty of determining "what comes first—the actual difference which registers itself in law, written or unwritten, or whether the law, the custom itself, produces and often creates the distinction and the difference" that set the terms for restriction.[13] "It would seem," Locke speculated, "that in the majority of instances, as soon as there is any recognition or sense of a difference, the law springs up to help confirm it and perpetuate [the difference.]"[14]

In Locke, as in Gilroy, practices of domination prepare the ground for what will become the common sense of "race." Locke's version of this claim proceeds from the fact that the "conception of 'inferior' races and 'backward' races and 'advanced' races or 'superior' races largely comes from the political fortunes and political capacity of peoples."[15] In Locke's formulation, the "ruling people" do not only dominate practically but also control what he calls the "actual class distinctions" that emerge and therefore make "almost all the subordinate status of race flow from their will and their traditions."[16] Locke's reference to "class distinction" indicates his refusal to divide race and class analysis theoretically, and also registers a characteristic emphasis on processes of marking and naming that accompany histories of domination. For Locke, racial designations follow patterns of domination and, at the same time, acquire semantic power through specific sociopolitical mechanisms.

Dynamic Nominalism contra Race Hierarchy

Locke understood law and custom (or social practices) as mutually constitutive. When he references the "stereotyping function of the law," he therefore includes in that category the range of accumulated customs and ways of thinking that organize a given social order. Locke asked his Howard students to think about the activity of category formation as coextensive with political and legal processes that stabilize "racial" demarcations and strictures. What Locke called the "stereotyping function of the law" is but one instance among many where Locke turns his attention to the work of labeling and the arrest of social circumstance through mechanisms of naming.

Concentrating on Locke's attention to labeling practices affords a rethinking of his work as a form of critical and dynamic nominalism. Ian Hacking's notion of "dynamic nominalism" posits that social change creates "new categories of people," but far from serving as "mere report," the categories conjured by the social world in turn create "new ways for people to be."[17] Hacking presses the analytic value of dynamic nominalism because it provides a means of analyzing processes he called "Making Up People." In Hacking's view, the promise of dynamic nominalism as an orientation has to do with the assistance it lends in assessing situations where "a kind of person came into being at the same time as the kind itself was being invented"—in those cases, in other words, where "our classifications and our classes conspire to emerge hand in hand, each egging each other on."[18] Dynamic nominalism allows Hacking to consider description more rigorously and to heighten the analytic purchase of several philosophical commonplaces about description. Hacking writes that in the realm of human action "what I am deliberately doing depends on the possibilities of description," but the larger point he emphasizes is that "if new modes of description come into being, new possibilities for action come into being in consequence."[19] Hacking's proposal encourages greater attention to practices of description and modulations in social arrangements and behavior instigated by such practices. He puts forth dynamic nominalism as the "only intelligible species of nominalism," insofar as it does not reduce the social world to discourses but also refuses to discount the effects of discourses on material and social processes.[20] Its basic supposition—"that numerous kinds of human beings and human acts come into being hand in hand with our invention of the categories labeling them"—provides a means of exploring divergent histories of naming, varied episodes of people making.

Locke's dynamic nominalism vis-à-vis "race" is perhaps most in evidence when he turns his attention to "modern race creeds," for it is the "modern commercial era" that ushers in the specific racial ideologies that concern him most. Maintaining that the "flowering of prejudice against Negroes is a plant the seeds of which were sown during the days of Reconstruction," Locke also argues that, amid industrialization, anxieties over class position and "compulsion for class monopoly seem to have sprung up along with this plant of color antipathy."[21] In his lectures, Locke presents racial ideologies as historical phenomena and as beliefs, or creeds, emerging from dominant patterns of race hierarchy and class antagonism. But what is arguably most interesting about the line of inquiry he initiates is the view that racial thinking can only be regarded plausibly in terms of "accidents and practices of history." Such contingency demonstrates to Locke the need to challenge the "basis of judgment" that undergirds both "race" and race hierarchy and convinces him that the act of challenging the "mere manifestation" of race hierarchy can all too often amount to yet another "concession to it." During the 1910s especially, work on the fallacies of race thinking and on the processes by which "race" enters and attaches to social and political practice constituted major preoccupations for Locke. He concluded, among other things, that to fail to concede to "race" but nevertheless refute its myriad social and political incarnations required historicizing race and recognizing the ways in which its dynamic discursive character was bound up with the intensified class antagonisms of the early twentieth-century United States. In emphasizing the importance of not conceding to "race," but instead deciphering its complex emergence, Locke delivers an early twentieth-century dynamic nominalism that explicitly renders "race" a problem not only of history but of social and political theory.

When he insisted that "race is not one thing—it is many things," Locke effectively theorized the historical contingency of all forms of race thinking. From that starting point, he developed arguments based on the conviction that "race" was not beyond analytical reach simply because of the commonsense status it achieves. Intriguingly, Locke held that race antipathy could well be "instinctive" but noted that by "instinctive" he did not mean "spontaneous." Indeed, this parsing affords another angle on Locke's dynamic nominalism, for Locke's "instinctive" can only follow from various processes of making and reproduction. Race antipathy achieves an instinctive character that is patently not spontaneous because it is "cultivated [. . .] and not only cultivated but controlled and modified."[22] It is amid practices of control and modification that racial ascriptions and race creeds come into being, conforming in large part to dominant social arrangements and made instinctive through habituation. Locke's focus on control and modification further his argument for the historical specificities of racisms, while also implicitly evoking an arena of contestation in which names and designations materialize along with, and not prior to, the activation of mechanisms that he considers constitutive of all situations in which race hierarchy organizes social life.

Locke's "social race" category stands at the center of his theoretical and cultural politics and is central to the dynamic nominalist character of his work. He discloses the most important dimension of his social race definition as his lectures draw to a close. Social race becomes relevant and valuable in the adjudication of modern problems only when understood as operating within a "civilization type or civilization kind." If, as Locke maintains, every civilization produces its type, one that imposes a "very arbitrary yet very natural obligation upon a man—conformity to its type," social race carries a nominal but not permanent, static, or settled significance in relation to a given civilization's assimilative processes.[23] The social race category, insofar as it aids an assimilative program, harnesses activities toward racial solidarity, yet this solidarity is always a "secondary race consciousness" that is finally subservient to the greater goal of civilization type and the necessarily imitative work it demands. "Society cannot maintain its exclusive standards and types free from imitation" and, indeed, it perpetually exacts conformity to civilization type from all of its members, Locke argued.[24] Race hierarchy in this schema is a contradiction, an aberration that interrupts what could be a more fluid and enriching process of social interweaving and translation.

Locke expresses confidence that with the careful and judicious development of "social race," or secondary race consciousness, "race type blends into 'civilization type.'" He connects such blending, the use of social race for broader civilizational ends, to the promise of "culture-citizenship."[25] Although Locke is associated with cultural pluralism, the lectures demonstrate that he is enthusiastic not about a readymade theory of cultural pluralism as such, but instead about the idea of culture-citizenship. ("Culture-citizenship is the thing!") For Locke, retaining "race" means retaining social race, a category that offers an efficacious secondary race consciousness that can be brought to bear instrumentally, and in contradistinction to racist lore and practice, to advance the goal of culture-citizenship for all. Here, social race blends one element into a larger civilization type, making possible a novel "homogeneity" that neither one would have been capable of "without the collaboration and the help of the other."[26]

Culture-citizenship for Locke is nothing if not a process, and its fluctuating, processual character means that it falls within the theoretical pattern of people making. Indeed, Locke's vision of cultural renewal is predicated on new peoples and new ways of being. For if people-making processes can result in hardened notions of racial difference that gain political and legal backing, "social race" and the ideal of culture-citizenship loosen up the process of naming, wrest "race" from race hierarchy, and present alternative models of sociality. "Race" retains meaning in Locke's work only as "social race" and accompanies supplemental terms—culture-citizenship among them—that communicate his antipathy to race hierarchy and his desire to bring into view a horizon beyond the conventional strictures and political practices of "race." Although social race figures in the overall design of Locke's theoretical intervention, his in many ways more robust commitment to culture-citizenship is notably free of racial ascription and does not in itself impart dependence on racial designation. Conjunctural pressures on Locke in the early twentieth century required a remolding of "race," given the semantic weight it carried, rather than any cancelling program. Yet culture-citizenship, as a kind of horizon beyond which social races acquire meaning and operate, seems to represent the location of Locke's genuine theoretic and political interests.

For Locke and Gilroy alike, to take part in the identification of existing and active race thinking is to enter an analytically complex and precarious terrain. "If you confront race prejudice as it is, in other words, if you argue with it or fight with it upon its own plane," Locke writes, "you have acknowledged it." For Locke, this scarcely amounts to a strategy of transformation. "Some of the most forceful arguments against race prejudice are guilty of the same fallacies [of arguing upon the same false] basis of judgment of which race prejudice is its expression," he writes.[27] Gilroy delivers the same caution when he observes that the very "attempt to make 'race' always already a meaningful factor, in other words to racialize social and political phenomena, may be itself identified as part of the 'race' problem."[28] Both critics refrain from attaching predetermined positive value to forms of racial thinking, and both pursue alternative vocabularies to address race hierarchy and the mystifications of "race." Many scholars note that Locke performed a complex "acceptance of 'race'" in his work. As I have suggested, in the case of Locke, such "acceptance of 'race'" is better understood as an instance of dynamic nominalism, a deliberate investigation of naming and racial ascription, in particular. That Locke's antiracist criticism gives "race" conceptual standing, if only of a limited kind, in no way diminishes the striking rethinking of racial ideologies that his brand of dynamic nominalism made possible. The conceptual work he believed "race" could continue to perform was predicated on the rejection of false and invidious "creeds of race," the basis for not a few "political crimes of nations."[29]

Writing in 1930, Locke expresses confidence that the "best chance for a new world lies in a radical revision [of the] idea of culture."[30] After the 1915–1916 lectures, Locke not only turns more to "culture" but also becomes more vocal about his hesitance concerning, and antagonism toward, ideologies of racial difference. Although he continues to work his reconfigured version of "race" into his interventions, the sense of frustration with "race" talk increasingly registers. Predicting Gilroy, Locke calls specifically for the "abandonment of the use of the idea of race as a political instrument."[31] Communicating in the future-oriented pulse advocated by Gilroy, Locke claims that "we are in a new era of social and cultural relationships once we root up this fiction and abandon the vicious practice of vested proprietary interests in various forms of culture."[32] Still, "race" could be interwoven harmoniously into "human culture" if freed from the political race creeds that gave rise to "theoretical and practical group supremacies," Locke continued. Here, Locke continues to envision an emergent practice capable of freeing "race" from political and historical encumbrances that have licensed and perpetuated its misuse. Yet such a process must be accompanied by an unmistakable refusal of the harms and hierarchies "race" has long helped to define. In pursuing the possibilities of "culture," therefore, Locke insists on abandoning the idea of "cultural purism" in much the way that the idea of a "pure race" had no place in his vision.[33] Locke's hesitant and revisionist invocations of "race" indicate that what I have called his dynamic nominalism was a doubled one, for it both foregrounds the processes by which "race" comes into social and political life and, through Locke's own conceptual renomination, brings "race" into being. Critically, his invocations or renominations are limited and transitional things, avenues toward cultural transformation rather than ends in themselves.

Gilroy, long familiar with Hacking's work, deliberately mobilizes dynamic nominalism as a practice. Dynamic nominalism is especially on display in Gilroy's commentaries on Frantz Fanon. Describing the antiracism that Fanon put forth as an "interventionist practice," Gilroy emphasizes Fanon's aptitude for identifying the ways racial difference "acquired specific capacities in the distinctive social and cultural relations of colonial society that have endured into the present."[34] Fanon's "Negro" emerges in Gilroy's retelling as "always a phantom," woven by historical circumstance and "picked up, acted upon, internalised, and fleshed out, with disastrous consequences for all stakeholders in these inglorious transactions."[35] Because Fanon calls attention to such patterns of making and historical contingency, he effectively "moved the discussion of race and identity towards what can now be recognised as a *dynamic* nominalism." For Gilroy, Fanon advanced the understanding of "race" as the product of dynamic nominalism, acts of labeling that come into historical being in tandem—"hand in hand," as Hacking puts it—with the people the labels are said to name. Gilroy appreciates that Fanon's dynamic nominalism does not offer the mystifications of "race" refuge and instead aims to bring into focus the means by which racial ascriptions gain social, political, and cultural traction. Expanding on Fanon's arguments, Gilroy contends that "race" is "best interpreted through the apparatus of a dynamic nominalism as racism's product rather than its catalyst or precursor."[36]

Given the extent to which Gilroy subscribes to an avowedly dynamic nominalist position in relation to "race," it is surprising that he draws upon the term so sparingly. In his most recent writings, the term primarily serves to indicate how he reads Fanon. He appears to maintain that a dynamic nominalist framework for the analysis of "race" and racism proceeds from Fanon's writing, that is, beginning with Fanon. Yet here several provisos seem in order. Although the dynamic nominalism that Fanon nurtures and develops as a critical idiom is one that Gilroy finds particularly compelling for his own reflections on contemporary cultural and political formations, many other dynamic nominalisms vis-à-vis "race" can be located alongside and prior to

Fanon's example. By bringing to the fore the model of critical reading that Locke instantiated, an earlier dynamic nominalism that has served Gilroy—and that arguably has grown only more important for him over time—comes into view.

Indeed Locke's future-oriented revision of "race" and his *avant-la-lettre* dynamic nominalism provide resources for thinking through Gilroy's work, from the powerful re-visioning of modernity presented in *The Black Atlantic* to the more recent arguments about the tasks of antiracist criticism. Certainly by the time of *The Black Atlantic*, Gilroy was already working within the parameters of a certain dynamic nominalism. The figures and texts that Gilroy brought together to build his account of the black Atlantic were admittedly "racialised examples," he wrote, but the point of revisiting the contradictory terrain from which they emerged had everything to do with a self-conscious "plea against the closure of the categories with which we conduct our political lives."[37]

For Gilroy, as for Locke, dynamic nominalism allows for a broadening of what counts as the political. Key to understanding dynamic nominalism as political intervention in Locke and Gilroy is the concept of "civilization," which represents a common term across the work of both critics. It is worth recalling that while civilizational discourses that rely upon racist suppositions are duly discredited by Gilroy, civilization as a generic concept holds a place in the architecture of his thinking. In Gilroy's *Postcolonial Melancholia* (published as *After Empire: Melancholia or Convivial Culture?* in the United Kingdom), an intermittent meditation on civilization emerges by way of Freud. Amid the destruction of World War I, Gilroy writes, Freud recorded the "flavor of the cosmopolitan response offered by powerless and disillusioned individuals who have cultivated a larger loyalty to civilization than their original nation-states could possibly contain or allow."[38] Gilroy puts forth commitment to civilization as a good that nurtures cosmopolitanism in much the same way that Locke posits commitment to civilization type as a social obligation that transforms racist culture. The civilization Gilroy advocates as a kind of horizon of possibility is defined by what he elsewhere calls "authentic, non-racial democracy."[39] In the essay that accompanies *Black Britain: A Photographic History*, Gilroy expresses his hope for the emergence of a "cultural history that refuses the dubious gift of a generic, U.S.-centered blackness and stays stubbornly tied to the broken edifice of our leaky nation state."[40] Gilroy endorses a version of loyalty to a compromised but salvageable nation-state, a designation not all that far from "civilization type." If Locke's vision of culture-citizenship was predicated on an industrial order marked by myriad antagonisms, Gilroy presents Britain as a postimperial civilization type in need of rethinking and renovation but also, and crucially, as a political arena worthy of intensified dedication. Locke's culture-citizenship is a capacious category linked to civilization but not intrinsically inimical to patterns of national belonging in its imaginative reach. When Locke writes that African Americans in the early twentieth century are willing "to conform to the very iota of the civilization type," he implicitly brings national belonging within the fold of civilization type. Locke's confidence that culture-citizenship can make "race type blend into 'civilization-type'" resurfaces in Gilroy's advocacy of a cultural history that can disabuse people of racial lore and weaken enduring strains of racism. Gilroy's "cultural history" proceeds by way of greater momentum toward collective cultural renewal, or what Gilroy increasingly calls "conviviality," a term he mostly reserves for descriptions of contemporary culture in Britain.

Locke's 1941 collection, *When Peoples Meet*, is nothing if not an early salvo in the intellectual and political work of anticolonial humanism of the kind that Sartre and Fanon, among many others, would advance. The book's intellectual reach brought within its scope a range of colonial situations and focused much of its attention on the problems of race hierarchy that Gilroy suggests are increasingly airbrushed or excised in today's accounts of colonial history. Produced amid the battles against the fascism of the Second World War era, *When Peoples Meet* noted "increased resort to theorizing about the nature of culture and civilization" but lamented that "far too much of it is mere rationalization of the claims and counterclaims of the various national and racial groups seeking partisan victory and glory."[41] To counteract this tendency, Locke urged a focus on racial thinking, or racialism, which in his view "had its worst effects and has bred its most sinister distortions as a source of general misconception about the nature of civilization and culture."[42] Gilroy's broadening of the scope of the Second World War, especially in *Against Race*, to include colonial history, draws upon many thinkers from the postwar era, notably Hannah Arendt. But Gilroy could have also easily invoked Locke, whose arguments dovetail with his own and who refused to limit the subject matter of his analysis to rivalry among nation-states. The Second World War, Locke writes, prompted the "intensification of the conflict of problems of national, ethnic and cultural groups." Yet "it is itself an intensified manifestation of previously existing conflicts, and so is more their symptom than their cause."[43]

Gilroy worries that current accounts of colonial history at times do "not even recognize the central place of 'race' as a dynamic political, historical, and economic concept during this period."[44] Such problems produce an additional impediment insofar as they limit the constructive analysis of a subject Gilroy considers critically important: "the possibility of a significant relationship between the sometimes genocidal brutality of the colonies and the later Nazi genocide in Europe." Reflecting on the nature of fascism represents a critical area of research and something more, for Gilroy posits careful scrutiny of the persistent appeal of fascism as a social imperative and sign of political health. He writes that pondering the nature of fascism is a principle in itself, one that "obliges us to scrutinize our own political philosophies, practices, and cultural predilections where they stray close to the dangers involved in becoming enamoured of power."[45] Locke, in *When Peoples Meet* and elsewhere, linked fascism, race hierarchy, and colonialism, and, from his earliest writing onward, regarded absolutist thinking as a mechanism of power that required scrutiny of the kind Gilroy urges. For "culture" to be a meaningful term, free of the lures of absolutisms and power, Locke writes, anticipating Gilroy, it "must constantly be self-critical and discriminating, and deplore its spurious counterfeits and shallow imitations."[46]

The Cultural Politics of Liberating Ordinariness

If there is much that unites Locke and Gilroy, there are instances when they arrive at notably different claims that undoubtedly have to do with the different historical moments to which they inevitably responded as critics. Where Locke fashions "social race" as a valid, if transitional, category from the cauldron of racist sentiment and racial ideology, Gilroy advances another position. "When the idea of 'race' becomes a concept," Gilroy writes, "it poses clear and incompatible alternatives." "Once we realize racism's alchemical power, we do have to choose," he adds.[47] Choosing means opting between two diametrically opposed alternatives: acceding to the "obligations of racial observance, negotiating them but basically accepting the idea of racial hierarchy and then, inescapably, reifying it," *or* discovering the "difficult but rewarding" means by which to "detonate the historical lore that brings the virtual realities of 'race' to such dismal and destructive life." Although others would describe the available alternatives in other ways, Gilroy's powerful framing mechanism is one that makes clear his distance, analytically speaking, from Locke. In his decision to recast, rather than relinquish, "race," Locke appears to choose the path of negotiation, presumably putting off what Gilroy would see as the more rewarding alternative. Yet, as Gilroy would likely concede, Locke's historical conjuncture presented a certain range of possibilities, and within those constraints, Locke presses a certain "racial observance," albeit dynamic and nominal, that he considers a counterpoint to racist ideology and hierarchy. Still, for all the ways this move on Locke's part seems peculiar to his time, a version of Locke's very intervention can be found in Gilroy's recent work, which returns directly to the question of antiracism.

Gilroy speaks in no uncertain terms of his "desire to see the end of raciology," acknowledging that he pursues an "unknowable future against the unforgiving present." This move on Gilroy's part takes the form of an openly utopian plea on behalf of a "heterocultural, postanthropological, and cosmopolitan yet-to-come."[48] The most striking dimension of the utopian expression carried in such formulations is the sense of practicality and viability that Gilroy develops in urging an end to raciology. His description of necessary work in the direction of the end of raciology relies upon a notion of emotional recalibration and, most important, the possibility of affective transformation that pivots on the term "antiracism" and the activities it names. Gilroy attaches importance to such seemingly negligible things as a "change in mood upon what used to be called 'antiracism.'" He similarly attaches significance to everyday activities that make "raciology appear anachronistic."[49] Gilroy's utopian strains are tethered to modifications in affective dispositions in relation to antiracism. Here, again, Locke offers a powerful parallel. His early to mid-twentieth-century antiracist criticism not only draws upon anthropology and social science to question longstanding ideologies of racial difference. Locke is intent on a project in which civilization type and culture-citizenship can work as affective levers that ultimately reconstitute social and political life. In such a transformed social order, the older, hardened race lines would no longer signify and the basis for raciology would dissolve.

What is antiracism in Gilroy's recent formulations? Increasingly, he proffers a dual orientation in relation to "race" that underscores, as in Locke, the value of addressing "race" as a "center of meaning" requiring analytical scrutiny in itself *and* a site of fluctuation demanding interventionist cultural politics. The first part of Gilroy's dual orientation follows from his hostility to the *racial nomos* as such, which in turn demands a return, not an evasion, of the history of empire and race hierarchy. Indeed, such histories become the basis for a range of pedagogical labors. A chronic inability to absorb and mourn past and ongoing histories of race and empire—"postcolonial melancholia"—renders those histories all the more vital as levers of political transformation. He continues to argue against the easy deployment of racial designations on the view that continued reliance on them indicates the compromised quality of contemporary political cultures and the diminishment of what Locke called "social culture."

The political visions generated by convivial cultures and the challenge they may represent to longstanding raciologies provide Gilroy with the basis for the second component of his dual antiracist orientation. Here the concept of the "ordinary" features prominently as processes capable of bringing notions of racial difference under the sign of the "ordinary" acquire political promise and function as a conveyer belt of sorts toward social cultures that no longer feel compelled to draw upon notions of racial difference as organizing principles. Gilroy refers to convivial metropolitan cultures as providing a privileged new angle on "race," one that reduces the "exaggerated dimensions of racial difference to a liberating ordinary-ness." Thus Gilroy's parallel tracks of antiracism include his longstanding hostility to the *racial nomos* and a privileging of processes aimed at the reworking of "race" along lines of ordinariness—processes that, more and more, render "race" trivial and further the possibility of depositing it in a dustbin of archaisms. If Locke considered the reading of texts and histories of "race" the necessary basis for antiracism, Gilroy, too, insists on a critical encounter with the center of meaning that is "race" and its assorted histories, episodes, and present-day refractions. And, just as Locke revises "race" in ways that might further a politics in which culture-citizenship represents a new horizon of possibility, so too does Gilroy endorse resignification of "race" as the stuff of ordinariness, a process that gestures toward a future in which putative "racial" difference connotes the mundane rather than the hazardous.

The critical likeness between Gilroy and Locke becomes especially evident around the question of the ordinary, for Gilroy's appeal on behalf of practices that render "race" ordinary shares many qualities with the revision of "race" that Locke undertook in his lectures. For if Locke wishes to posit a useful conception of "race" in opposition to scientific racism and the invidious logic of segregation, Gilroy also assigns "race" a social value, even if that value is the diminishing relevance he calls ordinariness. Such lack of practical serviceability is itself a kind of social good in Gilroy's vision of ordinariness as that which moderates and lessens longstanding racial antagonisms. Gilroy invokes the power of the ordinary to adumbrate a model of attenuation wherein, over time, "race" not only fails to license segregation and patterns of hierarchy but ceases to inform political life meaningfully at any level. Where the pedagogical dimension of Gilroy's proposed antiracism rests upon a foregrounding of race hierarchy, a reckoning with its material and discursive havoc, the model of attenuation Gilroy simultaneously presents rests upon the potential of "ordinary hybridity" to further a resignification process wherein racial designations become unworthy of special note amid the flourishing of convivial cultures. In this component of Gilroy's antiracism, "race" is neutered, rendered socially negligible and culturally powerless through the increasingly privileged prominence of conviviality and the power of ordinariness.

The relevance of the concept of ordinariness in Gilroy's recent writing has everything to do with the affirmation of a new antiracist project that "is prepared to break with the notion that racial differences are a self-evident, immutable fact of political life."[50] The activities and practices that Gilroy calls "ordinary hybridity" bring about "convivial cultures" that in and of themselves contest the "reification of race," operationalizing "effective work against racism." In Gilroy's revision-via-ordinariness, as in Locke's advocacy of social race for culture-citizenship, "'race' is nothing special, a virtual reality given meaning only by the fact that racism endures." Gilroy thus argues for the possibilities of an "ordinary hybridity" that makes a "strong sense of racial difference unthinkable to the point of absurdity." Of course, it was precisely the strong senses of "race" that Locke, too, was determined to discard. In remarkably similar ways, Locke and Gilroy address the question of how the strong senses of "race" can vacate social and political life. When Locke puts forth "social race" as an alternative that negates the stronger and invidious senses of "race," he effectively argues for a politics of ordinariness that serves larger ends of cultural renewal. When Gilroy delivers what amounts to a dual antiracist orientation, he argues vigorously for examining the past and present work performed by the logic of racial difference. But the other part of his antiracism, what might be thought of as the street-level part, sees ordinary hybridity, not the revisiting of colonial history, as the key to cultural transformation. Both Locke and Gilroy, despite the distance of time, emphasize the importance of antiracism not as a doctrine but instead as everyday practices that slowly but undeniably decompose the racist social order. Both see that the "political ontology of race is fatal to all democratic aspirations," as Gilroy puts it, and turn to quotidian pedagogies (Locke's "cultural pluralism" and Gilroy's "convivial culture" or "vernacular dissidence") as mechanisms to deploy against the intransigence of race hierarchy.[51]

Beyond US Race Talk, Beyond Culture

In his powerful conclusion to *Darker than Blue: On the Moral Economies of Black Atlantic Culture*, Gilroy could not be clearer about the bleak state in which he finds antiracism and the role of US cultural politics in its present quandary. "The goals of antiracism have been defeated, or perhaps more accurately undone, by strong theories of culture and identity and other race-friendly ideas which have been exported from U.S. history and culture." Where does Locke figure in this assessment? In at least certain ways, Locke's vision of culture-citizenship fits within the overall constellation of culture and identity practices and therefore part of the process by which antiracism was undone, in Gilroy's formulation. Yet Locke's early to mid-twentieth-century work emerges prior to the consolidated phase of identity politics that helped give shape to social and political life in the latter half of the twentieth century. To this extent, Locke stands outside Gilroy's argument about the undoing of antiracism. If debates about cultural pluralism locate Locke in a trajectory that extends into late-twentieth-century multiculturalism, he can only anachronistically and therefore inaccurately be said to advance "strong theories of culture and identity," to use Gilroy's formulation.[52] When Gilroy points to the problem of "race-friendly ideas," it may seem appropriate to attach Locke's corpus to that category. But such a catchall formulation is not very edifying. Gilroy's most recent work, especially his vocal distress about US identity and culture politics, in fact brings him closer to Locke and foregrounds the multiple points of intersection in their respective projects.

Gilroy argues that amid global and economic insecurity, "U.S. diversity management has begun to look unconvincing if not irrelevant."[53] The current conjuncture begs the question of what becomes of the "foundational absurdities of U.S. race talk." Looking ahead toward an avowedly cosmopolitan "new history of the postcolonial present," it is precisely such absurdities, as Gilroy has it, that need to be discarded and made irrelevant where they have yet to reach that status. Gilroy's focus on US race talk and diversity management has implications for how he brings his formidable knowledge of African American intellectual history and criticism to bear on his readings of contemporary cultures. Perhaps most remarkably of all, the concerted critical attention to American race practices throws Gilroy's relationship to Du Bois's concept of double consciousness into a kind of crisis. Where it once supplied one of the main categories of Gilroy's thinking, *The Black Atlantic*'s main term now fails as an interpretive implement and instead performs rather uneasily under the weight of its American provenance. Gilroy now writes explicitly about the "limits of double consciousness." He concludes that the "world-historic culture of freedom and freedom-seeking" that bequeathed the term to designate, among other things, the ability of black Americans to both render the meanings of, and transcend, the proverbial "color line," inadequately relates to current circumstances in which older notions of freedom no longer obtain. Thus, for all of its importance as part of the genealogy of human rights, double consciousness needs to be excluded from analysis of contemporary "racial" and postcolonial predicaments. Du Bois's term now emerges as a "pattern of basic doubling," a species of "superannuated dialectical rules" that only compounds problems he associates with the slipperiness of "identity" as a category in contemporary theory.[54] "As it loses its old power," Gilroy adds, "double consciousness" is best understood in terms of its nineteenth-century origins and relegated to that historical past. Bracketing "double consciousness," Gilroy reaffirms his commitment to the rejection of race thinking, and he does so through the very critical model that served Locke: he reads "race" as a center of meaning requiring political theorization and simultaneously converts "race" into a site of postimperial interventionist cultural politics in which the social and political efficacy of "race" is actively diminished.

The implied esteem for otherness carried by double consciousness cannot coexist with an American present that, for Gilroy, is captured in the political rise of leaders such as Barack Obama and Condoleezza Rice. Whatever their differences and qualities, he writes, Obama and Rice "don't seem to have been gifted with second sight or disabled by any inner doubleness."[55] Changes in American political culture whereby African Americans "acquire or operationalise their long-delayed membership in the national community" indicate a moment removed from the one that bestowed interventionist value upon double consciousness. In this new dispensation, double consciousness not only loses its relevance but indeed becomes a liability, a problem to be addressed. Here, Gilroy's reconfigured position resembles arguments presented by theorist Rey Chow, who has written that "in the valorization of non-Western 'others,' we have witnessed a kind of tendency to see all such non-Western 'others' as equivalent, as a mere positive, positivist idea devoid of material indebtedness and contradiction."[56] Gilroy's refusal of double-consciousness stems from a similar wariness of the positivist sameness it has the capacity to confer and the belief that such conferral misrecognizes present-day "race" politics. We thus see in Gilroy's rejection of double-consciousness as a perpetual analytical resource a desire to renew antiracism by resolutely ridding it of its theoretical encumbrances. In Chow's words, Gilroy's theoretical move is one that continues to "critique the legitimating structures inherent in the production of knowledge" by bringing within the scope of his even those categories that had earlier sustained interpretive practices.[57]

"There may still be things to learn from the U.S. acceptance of 'race,'" Gilroy contends, even as he creates greater distance between his critical practice and the US-derived vocabularies of antiracism. Yet any information to be gleaned has to follow from a preceding acknowledgment "of the damage done by racism" and a sincere commitment to staving off "blank resignation to the effects of racial hierarchy" that in Gilroy's view characterize the "U.S. acceptance of 'race.'"[58] The contractual character of Gilroy's formulations, in which the "U.S. acceptance of 'race'" is given a lifeline despite uncertainty as to whether Americans can fully concede the damage done by racism not only communicates a great deal about his views about contemporary U.S. "race" politics but also makes evident a distinct moment in Gilroy's corpus. They also engender an opening that permits Gilroy to redirect US intellectual and cultural work in ways intended to effect "our transition out of the neoliberal order." It is in the context of this alternative position, in which US race politics are rejected as a framework while American writings and practices retain theoretical, cultural, and pedagogical value, that Locke's contributions become especially salient for reading Gilroy's arguments.

Locke furthered an "acceptance of 'race'" that in fact functioned as a set of deliberations on racial naming and the work of undoing racism. Gilroy reprises Locke's cultural and theoretical politics when he claims that "conceptual innovations cannot bring racism to an end." Locke nowhere suggests that they can. Yet both Locke and Gilroy understand the limits of simply tracing the analytical patterns devised in earlier periods for making sense of racialized sociality. Gilroy agrees with Locke that preventing analytical atrophy means looking to the artistic imagination and the resources it presents for countering the alienation produced by a racialized social order. "Art itself and its multicultural institutions can play a role in promoting conversation, translation, and cosmopolitan recognition," Gilroy writes.[59] In this sense, if the interpretive agenda that Locke may be said to have bestowed upon Gilroy from within the tradition of African American criticism can be reduced to one word, it would surely be "culture." For it is around this nettlesome concept that Gilroy's affinities with and departures from Locke become most evident. From some of his earliest writings to the present, Gilroy poses culture as a problem to be worked out and a subject requiring rethinking.

Long a critic of appeals to culture that further rather than interrupt commitment to notions of racial difference, Gilroy continues to bring this theme into his commentary, as when he calls attention to the ways that "culture talk draws renewed power from the specifications of racial difference that are smuggled inside it." Yet whereas Locke considers culture a set of sites where "race" may function free of political dogmas, Gilroy effectively says "no." The political and the cultural bleed into one another, making the partitioning Locke put forth a starting point that Gilroy cannot adopt. His alternative position renders "culture" the space in which "race" may indeed acquire political salience and relevance, not a salutary arena of apolitical and beneficent reinvention. Where racial absolutism seems to emerge from political power alone in Locke's thinking, Gilroy understands absolutist thinking in "culture talk" and its related spheres of human activity among the very structures that can harden the political lines of racial difference. The political and the cultural enter the same space and become a palimpsest. Such a view contradicts Locke's notion that the work of culture-citizenship counteracted but did not become subsumed by the political.

Although it is seldom noted, Locke himself later questioned many of the suppositions that guided his cultural pluralism in the 1910s and 1920s. Indeed, simplistic associations of Locke with cultural pluralism obfuscate his post-cultural pluralist critiques of "culture," critiques that once again prefigure many of Gilroy's arguments. "Culture is not related functionally to definite ethnic groups or races, but varies independently," wrote Locke.[60] Gilroy's criticism of static notions of culture reaffirm Locke's formulations. And both critics draw in various ways upon a European tradition of inquiry that encompasses Walter Benjamin, for whom the "concept of culture as the embodiment of entities that are considered independently" is nothing if not "fetishistic," a misconception in which "culture appears reified."[61] Gilroy's work has served to disabuse "cultures" of fetishistic notions of racial difference and thus alert them to racisms and systems of race hierarchy that wreak havoc on social life. His reliance on the concept of culture has always been an ambivalent one—an ambivalence increasingly on display in his writing. A similar attitude also entered the work of Locke, especially in the 1940s. In 1949, Locke wrote: "First a word or so about culture itself. It was once a favorite theme-song word for me. Now I wince at its mention and frankly would like to keep silent on the subject—so great have the misconceptions and misuses been. I recall how focal the word culture was for many movements I have been interested and involved in."[62] Although not a repudiation of the concept, Locke's reflections on the place the culture concept once held in his thinking brings to mind Gilroy's own cautious handling of the term. Locke may be said to supply Gilroy not with a neatly packaged cultural pluralism but with the difficulty of "culture" formed at the exasperating juncture of belongingness and race hierarchy in the modern West.

In Gilroy's menu of terms for thinking the current conjuncture—postcolonial melancholia and conviviality, among others—one continues to find invocations of "culture," but it is a noticeably diminished term, as if the ways in which it has been compromised cannot altogether be undone. The "culture" of cultural studies, of critical reading that can intervene in the reified social order, and as the name for dynamic processes that bring the present into being, retains analytical value but only of a limited sort in his interpretive practices. Although he does not go as Michel-Rolph Trouillot, Gilroy's reworked, disenchanted relation to "culture" is largely of a piece with the observations of the anthropologist and critic. In his provocative essay, "Adieu Culture: A New Duty Arises," Trouillot claimed that the category "is now in an orbit where chasing it can only be a conservative enterprise." Trouillot argued that the word itself needs to be abandoned even as its "conceptual kernel"—the structuration and symbolic dimensions of human behavior—is defended.[63] Such a defense may make possible fresh intellectual and critical practices that preclude "culture" as a "theoretical refuge."[64] Gilroy has arguably already made the shift advocated by Trouillot, even if his writing retains a certain allegiance to the concept of culture. In his most recent work, Gilroy continues to make "Black Atlantic culture" his subject but works assiduously to render its status as a self-evident and synchronized unit of analysis suspect. His current practice reaches for the meanings and connections once called "culture" by dislodging and reframing alleged unities. More important than "cultures" as such are the analytical possibilities promised by the adjectives appended to them, as in "convivial culture." Along this trajectory, he strengthens his commitment to what Trouillot calls the "changing heads of the hydra we once singularized."[65]

In his recent work, Gilroy invokes Locke's thought primarily to emphasize temporal and analytical divergence. Yet Gilroy's conceptual departures, for all their significance, are already inscribed within a relation of intellectual affiliation and consonance. In *Darker than Blue*, Gilroy briefly turns to Locke in order to reflect upon black cultural politics and certain of its musical analogues from the last decades of the twentieth century into the present. Locke's 1936 book, *The Negro and His Music*, describes the Negro as "America's troubadour" and deems modern black peoples the "songsters of the western world." Yet, for all of its insights, Locke's work serves Gilroy's purposes primarily as an artifact through which to set apart his interpretations of contemporary cultural politics. "The Negro monopoly on popular song has expired," Gilroy reports, even as he expresses admiration for the "special period" in artistic production that Locke's book brought into historical view.[66] Gilroy accurately identifies Locke's commentary in *The Negro and His Music* as the product of a "Germanic view of how folk cultures could be elevated into the higher, classical forms which corresponded to the ideal configurations of nationhood." He locates Locke's observations in the receding historical distance and alludes to the political obsolescence of the cultural forms at the center of Locke's book.

Yet such distancing necessarily introduces questions about Gilroy's reliance upon African American letters and about the ways distancing can itself reveal the complex character of reliance and influence. What Gilroy retains from Locke are precisely those conceptual problems that Locke addressed through his own imaginative and critical faculties during the first half of the twentieth century. The questions and ways of thinking that Locke put forth were marked by the steadfast rejection of racisms and a dynamic nominalism vis-à-vis "race," and it is these defining features that mark Gilroy's own ongoing encounters with the present. The current instantiations of Gilroy's "Black Atlantic" critical idiom suspend aspects of the African American intellectual tradition, but they continue to demonstrate an enduring indebtedness to that tradition. Locke's writings provide ways into the story of that debt.

Notes

1. Paul Gilroy, *The Black Atlantic: Modernity and Double Consciousness* (Cambridge: Harvard University Press, 1993), 91.
2. Alain Locke, *Race Contacts and Interracial Relations: Lectures on the Theory and Practice of Race* (Washington, DC: Howard University Press, 1992).
3. Ibid., 2.
4. Houston A. Baker, Jr., *Modernism and the Harlem Renaissance* (Chicago: University of Chicago Press, 1987), 74–75.
5. Louis Menand, *The Metaphysical Club* (New York: Farrar, Straus and Giroux, 2001), 394.
6. Ibid., 397.
7. Ross Posnock, *Color and Culture: Black Writers and the Making of the Modern Intellectual* (Cambridge: Harvard University Press, 1998), 197.
8. Leonard Harris, ed., *The Philosophy of Alain Locke: The Harlem Renaissance and Beyond* (Philadelphia: Temple University Press, 1989), 53.
9. Locke, *Race Contacts*, 84–85.
10. Ibid., 11–12.
11. Ibid., 66.
12. Paul Gilroy, *'There Ain't No Black in the Union Jack': The Cultural Politics of Race and Nation* (Chicago: University of Chicago Press, 1987), 236.
13. Locke, *Race Contacts*, 48–49.
14. Ibid., 49.
15. Ibid., 22.
16. Ibid., 23.

17. Ian Hacking, *Historical Ontology* (Cambridge: Harvard University Press, 2002), 162.
18. Ibid., 165.
19. Ibid., 166.
20. Ibid., 170.
21. Locke, *Race Contacts*, 69, 65.
22. Ibid., 54.
23. Ibid., 89.
24. Ibid., 94.
25. Ibid., 100.
26. Ibid.
27. Ibid., 71.
28. Gilroy, *'There Ain't No Black in the Union Jack,'* 116.
29. Harris, ed., *The Philosophy of Alain Locke*, 203.
30. Ibid., 204.
31. Ibid., 218.
32. Ibid., 203.
33. Ibid., 213.
34. Paul Gilroy, *Darker than Blue: On the Moral Economies of Black Atlantic Culture* (Cambridge: Harvard University Press, 2010), 161.
35. Ibid., 161.
36. Paul Gilroy, "A Response," *The British Journal of Sociology* 60, 1 (2009): 33–38; 34.
37. Gilroy, *The Black Atlantic*, xi.
38. Paul Gilroy, *Postcolonial Melancholia* (New York: Columbia University Press, 2005), 68.
39. Paul Gilroy, *Black Britain* (London: Saqi, 2007), 241.
40. Ibid., 306.
41. Alain Locke, ed., *When Peoples Meet: A Study in Race and Culture Contacts* (New York: Hinds, Hayden and Eldredge, 1946), 3–4.
42. Ibid., 5.
43. Ibid., 5.
44. Paul Gilroy, *Against Race: Imaging Political Culture Beyond the Color Line* (Cambridge: Harvard University Press, 2000), 141.
45. Ibid., 146. In his reflections on power and fascism, Gilroy cites Michel Foucault's preface to Deleuze and Guattari's *Anti-Oedipus*. Foucault writes that *Anti-Oedipus* has several targets, but its "strategic adversary is fascism." Foucault continues: "And not only historical fascism, the fascism of Hitler and Mussolini—which was able to mobilize and use the desire

of the masses so effectively—but also the fascism in us all, in our heads and in our everyday behavior, the fascism that causes us to love power, to desire the very thing that dominates and exploits us."

46. Harris, ed., *The Philosophy of Alain Locke*, 179.
47. Gilroy, *Postcolonial Melancholia*, 32.
48. Gilroy, *Against Race*, 334.
49. Ibid., 334–35.
50. Gilroy, *Postcolonial Melancholia*, 45.
51. Ibid., 99.
52. Gilroy, *Darker than Blue*, 162.
53. Ibid., 175.
54. Ibid., 153–53.
55. Gilroy, *Darker than Blue*, 153–54.
56. Rey Chow, *Ethics after Idealism* (Bloomington: Indiana University Press, 1998), xxi.
57. Ibid., 12.
58. Gilroy, *Darker than Blue*, 176.
59. Ibid., 164.
60. Locke, ed., *When Peoples Meet*, 6.
61. Walter Benjamin, "Eduard Fuchs, Collector and Historian," *One-Way Street* (London: Verso, 1979), 360.
62. Harris, ed., *The Philosophy of Alain Locke*, 320.
63. Michel-Rolph Trouillot, *Global Transformations: Anthropology and the Modern World* (New York: Palgrave, 2003), 115.
64. Ibid., 104.
65. Ibid., 116.
66. Gilroy, *Darker than Blue*, 120–21.

8

Black Humanitarianism

TAVIA NYONG'O

Introduction

Although the work of Paul Gilroy has proved central to debates around diaspora, cosmopolitanism, and postcolonialism, its relation to the field of human rights has not yet been extensively discussed.[1] This is so in part, as I argue in this chapter, because his stance taken toward that field and the discourse it mobilizes is characteristically ambivalent. His two most recent books, *Postcolonial Melancholia* (2004) (published as *After Empire: Melancholia or Convivial Culture?* in the United Kingdom) and *Darker than Blue* (2010), contain his most extensive commentary to date on human rights, and I focus my present discussion on them.[2] However, these statements clearly draw upon prior formulations—such as the "planetary humanism" of the final chapter of *Against Race* (2000) (published as *Between Camps* in the United Kingdom), and the twinning of "utopia and the critique of capitalism" in *'There Ain't No Black in the Union Jack'* (1987). So while it is in recent years that a direct engagement with human rights has emerged most forcefully in his work, that emergence is also an opportunity to revisit early work from a slightly different angle. In these recent statements, Gilroy has taken a contrarian stance to the almost rote leftist dismissals of human rights for its complicity with capitalism, neoliberalism, and empire. He has spoken with critical sympathy about "the movement aimed at extending and consolidating human rights."[3] But his is no liberal humanist defense of the present state of that movement either. Instead, Gilroy calls for a longer history of human rights that would link human rights more substantively to the centuries-long struggle of black and other racialized people to win "the right to be human." Without engaging the history of slavery, colonialism, and the black struggles against both, he argues, "cosmopolitan" human rights is destined to remain defanged. Gilroy's genealogy of race and infrahumanity thus urges contemporary theorists and activists toward a new reckoning with that history, albeit one that would entail a wholesale reconstruction, rather than an outright dismissal, of human rights as a project. Gilroy therefore presents a challenge for the humanitarian and human rights Left, in terms of the limits he presents to the liberal humanist jurisprudence of human *being*. At the same time, he also presents a challenge for the posthumanist Left, one which refigures rather than rejects liberal humanist presuppositions and opens a path to black radical *becoming*.[4]

Wither Human Rights?

The human rights field has been increasingly split off from the left in recent years, as a post-1989 moment of potential rapprochement floundered on the shoals of "humanitarian intervention" during the Clinton-Blair era and decisively gave up the ghost in the wake of Bush-Blair's cynical use of human rights to legitimate invasions of Iraq and Afghanistan. And when human rights rhetoric has not been castigated for directly colluding with US foreign policy, it has been lambasted as a discourse for dupes, part of a soft "human rights imperialism" that replaces sober geopolitical thinking with sentimental and misguided moralism, leaving those it seeks to aid worse off than before. Former *New York Times* reporter Stephen Kinzer, for instance, has denounced the movement he once entered his profession to further:

> Founded by idealists who wanted to make the world a better place, it has in recent years become the vanguard of a new form of imperialism. Want to depose the government of a poor country with resources? Want to bash Muslims? Want to build support for American military interventions around the world? Want to undermine governments that are raising their people up from poverty because they don't conform to the tastes of upper west side intellectuals? Use human rights as your excuse! [. . .] The human rights movement lost

> its way by considering human rights in a vacuum, as if there are absolutes everywhere and white people in New York are best-equipped to decide what they are.[5]

Kinzer's biting critique demonstrates a self-reflexivity not often seen in Western journalistic circles. At the same time, his laudable denunciation of "an absolutist view of human rights permeated by modern western ideas that westerners mistakenly call 'universal'" plays directly into a well-rehearsed debate that is equally absolutist and increasingly stale.[6] Casting the stakes as a contest between universalism and cultural relativism perpetuates the ahistorical framework that scholars of human rights have sought to challenge. In *Postcolonial Melancholia*, Gilroy offers a less caustic but equally devastating assessment when he points to the declension from socialist and feminist internationalisms of the nineteenth and twentieth centuries to the current "political environment where cosmopolitan and translocal affiliations become suspect and are now virtually unthinkable outside of the limited codes of human-rights talk, medical emergency, and environmental catastrophe."[7] Gilroy's point reintroduces history into the pernicious binarism Kinzer's well-meaning critique nonetheless leaves standing, clearing the ground for a more thoroughgoing assessment of what those "limited codes" have historically meant and potentially could come to mean. I discuss two representative left critiques of those codes of human rights talk, before returning to Gilroy to explore how he proposes refashioning human rights discourse in *Darker than Blue*, in part by deepening their historical genealogy and apprehending the black radical imagination at work in nineteenth-century proto-human rights activism and ideology.

The work of Randall Williams and Costas Douzinas (among others) has pointed to the need for the Left to situate human rights within the broader horizon of modernity, precisely in order to grapple with *how* contemporary regimes of violence become either represented or omitted, legitimated or denounced, within the field of human rights discourse.[8] In *The Divided World*, Williams opens his critique by recounting W. E. B. Du Bois's skeptical attitude toward the post–World War II attempts to enshrine human rights in international law. As Williams shows, Du Bois immediately saw how such worthy efforts to make another Holocaust impossible nevertheless were proceeding without directly confronting empire or the color line. Commenting on one draft Declaration of Human Rights from 1944 he was asked to support, Du Bois responded that while he agreed that it addressed the prevention of future genocides and protected the rights of stateless persons, it failed to connect those modes of violence against humans with other kinds, such as the violence done by settler colonialism and racial segregation. It did so, furthermore, at a moment when the anticolonial movement was embracing revolutionary violence. In the face of revolution, human rights were a gift of the free world, led by the United States. As such, they stood diametrically opposed to the self-endowed freedom that revolution promised subjugated peoples. Without establishing a basis of transnational connection between anticolonial struggle and the struggle against the color line, Du Bois noted, human rights talk could not hope to command the enthusiasm of the black and brown masses.

In his materialist and philosophical critique of rights discourse, Costas Douzinas has shown how entrenched this aporia of violence in rights talk is. Rights, he argues, following Marx, are a discourse founded in a property relation that must cloak its violence in legitimating rhetoric and ritual, and which must deny the legitimacy, in the name of "human rights," of a right of resistance to the rule of property.[9] Noting the consistency with which Marxist intellectuals, with the salient exception of Ernst Bloch, have maintained a skeptical distance from human rights, Douzinas explores how revolution and rights became increasingly decoupled in the aftermath of the French Revolution and its Declaration of the Rights of Man and Citizen.[10] One need look only to the fate of the black Jacobins of Santo Domingo, and the reaction against their claiming the emancipatory rhetoric of the Parisian revolutionaries for their own, to understand how the universal extension of the rights of man to enslaved blacks was literally unthinkable.[11]

Extending this critique from the historical to the philosophical, Douzinas has crisply noted the deficits of human rights reasoning. However noble sounding, Douzinas notes, the Rights of Man "turn real people into abstract ciphers. The abstract man of the declarations has no history or tradition, gender or sexuality, colour or ethnicity, those elements that make people real. All content is sacrificed at the altar of abstract humanity."[12] Williams similarly notes how W. E. B. Du Bois "recognized a looming danger: the new universal human was remarkably similar to previous ideological iterations of the Rights of Man."[13] In a divided world, Williams and Douzinas both argue, human rights has more often than not served as an imperial instrument, proffering a liberal alternative to the internationalist rhetoric of decolonization and communism that might reanimate the revolutionary kernel of the Rights of Man and extend them beyond the cordoned zone of their approved contemporary application.

This cautionary account of human rights discourse is, however, not the end of the tale. The very fact that Du Bois sought to engage in the shaping of human rights instruments at all, striving to make them live up to the aspirations of racialized and colonized peoples, reflects his own considered judgment that such an attempt was worthwhile. And, in his brief but notable reconsideration of Ernst Bloch's *Naturrecht und menschliche Würde* (1961), which he considers "the most advanced Marxist reading of the history and philosophy of human rights,"[14] Douzinas points out that "Bloch retains the main elements of Marx's critique of rights but discovers in the tradition of natural law the historically variable but eternal human traits of resisting domination and oppression and of imagining and fighting for a society in which 'man will walk upright.'"[15] While rights discourse indeed originated in property right, the power of human rights, according to Bloch, lies nonetheless in the potential transformation of right from its "monolithic, authoritarian normative" regime into "the subjective catchword of the revolutionary struggle."[16] In my conclusion, I return to and expand on this notion of a "subjective catchword" and redescribe it in black radical terms that seek to move beyond both subjectivity and language and toward a new materialism that encompasses both. At this stage, I want merely to highlight the contrast between "realist" perspectives that would read history as a predictable tragedy, with human rights talk its farcical narration in and for "polite society," and Douzinas's citation of Bloch's utopianism. I can only signpost here the work that has been done in this area on Bloch's notion of concrete utopia, not as a programmatic plan or realized totality but as anticipatory illumination, a community (and humanity) to come. This utopianism not only jibes with Gilroy's early and consistent attention to the utopian, otherworldly, and transfigurative elements of black popular culture, it also resonates with the speculative approaches to the past manifested in the work of queer theorists like José Muñoz and black feminist theorists like Jayna Brown.

Muñoz, in his queer reading of black radicalism in the early plays of LeRoi Jones / Amiri Baraka, cites Bloch's "unorthodox and messianic Marxism" as enabling a perspective on the past that, by pointing toward what is missing in the present, opens out a future potentiality. Aligning this move toward "concrete utopia" with queer temporality,[17] Muñoz suggests that "if the condition of possibility for blackness is a certain radicalness in relation to capitalism's naturalizing temporal logic, the black radical tradition is engaged in a maneuver that helps elucidate queer futurity."[18] The critical recuperation of the history of black and radical contestations of human rights may prove one such maneuver, (and I'll speculate that it may even help, in ways that we cannot yet spell out, in rearticulating the struggle for human rights for queers in the Global South. In light of Muñoz's approach, we can look to Du Bois's intervention as an instance of the Blochian "no-longer-conscious": a past moment that points to an absence in the present arrangement, gesturing in turn toward the future as the "not-yet-present."[19]

Homi Bhabha, while not citing Bloch, similarly posed the past as an indictment of the present that might pave the way for a redeemed future, in the final pages of his now classic *The Location of Culture*. Turning, as Muñoz does, to the Black Arts Movement as the no-longer-conscious, Bhabha cites a poem by Sonia Sanchez that ends:

> life is obscene with crowds
> of white on black
> death is my pulse.
> what might have been
> is not for him/or me
> but what could have been
> floods the womb until I drown.[20]

For Bhabha, the "marginalized disjunctive experience of the subject of racism" can be heard in the split temporality of this poem, which oscillates between "the conditions of an obscene past—*might have been*" and the "conditionality of a new birth—*could have been.*" This temporal trope produces what Bhabha terms a "projective past," in the process "erasing the compliant past tethered to the myth of progress."[21] I want to highlight the formal symmetries of such a past projecting itself into the present with Bloch's notion of the no-longer conscious. Like Bloch, then, Bhabha finds in Sanchez's grief-stricken lament not a figure of the past as loss, but one of projective, interruptive, performative haunting, a death that courses through the body like living blood, a past that is also already a future in embryo but one whose imminent arrival presages not the compliant *reproduction* of present conditions but a cataclysmic flood that threatens to undo the egoistic "I." Following upon the suggestions of Cathy Cohen, Evelynn Hammonds, and other black feminist theorists that we not see black female sexuality as automatically heteronormative,[22] even when figured through tropes of heterosexuality and reproduction, I would see this projective past as a figure of *queer* birthing, one that does not necessarily reinscribe "reproductive futurity."[23]

The subject of Sanchez's elegy, as it turns out, was Malcolm X, which provides a convenient connecting thread back to the subject of human rights talk. Toward the end of his life, Malcolm X began tactically to evoke human rights as a more internationalist premise for the U.S. black freedom struggle to base itself upon than civil rights. In his 1964 speech "The Black Revolution," Malcolm argued (referring to the United States using the feminine pronoun): "She has not only deprived us of the right to be a citizen, she has deprived us of *the right to be human* beings, the right to be recognized and respected as men and women. In this country the black can be fifty years old and he is still a 'boy'" (my emphasis).[24]

Although couched within a gendered language of emasculation—in which America is depicted as a castrating mother denying adult men the dignity of their manhood—Malcolm invited his audience to think beyond the constraints of the nation-state as a horizon of redress, precisely by converting human rights into a "subjective catchword of the revolutionary struggle." Implicitly, and reading somewhat against the grain, Malcolm even presents an oedipal scenario of castrating mothers and emasculated "boys" as a dystopian present to be *transcended* by a future in which we are, finally, human beings. Not only is this future co-gendered ("men and women") but the black radical imagination at work in the right to be (or become) human casts its sights on a horizon beyond oedipal gender. In "The Ballot or the Bullet," a speech given in that same year, Malcolm said:

> Whenever you are in a civil-rights struggle, whether you know it or not, you are confining yourself to the jurisdiction of Uncle Sam. No one from the outside world can speak out in your behalf as long as your struggle is a civil-rights struggle. [. . .] But the United Nations has what's known as the charter of human rights, it has a committee that deals in human rights. You may wonder why all the atrocities that have been committed in Africa and in Hungary and in Asia and in Latin America are brought before the UN, and the Negro problem is never brought before the UN. This is part of the conspiracy.[25]

Now, Paul Gilroy's work has taken strong and consistent exception to the nationalism and masculinism of organizations like the Nation of Islam, as well as the paranoid style of Malcolm's rhetoric.[26] But, at least to my ears, something of Gilroy's "strategic universalism" is audible here in Malcolm X's appeal to human rights as a broader and more critical basis for an international struggle that would link black nationalism in the United States to movements for self-determination in the Third World and beyond. For Malcolm, the right to be a human being had been patently abrogated by the world's leading advocate for human rights. Bringing a case before the United Nations, the "case of blackness" as it were, could expose the tension between decolonization and human rights, short-circuiting the hegemonic liberal order with political energies routing themselves along prohibited channels.[27] For Gilroy, this right to *be* human—to interrupt and make trouble within the quiescent and orderly *being* of humans—draws upon antinomian traditions of popular struggle dating back for centuries but taking especial shape in the transnational abolitionist movement of the late eighteenth and nineteenth century.

Abolitionism as a Human Rights Campaign

Consistently challenging scholars whose historical accounts of modernity continue to omit slavery and colonialism as constitutive of its order, Gilroy's genealogy of human rights looks past the familiar historical landmarks of the French and American revolutions, which continue to magnetize most commentators. Beginning with his reading of Frederick Douglass in *The Black Atlantic*, Gilroy has frequently looked to abolitionism as a counter-culture to modernity, one whose historical legacy constitutes a Foucaultian "counter-memory" to the official past, even or especially the official past that incorporates abolitionists as figureheads of an accomplished, as opposed to ongoing, process of liberation. Where Douglass is now so politically neutralized a figure that the far right media personality Glenn Beck can open his cable TV show with a montage of historical icons that include him and Harriet Tubman, Gilroy's most recent book insists upon retaining Douglass within an uncompromisingly radical, internationalist lineage: "Douglass' political record suggests that, in demanding equality before the law based on natural rights and exploring the relationship of debased citizenship and tainted law to racialised life, he was drawing upon the thinking of an earlier cohort of abolitionist writers. [. . .] These thinkers and activists had a wholesale transformation of U.S. society in mind."[28] Among those thinkers Gilroy discusses is Angelina Grimké, the pioneering American Quaker feminist who "connected the notion of divinely instituted human rights to a growing sense of what it would mean for women to acquire political rights."[29] This, Gilroy insists, was not an analogical or metaphorical comparison between the subjection of women and chattel slavery. Nor was it precisely a politics of formal equality and identity, although certainly there were strands of such thinking in the movement. But the strands Gilroy seeks to tease out and retain involve a politics of thinking and feeling through difference in order to grapple with the root causes of hierarchy and degradation. In a particularly pointed comment, Gilroy laments the eclipse in prestige that sentimentalism has suffered in the face of

> the righteous repudiation of humanism which was common among "poststructuralist" and leftist thinkers during the Cold War years. To account for the origins of that antihumanism is beyond the scope of the present argument, but we should note emphatically that it does not follow the paths developed by post-1945 critics of liberal humanism, whose hostility to that doctrine included its relationship to the history of colonialism, imperialism, and racism.[30]

With this brief for anti-antihumanism, Gilroy proceeds to reconsider the counter-cultural legacy of American abolitionism's diceiest properties, Harriet Beecher Stowe's *Uncle Tom's Cabin* (1852), from a cosmopolitan perspective. James Baldwin famously savaged the novel and the sentimental protest tradition it stood for (while later on admitting its formative influence on his worldview) in "Everybody's Protest Novel." With the recent 150th anniversary of *Uncle Tom's Cabin*, the critical pendulum has swung so far in the direction of Baldwin's indictment that it is sometimes hard to imagine what in it might have moved uncounted readers into action in the first place. If so, Gilroy's account helps remind us:

> The bibliographic note included in the repackaged 1879 edition was compiled by George Bullen, a curator of books at the British Museum. He revealed that almost three decades after its first publication, Stowe's novel had been translated into numerous languages, including Bengali, Farsi, Japanese, Magyar, and Mandarin. Fourteen printings had been issued in the German language during the first year of publication; a year later, seventeen printings in French and a further six in Portuguese had also appeared. In Russia, the book had been recommended as a primer in the struggle against serfdom and was duly banned by the authorities. The first book to sell more than a million copies in the United States, Stowe's novel was a world-historic event when it was published. Though it cemented some deeply problematic conceptions of slave passivity, redemptive suffering, and

> indeed of racial type, it was also instrumental in spreading notions of black dignity and ontological depth, as well as an antiracist variety of universal humanism. This combination merits recognition as a potent factor in the circulation of a version of human rights that racial hierarchies could not qualify or interrupt.[31]

I have quoted Gilroy at some length here to convey a sense of the rhetorical force of his argument, which serves as a kind of metacommentary on the current conditions of politics and discourse that make such a balanced assessment of Stowe's novel hard to swallow. Like Bloch, Gilroy here is unafraid to look to notions of dignity, ontological depth, and even universal humanism, as something deeper, finally, than tactics, redeeming their use in a struggle to, as the late philosopher Emmanuel Eze once put it, "achieve our humanity."[32] Certainly, *Uncle Tom's Cabin* does not belong to the canon of black literary self-representation—much of that canon, indeed, was written implicitly or explicitly against it, beginning with Martin Delany's *Blake: Or, The Huts of America* (1859–1861). Stowe's novel must instead form a kind of uncommon memory, a historical counter-memory that does not consolidate but instead disperses identity across gender, racial, and national lines.

One might also note, in passing, how the rhizomatic dispersion of the text into so many editions, languages, and nations was enabled by a lax regime of "copyleft" *avant la lettre*. The ability of texts to circulate not as private property but as a political, affective, and imaginative commons is crucial to an account of the dissemination of *Uncle Tom's Cabin* that focusing solely on its sentimentalized, sacralized storyline might miss. Gilroy is not calling for a simple reclamation of the text, as if we could still read or be guided by its dated portraits of "redemptive suffering." Instead of a close reading of the text's ideological effects, his "distant reading" of Stowe's world-historic impact invites us to consider the no-longer-conscious revolutionary energies of that moment and to wield it as a critique against the imaginative enclosures of the present.

The occurrence of the phrase "human rights" in abolitionist literature is too extensive to need more commentary than a simple reminder that this was more than a century before the United Nations charter. It is not, as I've already noted, a language shorn of ambiguity, and placing abolitionism in the genealogy of human rights talk is emphatically not a gesture of liberal contributionist historiography. Rather it is the opposite: an opportunity to expand and refine our critical consciousness of the profane tools with which activists then and now sought to create a politics that would transfigure their present order. Consider this extract from *The Colored American*, one of the earliest black radical newspapers, explaining to its readers, in 1837, the sins of slavery:

> What is that but a sin, which sinks to the level of brutes, beings ranked and registered by GOD, a little lower than the angels, wrests from their rightful owners the legacies which their Maker has bequeathed them—inalienable birthright endowments, exchanged for no equivalent, unsurrendered by volition, and unforfeited by crime—*breaks open the sanctuary of human rights, and makes its sacred things common plunder*, driving to the shambles Jehovah's image, herded with four-footed beasts and creeping things—and bartering for vile dust the purchase of a Redeemer's blood, and the living members of his body?[33] (My emphasis.)

The Christian theological reasoning is starkly evident, as is the case with many other popular struggles against the wealthy and privileged in Anglo-American history. This is not an avenue, incidentally, down which Gilroy's thought frequently travels. What I want to note here, however, is how the property logic of rights, which Marx rightly critiqued, is in this antebellum text already socially transfigured. Chattel slavery, the holding of property in humans, is recast through the language of human rights as a profanation of a sacred order and the making of an ersatz common. The defense of property right, in legal and religious terms, is used against the legal, religious, and property system under which black people were held in slavery. Human rights here had already become a "subjective catchword" of a struggle that, as the American Civil War made evident, would indeed become revolutionary.

Humanity and Utopia on the Lower Frequencies

Even in his earliest formulations, Gilroy was pointing toward a conception of blackness that employed the multivalence of political languages as a redemptive force in human history. In *'There Ain't No Black in the Union Jack,'* he argued that black cultures

> have been created from diverse and contradictory elements apprehended through discontinuous histories. They have been formed in

> a field of force between the poles of under- and overdevelopment, periphery and centre. Their *bi-lingual character* expresses these origins and dislocates the languages of sometimes antagonistic political formations—black and white, slave and slave-holder, class, people, nation and locality into new meanings. [. . .] The outcomes of this cultural and political interaction reconstruct and rework tradition as they pursue their particular utopia. *A vision of a world in which "race" will no longer be a meaningful device for the categorization of human beings, where work will no longer be servitude and law will be disassociated from domination.*[34] (My emphasis.)

The vision of a world beyond race has proved most contentious for some readers who see in it only the threatening prospect of an indefinite extension of the colorblind racism of the present. But in noting the triadic conception of liberation from race, work, and the law, I want to highlight the manner in which Gilroy's utopian conception of black radical becoming is not based on any affirmation, in whole or in part, of the achieved circumstance of present-day cosmopolitanism. This "vision" is in some sense beyond view, it is not yet present, not yet conscious. And while "the right to be human" does not yet appear at this stage in Gilroy's thinking, the concept of utopia he articulates here signals a commitment to thinking beyond the terms of the present political order, including its legalistic conception of human being. When he speaks subsequently, in *Postcolonial Melancholia*, of "the disenchanted acquisition of what are now called human rights by peoples who had only recently been accepted by their colonizers and racial betters as human beings," he is clear regarding the chasm between the world as it is and the world as it must become.[35] Put another way, it is not the case that Gilroy has argued that "race" or race thinking can be overcome without also liberating humanity from the domination of capitalism and sovereignty, without, that is to say, profaning the bases upon which rights have been sacralized. The human rights talk he would champion would only occur in a space where they took up a politics of transfiguration, rather than one of fulfillment.

Drawing on Seyla Benhabib's classic distinction between politics of fulfillment and transfiguration, Gilroy has described, in one of *The Black Atlantic*'s oft-cited passages, the role of black music and performance as a counterculture to modernity:

> The issue of how utopias are conceived is more complex not least because they strive continually to move beyond the grasp of the

> merely linguistic, textual, and discursive. The invocation of utopia references what, following Seyla Benhabib's suggestive lead, I propose to call the politics of transfiguration. This emphasises the emergence of qualitatively new desires, social relations, and modes of association within the racial community of interpretation and resistance *and* between that group and its erstwhile oppressors. It points specifically to the formation of a community of needs and solidarity which is magically made audible in the music itself and palpable in the social relations of its cultural utility and reproduction. Created under the very nose of the overseers, the utopian desires which fuel the complementary politics of transfiguration must be invoked by other, more deliberately opaque means. *This politics exists on a lower frequency where it is played, danced, and acted, as well as sung and sung about, because words, even words stretched by melisma and supplemented or mutated by screams which still index the conspicuous power of the slave sublime, will never be enough to communicate its unsayable claims to truth.*[36] (My emphasis.)

I call this passage oft-cited, but probably it is the final sentence that is most frequently, and justly, celebrated. There is, in that sentence, an irony upon which we could dwell, one involving the virtuosic deployment of language to point to that which language cannot perform. It may be what Eve Sedgwick termed a "peri-performative" sentence, a sentence that places itself in relation to what it cannot do, that convinces us how its effort at communicating "will never be enough to communicate," one that mines, in its repetitions and acts of supplementation, the very improvisatory and melismatic musical energies to which it pays tribute.[37] Gilroy's surprising gesture here is toward both "magic" and "invocation," as the means by which the sublime energies of the lower frequencies may engender a politics of transfiguration reflect this peri-performativity of language. There is a sense of language being on the border of something else.

The politics of transfiguration, that is to say, is not only ambivalent, in terms of its capacity to render pliable the subjective catchwords of revolutionary struggle. Its revolutionary litany must also, in turn, be placed in the service of a performed politics—performed not *instead* of being spoken, written, and so forth (which would be a very retrograde and primitivist gesture) but performed in speech, song, text, music, and struggle because they figure the no-longer-present (the slave sublime) as a negation of the present that might clear an opening to the not yet present.

Conclusion

"Nostalgia," the philosopher Stanley Cavell writes appositely, "is an inability to open the past to the future, as if the strangers who will replace you will never find what you have found."[38] What might it mean to "open" the past? And why would such an ability, both in Cavell's formulation and, I believe, also in our ordinary language, be cast in the form of a double negation, *not nostalgic*? I have already suggested one route through this question, via Sonia Sanchez and Ernst Bloch, and I want, in closing, to speculate on how nostalgia emerges as a problematic in Gilroy's latest reconsideration of the black musical tradition.

Nostalgia, of course, like kitsch, is an accusation. Someone always stands *accused* of being nostalgic, even if they are self-accused. But nostalgia is also an act of identification, against the grain of the times. Hence the desire to find another word for it, another way of moving sideways along the groove into which our reminiscence might settle us, like the grooves in a record that, by drawing the needle forward in ever tightening circles, pulls out an emanation of song that casts us forward, expectantly, into itself, still yearning for what we might call, after Cavell, its *opening*.

What might it mean for a song to open the past to its future, such that the stranger who will replace us would find in it what we have found? He does not say so in so many words, but I believe that a question very much like this one animates much of what Paul Gilroy has written about black music. His most recent volume of criticism, *Darker than Blue*, raises the aesthetic and political stakes of this question anew. Returning in an almost incantatory fashion to his longstanding musical exemplars—Jimi Hendrix, Curtis Mayfield, Bob Marley—he asks of them the nigh impossible, which is that their struggle and achievement might redeem our future. Speaking personally toward of the end of his book, Gilroy comments:

> I do not wish to capitulate to the pressures which dictate a nostalgic relationship to the latter part of that departed golden age. And yet, at the same time, I can recall the glorious parade of black Atlantic performers that flowed through London's musical scenes between 1969, when I first started going out to enjoy live music, and the more recent point, when deskilling, aesthetic stagnation, and what can politely be called "recycling" all intervened to make live performances less alive and less pleasurable than they had been before.

> I cannot avoid the sense of loss that results from having lived through that rare period. Responding to black culture's changes of moral tone and social orientation involves grieving for a certain fragile, precious relationship between music and political ethics in which the former amended, stretched, and enriched the latter [. . .]. My sadness at these changes is also connected to a desire for the restoration of a public culture in which art and social life, those different dimensions of our complex practice as a collectivity, could dissolve easily and pleasurably into each other.[39]

Couched in the idiom of the "not nostalgic," *Darker than Blue* seeks a melancholy equal to the task of marking the lost as lost while still opening (Gilroy's word is "restoration") the past to a future in which what was immanent to it could unfold once more. This entails a doubled move of historical and aesthetic reconstruction that resembles but need not be nostalgia, if its purpose is not to close but rather to open the past, as past, to present use. The past is dispossessed as a personal property and opened as a space of virtuality and becoming.[40] The historical predicament of the "golden age" of soul must be adequately restored to mind, while its limits and failures are never out of sight. The aesthetic mode Gilroy insistently aligns with the pleasure of being alive—a pleasure that always takes on the radical character of the insurgent drive in black culture—must be patiently described and defended against any critical shorthand that could miss its complexity and precarity. The indiscernible "it" for which nostalgia is never an adequate tribute is attached to the liveliness of the world making of black sonic cultures, the audiotopic moment of *jouissance*, rendered here not just as aesthetic rapture but as one attached specifically to the political character of music, what Gilroy chooses to call its "moral economy."

Many, including Gilroy himself, have noted the affinity between his thought and the melancholic tonalities of Adorno. Their shared willingness to tarry with the negative can be misread as nostalgia. For either to be guilty of that charge, however, one would have to seriously believe that they could have confused the catastrophe of history with a naïve belief in some prelapsarian idyll. One of Gilroy's more interesting and quirky recent interlocutors, João Costa Vargas, has instead suggested that we look to the black musical tradition as a source of black radical *becoming*, as unfinished and contingent. This, he usefully notes, may prove a way around the depressing choice of either abandoning its inheritance or accepting the logic of "no alternative" to the hypercommodified capitalist present. As Vargas writes:

> We are black insofar as, having more or less survived the constant assaults on our humanity, we recognize and draw on a collective reservoir of resistance, pride, and hopes. Thus, because blackness is a process marked by time, space, and power, and because this collective reservoir is not only constantly changing but also can be accessed through countless routes (politics, art, and spirituality, for example) We are always *becoming* black. It is the immanent revolutionary potential of becoming that interests me—it is the revolutionary component of Blackness that is capable of generating theories and practices that project a nonhierarchical lifeworld, one that does not depend on tropes of difference associated with vertical scale of power and humanity.[41]

Vargas differs from Gilroy in terms of his tolerance for what he terms the "necessary, but partial" truths of race.[42] But he joins Gilroy in looking to black music—in his case, John Coltrane's *A Love Supreme*—as a truth procedure where black radical becoming leads, beyond words, toward an ineffable vision of utopia. For Vargas, both blackness and humanity are placed in the present and future tense: these are not identities we can fall back upon or a world of rights into which we are born. They are a project that looks both forward and backward in its effort to redeem and restore the past, without nostalgia, while remaining open and self-critical.

Gilroy's call for human rights discourse to grapple more seriously with the implications of grounding itself in an alternate genealogy of abolitionist and black radical movements is persuasive and timely. What the outcome of such a grappling might be is less clear. Jodi Melamed's portrait of a neoliberal present in which everyone is officially antiracist, but racial inequalities are metastasizing, is sharp.[43] Official statements of antiracism, Sara Ahmed notes, increasingly take on the cast of the "non-performative" speech act, words that do not accomplish what they say they accomplish.[44] The assumption that human rights operates in a post-racist context, as Gilroy constantly reminds us, preserves the racial innocence of its predominantly white and Western agents, even or perhaps especially when they present their work as "enabling" or "giving voice" to others in distress. But the answer is not to retreat to a defensive identitarian stance. Nor is the answer to this predicament to throw up our hands but to learn to live with the ambivalence. And if ambivalence sounds like a crippling state of psychic stasis and indecision, it need not be. Zygmunt Bauman, in *Modernity and Ambivalence*, defines ambivalence as "the possibility of assigning an object or an event to more than one category [. . .]

a failure of the naming (segregating) function that language is meant to perform."[45] This is a different sort of failure than the nonperformativity Ahmed identifies. It is perhaps not right to call it failure, at least not without recoding what failure is or can do. Learning to live with ambivalence, as Bauman suggests, could mean the very opposite of stasis, for it could provide the conditions for radical becoming. The impossible of a stable, segregating naming is what guarantees and is guaranteed by this movement of the human.

Gilroy's characterization of the black Atlantic as "rhizomorphic" reflects such a sensibility. "I have suggested," he writes, "that the critiques of modernity articulated by successive generations of black intellectuals had their *rhizomorphic systems of propagation* anchored in a continued proximity to the unspeakable terrors of the slave experience"[46] (my emphasis). Such rhizomorphic genealogies of black critique, propagated within and without, over and underneath, profaning and making usable the sacred languages of rights, call attention to the ongoing capacity for a struggle over the terms of human rights and the right to be human.

Notes

1. One exception is a passing mention in Hope Lewis, "Reflections on Blackcrit Theory: Human Rights," *Villanova Law Review* 45 (2000): 1089–1090.
2. I refer to the U.S. edition of both volumes throughout this chapter.
3. Paul Gilroy, *Postcolonial Melancholia*, xvi.
4. I take the phrase "black radical becoming," discussed later, from João Costa Vargas, *Never Meant to Survive*, 137–57.
5. Stephen Kinzer, "End Human Rights Imperialism Now."
6. Ibid.
7. Gilroy, *Postcolonial Melancholia*, 5.
8. And more recently, Eyal Weizman's haunting and magisterial *The Least of All Possible Evils: Humanitarian Violence from Arendt to Gaza*.
9. "The first epigrammatic article of the Universal Declaration of Human Rights (1948) repeats the French statement of equal freedom. Yet no right to resistance is found in the much longer epigonal recitation. On the contrary, the preamble states that these rights are given in order to prevent revolution, and article 30 prohibits radical challenges to the political and legal system." Costas Douzinas, "Adikia: On Communism and Rights," 92–93.

10. Douzinas, "Adikia: On Communism and Rights."
11. On the unthinkability of the Haitian revolution, both at the time and subsequently, see Trouillot, *Silencing the Past.*
12. Douzinas, "Adikia: On Communism and Rights," 83.
13. Randall Williams, *The Divided World*, xiv.
14. Douzinas, "Adikia: On Communism and Rights," 86.
15. Ibid., 85.
16. Ernst Bloch, *Natural Law and Human Dignity*, 217.
17. Queer temporality is the critique of conceptions of time that take for granted and thus naturalize heterosexuality and human reproduction. A common critique is of "reproductive futurity," or the reduction of the future to that which can be made safe for or sufficient unto an imagined child. Another temporal critique is of the presumption that because queers "don't reproduce," queer existence is somehow parasitical on straight existence and has no transgenerational or historical depth of its own. See Edelman, *No Future.*
18. Muñoz, "Cruising the Toilet," 356.
19. Other scholars of black performance who have recently turned to the work of Ernst Bloch include Jayna Brown, "Buzz and Rumble."
20. Homi Bhabha, *The Location of Culture*, 363.
21. Ibid.
22. Cohen, "Punks, Bulldaggers, and Welfare Queens"; Hammonds, "Black (W)holes and the Geometry of Black Female Sexuality."
23. On reproductive futurity, see Edelman, *No Future.*
24. Malcolm X, *Malcolm X Speaks*, 50–51.
25. Ibid., 34.
26. Malcolm X announced his break from the Nation of Islam shortly before giving the two speeches mentioned here.
27. I borrow the phrase, with apologies, from Moten, "The Case of Blackness."
28. Paul Gilroy, *Darker than Blue*, 62.
29. Ibid., 63.
30. Ibid.
31. Ibid.
32. Eze, *Achieving Our Humanity.*
33. "Declaration of Sentiments, on the Sin of Slavery."
34. Paul Gilroy, *'There Ain't No Black in the Union Jack,'* 218.
35. Gilroy, *Postcolonial Melancholia*, 36.
36. Paul Gilroy, *The Black Atlantic*, 37.
37. Eve Kosofsky Sedgwick, *Touching Feeling.*

38. Stanley Cavell, *Philosophy the Day after Tomorrow*.
39. Gilroy, *Darker than Blue*, 122–23.
40. On the virtual past, see Henri Bergson, *Matter and Memory*.
41. Vargas, *Never Meant to Survive*, 138.
42. Ibid.
43. Jodi Melamed, "The Spirit of Neoliberalism."
44. Sara Ahmed, "Declarations of Whiteness," 52.
45. Zygmunt Bauman, *Modernity and Ambivalence*, 1.
46. Gilroy, *The Black Atlantic*, 72–73.

9

A Dialogue on the Human

An Interview with Paul Gilroy

EDITED BY
REBECKA RUTLEDGE FISHER AND JAY GARCIA

In fall 2007, William "Sandy" Darity and Jay Garcia team-taught a graduate seminar on Paul Gilroy's work. On January 16, 2008, members of that seminar engaged Gilroy on a number of issues emerging from his work. The interview was moderated by Rebecka Rutledge Fisher.

TATIANA MARGITIC: The contribution *The Black Atlantic* has made generally and continues to make as a theoretical paradigm for studying transatlantic black cultures is well known. Could you nevertheless speak to how you understand the impact you were trying to make with that work? Along similar lines, how did the selection of main figures in *The Black Atlantic* take place? Most are men; few black women, black women intellectuals who also crossed the Atlantic, enter the book. I was wondering if you could speak to this point at the same time that you revisit the larger set of aims that led to the book.

PAUL GILROY: Well . . . I hope that the greatest inspiration that my modest contributions might offer people is the courage to write the books they want to read. So the arbitrariness of my own work isn't supposed to preclude anybody else doing other things that are better, richer, more timely, more important. *Black Atlantic* was a book that was written to respond to certain kinds of "conjunctural problems" and also as a book that was written to try and get me a proper job, which I didn't have. So, unlike some, I wasn't cooling my heels in Oxford or anything like that. I feel like Jude the Obscure when I go there, to be truthful. I was really just wondering—from the vantage point of South Bank Polytechnic—whether having a life as a scholar was going to be possible for me. That's where a lot of the neurotic energy of *Black Atlantic* comes from.

With regard to my choices, I also wanted to write a book I could finish. You've asked me specifically about women. The one whose life I was most acquainted with, whose travelings and imaginings and reflections and whose political culture was most appropriate, was Ida B. Wells. At that time, Vron Ware had been going through the archive and working on her book about that, and I didn't feel I should trespass upon it. [Richard] Wright was chosen because his work crosses the language barriers and political idioms between the English and the French. [W. E. B.] Du Bois was chosen because he functions . . . to me and to many, then, as I think he functions now, as custodian of a kind of core project of African American political or liberation thought. You know, as a cipher of the modern phase of that.

Obviously, Toni Morrison is someone who figures in the book, and through my own work as a journalist, I had interviewed her and James Baldwin at some length during the time the book was being written. And there is something of my conversations with both of them I think that was folded into it. I can't even remember who the third, "case-study" person actually *was* now? It's in the book? Is there a third . . .? [Someone from panel says: "Douglass, Douglass and Delany . . ."] Obviously the question that bothers me now, which is something that Marshall Berman made me think about in relation to Margaret Garner, was what he calls the Masada question. It highlights my failure to be sufficiently alert to the idea that killing your children is not killing yourself. There are all sorts of reasons why people might kill their children when they could be killing themselves. Anyway, those are the reasons why I chose Wright and Du Bois. If I were doing it now, I'd include a chapter on Anna Julia Cooper.

How [*The Black Atlantic*] functions, I have no idea. In fact, I'm the last person . . . I probably should start as I said I was going to do this morning, only half jokingly, talking about "Gilroy." Because "Gilroy"—there are certain things "Gilroy" did, and I don't necessarily recognize myself in the "Gilroy," so it frees me somewhat if I lapse into speaking about "Gilroy." Perhaps that will help you. You know, "Gilroy" is someone who does other things than I do and whose books have other lives. Books have their own lives. They are like children in that sense—they go off into the world, as Mary Shelley put it. You know, "Gilroy" reads Fanon as though Fanon was a doctor and put his hands on people and doctored them. "Gilroy" reads *The Wretched of the Earth*, read it, let's say, sorry, past tense—"Gilroy" read it as though there were case studies in the back of the book. "Gilroy" thinks there isn't any politics in the colony. So when we start asking questions about the political, as was coming up toward the end here, we are in danger of missing the whole point. There is no politics in the colony. There's something else—but it's not politics. It might be violence. So I think all those questions have a bearing really on the travels of the book. I was very humbled by the whole thing that's happened with the book's success. I don't need to go further into that, but let me say that it was modeled on *Orientalism* and my own understanding of that intervention by Edward Said. I didn't want to make a sort of sausage machine that anybody could put whatever they liked into. You know, put—what's the phrase?—"mechanically recovered meat" into it and produce sausages of their own particular kind. I wanted to offer a set of tools with which people could think differently about culture and history, politics and social life.

Okay, so that's the sort of surface version. The other thing is, and this has a bearing on those choices you asked about, that there was a kind of quarrel, really, about the direction of theory. My partner and I had briefly become friends with Cedric and Elizabeth Robinson when they were living in Radwinter near Cambridge and [Cedric was] writing that beautiful book, *Black Marxism*. Conversations with Cedric referred me to dimensions of African American political thought and philosophical thinking that I had no knowledge of previously and I was very grateful to him. At the same time as I was, you know, thinking about C. L. R. James, whose work I knew quite well and had some contact with. I didn't know C. L. R. James until the early period leading up to the leavening of this book. So, I think there was some sort of sense of *Black Atlantic* as an intervention. I said it was conjunctural, which may be why it has other uses now. It was directed toward an argument about the relationship between traditions of radical thought within that, broadly speaking, pan-African frame that were not simply and straightforwardly Marxist. Fanon calls it a stretched Marxism, and actually Wright described Marxism as "but a transitory makeshift pending a more accurate diagnosis and containing within it a definition of man by sheer default." That was in his "Blueprint for Negro Writing." At the same time, a certain set of nationalist forces, and I do mean forces, was very much alive. This was the moment of Public Enemy marching around in uniforms on stage. I was approached—at that time I was doing a bit of expert witnessing and talking to people in certain court cases as an expert. And there was a court case that arose from the arrest of some young black men outside a Public Enemy *concert* at Hammersmith. They had been marching around doing their militarized thing and the police had arrested them. When they got into the police van, they were beaten up. And while they were being beaten up, the equally young policemen said to them: "They've got guns in there, we've got guns out here too. We're a posse too you know." That was something that underlined for me the possibility that there was a certain kind of continuity in the way fraternity was being imagined. This, after all, was leading up to the historic moment of "Malcolm, Marley, Marcus, Mandela *and ME.*" The kind of narcissistic impulse, Fanon calls it the dual narcissism, the implodedness in which the integrity of the whole community becomes the integrity only of masculinity. I wanted to damage that a bit. That's why I chose those people, because I felt they were the best resource. Their lives yielded the best resource to damage that moment.

LAURA SIMS: In *The Black Atlantic* and *Against Race*, you rely heavily on African American history and politics as a model of black experience, yet in your most recent work, including the article "Multiculture, Double Consciousness and the 'War on Terror,'" you clearly begin to distance yourself from this tradition and decide that, I'm quoting you: "US history and the field of racial politics need not represent the future of Europe's minorities." You have suggested that, in your next book, you will explore even further the limits of Du Bois's notion of double consciousness in today's world. Can you discuss the shift in your thinking and some of its implications?

PAUL GILROY: My friend and colleague in London, Chetan Bhatt, has developed the concept of "xenology." It identifies the ways we talk about strangers and the discourse of reflection on strangers and strangeness, perhaps also on estrangement as a subset of those. I suppose I would say that I found my conceptual approaches to be incompatible with certain features of the local xenology. I didn't fit with what some people call the authenticity question (I don't always refer to it as that because I think that formulation is not complicated enough). The premium on authenticity and insiderism meant that I've been identified as an outsider and shut out from African American political thought and culture. Happily, I'm not in any melancholic state about that expulsion. I have embraced it in the same way that I was happy when the United States excluded itself from the Durban Conference on race, racism, and oppression in 2001. It's not that I feel I want to put energy into provincializing the United States, because very often the conversation we have about these issues is already polarizing and provincializing. I don't have to add any salsa to it in order to demonstrate the dynamic in which racial Americana provincializes itself.

I said earlier—was it last night?—that there has been a great shift from an East/West to North/South dynamic in the way that black political culture is being thought and lived. That's a timely thing. It connects with the authenticity problem again in ways that should be obvious. I feel a bit ashamed that I've kept on repeating things that I've written about, that you've read already, so it seems really silly to use our time today in quite this way. But, there's a sense in which the engagement with Africa, which underpins, historically, the notion of an African American identity—when the hyphen is not a minus sign—has been completely transformed. In the moment that *Black Atlantic* was addressed to, Africa wasn't allowed to inhabit the same present as the overdeveloped world. I remember the first time I came to Duke twenty years ago. I was very happy to meet [Valentin Y.] Mudimbe. I had never met him before. I don't know if he still works in the area. I remember Mudimbe telling me that he had some experiences in which he had been bruised by the notion that, in some US circles, perhaps some of the more flamboyantly Afrological scenes than the ones we normally move in, he had encountered being interpellated as the wrong variety of African. I remember Manthia Diawara saying some similar things. I remember also Kwame Anthony Appiah saying that he had, at a certain point, felt himself being drawn into somewhat similar sorts of conflicts. In that occult company, Africa was alright as long as Africa followed a particular script that originated locally, in the USA. These things, you know, probably go back a long way. In *Black Atlantic*, they seemed to go right back to Martin Delany. What was Delany doing in the Niger Valley? His lofty, sometimes impatient responses to empirically existing Africans were deeply problematic. Similar patterns are evident in the history of Liberia and go back to unsettle the very notion of being a returnee to Africa. So much of the time when Africa arises, Africa isn't in the same present. Africa isn't allowed to be there. I don't recall whether I said this already: *Black Atlantic* began when I was walking through the Valley of the Kings in Egypt and I bumped into a posse, sorry, a party of African American tourists who were doing one of those tours led by Doc Ben [Yosef Ben-Jochannan]. I'm sure you all know who Doc Ben is. Doc Ben or his team was leading them through the Valley of the Kings, and there they were with their camcorders and all the rest of it. I was, like them, awestruck. Anyway, the last chapter of *Black Atlantic* grew from there. A lot of my sense of the conjuncture derived from that tantalizing, extraordinary interaction with them in that special location. My sense of our connection to the place in which we were standing became acute. Our relationship to the histories, memories, and historiographies, and then the tourism, all of those things, was something that was being actively negotiated in real time, face to face. A little bit, I suppose, later on, I discovered comparable parties of African American tourists in Cachoeira, going to the sisters of the Boa Morte Festival there that they have in August, dancing a special samba. Their finding Africa in Brazil involves something of the same notion of return to a familiar past.

I found this fascinating, and I was interested to see how it connected to the larger issue of Delany—which is the issue of how one returns to Africa, not as a colonist, which is slightly fudged in the notion of being a returnee, but as a recovering diaspora. You know, Delany had various schemes, he was going to . . . I'm sure you all know what he was going to do with African grown cotton and locomotives and building the transcontinental railway and all this kind of stuff. I guess that some people might think of his plans as a colonial intervention in the social and economic life of Africa. So in that sense, Africa did not exist in the same present as his modernity. When we were all kings and queens, that may have been okay, but Africa now really wants help and solidarity to deal with what's going on. I'm sure, of course, there are Africans here who may want to speak to these questions directly. Let's say that there are issues about where the African content in African American identity comes from and how it's going to be specified and where the issue of authenticity bites that particular question of identification.

MURAT ES: After two days of conference-going, the tidy question I had has gotten all messed up. So I will do my best to make it intelligible somehow. Throughout the semester, when I was reading through your work, I considered ways of appropriating or redirecting your critique of race to my own work, which focuses on religion. You have consistently focused on the category of race throughout your career as the central concern of your intellectual endeavor, and this is pretty much based on your own experience within the British context. Thinking of my own experience in the context of Turkey, or others who are looking at places where there's no direct experience of colonialism or there are other registers of difference that are operating, constructions of difference—I'm thinking of linguistic differences, religious differences, or regional differences. Within this context, I was wondering, can you reflect on this privileging of race in your thinking especially over these other categories? And within the context of the planetary humanism you invoke, does race become an analytical category that can be taught universally on a planetary scale?

PAUL GILROY: Well, I hope it does not. I mean, I wouldn't want race to play that role. I am less interested in race as a variety of political ontology than I am in the history of racism(s). There are people who do see race in that way and they have been around for a while. We know the history of their geopolitical aspirations, and we can read their work through a genealogy that we have. We all know that genealogy here. We know where race thinking and pragmatic anthropology arose in the eighteenth century, we know where they became scientific, we know where they correspond to the historical monopoly of agency and progress by Europeans, we know where that history was cut by conceptions of time that transformed the relationship between self and other—so that it could be articulated not as a relationship between parent and child but, along the lines of Darwin and Lyell, through a notion of geological time that assembled otherness—the primitive—as belonging to another time. Whites were in a different time. And, of course, we know where they fell out with each other and started to ask whether we were all on the same linear journey to the same teleological destination and so on. We know where the colonial project cuts history. We know where the Congo Conference happened. We know *why* the Berlin Conference happened. We know where the lines were drawn on the earth. So we can tell a story of the making of the modern world that is centered on those questions. I'm sorry if I seem neurotically overinvested in that sort of story. I guess I am neurotically invested in it. I think that's because there's a kind of corrective intervention that's necessary because it's still not thought to be something that's worth talking about. *We* think it's worth talking about, but most of the time in universities, most of the time in educational institutions, it is a disreputable, dishonest, and unserious thing to be interested in. Where vindication is a project or a sort of therapeutic activity, one is allowed in under the umbrella of university life—that's sort of accommodated. But in the sense of scholarship and intellectual life, that's still an image people aren't able to be interested in. The category of infrahumanity is central to my understanding. I'm interested in the prospect you describe, and we've known about this problem since Genesis, I suppose. Certainly, it's been familiar since thinking about Freud and Freud's sense of the problems that arise when a people or nation takes itself as its preferred object of identification. It's a problem that exceeds the issue of the Atlantic system of racial slavery, of the colonization and destruction of the world by European powers. I think we need to have a worldly and a cosmopolitan conversation about that, you know, so when the Dalits write to me and say, "Oh we want to translate some of your work into languages that will make it useful for us to think about what we're doing," or even when the Dalits, as I've heard they're also doing, translate the Combahee River Collective Statement. Whenever I hear or think of the Combahee River Collective Statement, I remember June Jordan's opinion of it. But even if the

Dalits want to do that—I think that's good and I think that it could be part of promoting a worldly conversation about these things that is something that we've only relatively recently been able to do. We need to do more of that and we don't know what the outcomes of that conversation will be. We don't know, so I just want to feed it. I want to feed that possibility. We have the technological means, although we have to remember that half the people on earth have never heard a dial tone, and that many people have other things to do than play with the latest yuppie toy they've got in their pocket. I'm worried, in the discussions that we have, that we don't always remember that. Without wanting to sound like a hair-shirt socialist—I'm not a hair-shirt socialist—but without wanting to sound like a hair-shirt socialist, I believe that we who live in the overdeveloped world have to face that question and that's the responsible thing for us to do. If we want to have a worldly conversation about these matters—that's the price of admission to that conversation: that we address the global dimensions of that inequality and we articulate the concerns of this, you know. Here we're doing the *Black Atlantic*, whatever, in the context of a different sort of idiom. I can't remember if I said this to you or whether I said it before, or who I said it to, and I'm sorry if you're hearing it a second time—but for me the issue becomes how to make a map of the black Atlantic that includes Guantanamo Bay and Diego Garcia and Bagram Air Base. And that speaks to the issue of the infrahuman, but it also speaks to why Guantanamo Bay was in Cuba in the first place.

Denise Thorpe: In your work, you acknowledge the importance of remembering and honoring the suffering that has been endured by many people because of the imposition of racial categories. You are skeptical of the modern nation-state, of religious institutions, and of political and social groups formed around race identity. Given your commitment to practices of remembering and your skepticism of current institutions and identity groups, I am interested in the locus of these practices of remembering. Where do the practices of remembering take place beyond biological family, and how are children and adults formed for such practices? Also, what is the relationship between personal memories and the broader, socially consequential forms of remembering that you espouse?

Paul Gilroy: I think that history and memory are not friendly presences within the social and technological environment that we inhabit, so this is a wonderful question. Answering it depends on who you are and where you are and the institutions in which you move. I don't believe those processes happen in households always or in kin groups, necessarily. I think that the creation of a sort of civil order among down-pressed people is important, as is the responsibility of those who act to socialize and radicalize and even to resist the way that power writes itself in people's lives so miserably. All of those things attend the question of memory.

Now the issue of religion has come up a lot, sometimes in ways I can understand, sometimes in ways I can't. Of course, if we are talking about African American racial identity and those histories of suffering, the church would be one of the places where that memory has been cultivated. It is, loosely speaking, within traditions of worship and church life. I also try to show that those cultural developments change over time and that there are profane successors to that sacred memory-work and there are secular ones also—which are not the same as the profane ones. So then the question becomes where is that process going now and how does it work? What is the balance of forces and how does it promote a relationship to the past? What demands do we place upon power to accommodate that memory-work and to accommodate that history of suffering and make a public acknowledgment? At that point, we end up having a different kind of conversation about educational institutions and curricula in public schools, what we expect people to know and how we educate people, and how people are made and kept ignorant, and where the responsibility for that situation lies. Some of it, I believe, rests with the victims as well as that which lies with the people who victimize them. One does not have to embrace that condition of ignorance. There are always choices. That is why I'm now so interested in literacy. Mark Anthony Neal spoke movingly the other night about his father's functional illiteracy. I was thinking a lot about that and how we cultivate multiple forms of literacy: cultural, philosophical, political, and historical literacy in a cosmopolitan way. That involves negotiating a new concept of culture—that point came up earlier on, too. Perhaps it means seeing culture in forms that aren't amenable to being held as the particular, private property of groups.

Let me give you a practical example. I mentioned the problem of Holocaust piety last night. We have, in England, a Holocaust Memorial Day. It's about to happen, actually. It's in January. This is a new development promoted by the Labour government and Tony Blair. There's been a very controversial response to it in which Rabbi Jonathan Sachs and others have been very active. It connects also to the question of Sharia law and how that compares to the uncontroversial, supplementary operation of Beth Din courts. This is something that has been used to, I won't say, politically dispose of multiculturalism but to query the democratic credentials of certain Muslim groups who object to that particular history of Jewish suffering being singled out and accorded the universal recognition involved in a national day on which everybody is asked to turn their attention in that direction. I'm saying that for some people, that invitation doesn't look like an opportunity. For some people that looks like a selective memory especially in the context of Britain's amnesia and patterned postcolonial forgetting and something more than that, because amnesia often refers to an accidental development. I'm talking about the refusal to acknowledge other histories of suffering, a refusal to open oneself to the claims of shame-inducing memory. You know, there are a whole raft of political questions that arise. I'm sure you know that these are not parochial matters. I think we need more conversation about these universal things. That, of course, means opening up that historic "never again" that I spoke about last night[1] to a larger set of meanings and dealing with the people who think it should be confined to particular groups. The "never again" should mean "never again for anybody." The majority believe that the injunction "never again" should have a broader applicability. So I think all of these things are relevant to this calculation of how that memory-work is to proceed.

PATRICK HORN: Hello again, Dr. Gilroy—Patrick Horn from the Department of English and Comparative Literature and an aspiring champagne anarchist.

PAUL GILROY: I must emphasize that my passing reference to champagne anarchism was a joke—just so you know. I don't want it to spread around that "Gilroy said he was a champagne anarchist and that's the proof of the fact that he hates black people." That really was a joke. I should have a hat or something I put on when I'm being humorous. Sometimes when I was reading the papers,[2] I will say I did wonder what it must be like to lead an irony-free life. But that's another story that I shall develop at length in my footnotes when I write my response.

PATRICK HORN: In *Postcolonial Melancholia*, you describe British nostalgia for the perceived or imagined moral simplicity of World War II, a world in which heroic British (and American) troops rescued Europe from the threats of Nazism. Similar forms of nostalgia can be found in the United States, particularly in relation to World War II and the Cold War. Can you discuss how these forms of nostalgia work today amid the war on terror? Does the war on terror depend upon particular forms of nostalgia? Do you see links between the Manichaean thinking that shapes nostalgia about World War II and the Manichaean thinking at work in the war on terror?

PAUL GILROY: Yes, yes, and yes. I know that the point is to do some creative gymnastics with all these questions, but I mean that one answers itself. Let me go at it at another way. Of course that's true, and "who's Hitler?" is the first point of departure, right? You know, Saddam is Hitler, Ahmadinejad is Hitler. There are suddenly a lot of Hitlers around. And the point of there being a lot of Hitlers is that the Manichaeism that generates them is a way of reinstating not just an American position but a moral order that corresponds to the deployment of legitimate violence in pursuit of a cleaner, tidier world. Actually, that enterprise is noble. Part of that is absolutely noble. But one problem about it that we haven't talked about yet and that I was thinking about earlier on—this is one of my things that I wanted to say earlier on—is that is that you all talk as if fascism were just a historical problem. You all talk about it as though it's something that's ended forever. When I was writing *Between Camps*, I was thinking a lot about that. I was reading George Jackson again, thinking about George Jackson's view of a "friendly fascism." I was thinking about what I discovered as Abercrombie fascism, right? And [the photographer] Bruce Weber and all of this ideal, Charles Atlas physicality. You know, not too many of you are as ripped as you should be. I'm sorry—you'd be better off spending your time in the gym rather than listening to this conversation. [Just] as me, of course, I'm in the same category. So I think, you've got to stop thinking about fascism as a historical thing. I read Naomi Wolf's essay she wrote last April [for *The Guardian*] about fascism,[3] and immediately a host of people got up to say: "But that happened in the 1930s, and the state did this and the corporations did the other and really, you know, it's completely irresponsible to raise it as something relevant today." Well, okay, you're not going to persuade me. I've read those books. I've read the history. I've read the legal books, I know those arguments and I always thought, since the very first moment I opened Gramsci's *Americanism and Fordism*, actually, and considered the historic figure of Henry Ford and thought about what he was saying about this new worker who was being created. That was at a time when a life of indentured consumerism (what we do) hadn't even been a glimmer in the boardrooms. It's not just about Lenin, there are things to be said about the way that radio worked to promote particular forms of social bonding and political solidarity. So it's not the nation-state that we should be thinking about, I think. It's the national state and the principle of nationality as political order. I want to suggest that we also try to incorporate into our reflections on this question, the *Saving Private Ryan* question, if you like. What is it to admit fascism into the present? I thought Naomi Wolf's list of ten things that should make you return to debate this question was compelling. It was a very admirable and brave attempt to just start a worthwhile inquiry. I remember when in the 1970s, when it looked as though in our country, the fascist ultra-right forces were going to make an electoral breakthrough, some people in the black movement, if I can call it that, thought that taking or importing George Jackson's notions of friendly fascism into our own discussions of what was going on in our own country was the right thing to do. They were immediately stamped on and told they were stupid, ignorant, and unsophisticated, that they hadn't really thought about things in the right way. I have a certain sympathy with some of those views that correspond, not only to Jackson's personal experiences, but to Gramsci's personal experiences, too. So, I say let's think about fascism in the present and not just as the primary mechanism for reinstating a kind of Manichaean order, in which the deployment of violence without limit is legitimate.

KWANGTAEK HAN: I am not American. I am Korean, and I am reading against multicultural identity in the American academy. In your recent work you discuss what you call "multicultural ethics and politics," which sounds hollow because, due to the very dissenting nature of historical, religious, ethnic, cultural, and political opposition, it becomes much more difficult to apply one justifiable "multicultural ethics and politics" to those conflicting entities. For many non-Western people, "the multicultural ethics and politics" proposed by Western people for their harmonious multiculturalism seems to rely on Westernized (and Westernizing) ethical values and moral standards. In your view, what are "multicultural ethics and politics"? What kind of ethical value and moral standard can serve as the most proper principle of multiculturalism for a diversity of historical, religious, ethnic, cultural, and political others?

PAUL GILROY: You must know that's an impossible question to answer. You must know that. [Laughter from audience.] So the issue is: why are you asking me that question and what do you expect me to do when you know that's an impossible question to answer. If you know the answer to this question—please tell us, actually, because I would really like to hear it, you know. I really would like to know. [Laughter from audience]

[. . .] Obviously I'm speaking from somewhere where multiculturalism had a particular set of historical meanings that are different, I must admit, from the mosaic (in the sense of concrete tiles rather than the biblical sense) pluralism that is the foundation of US social and economic interaction. So I speak from somewhere and I'm very clear about where that is because I might go on about rootedness and all the rest of it, but I've lived all but ten of my fifty-one years in the same place, actually, so I do understand. I do understand the obligations that fall to one for living and speaking from somewhere and for where one speaks. We all know about the perspectival nature of truth. It means that from this or that angle of vision there are certain things I can see and other things I can't. I've tried to place an emphasis on conviviality precisely to accommodate the plurality—Stuart Hall would say the difference—that won't go away, the one you invoked a moment ago. The fact is that there are Koreans and other people who might not recognize themselves as Western. I know that in Korea, that designation can be a contentious one. The question of whether Korea is part of the West and at what point it became such and so on is something one might want to interrogate a bit more carefully than we have the chance to do right now.

So I think one can speak from a range of different places. And that's why I said earlier on that I think we need to have a worldly conversation about these things and we're in a position to do that. And obviously, if you're a Japanese person asking the question of whether or not Korea is part of the West—you'll get one answer. If you're a Korean born in Japan to Korean parents who can't get Japanese citizenship, you might answer that question differently. And if you're a Korean from the North, you will answer it, perhaps, in a slightly different accent. And if you're a Korean from the South you will answer it differently again. So I recognize that problem and I recognize the stubborn adhesion of difference. I also think, and this goes back to something else that came up earlier on—the point emerged very sweetly in some of the earlier discussion: strongly held group identity can't be and shouldn't be wished away. I mean, trying to dispose of that is like trying to tell the snow not to arrive. It's not gonna happen. I'm not quixotic to that degree. What I am trying to say is that those strongly held group identities don't, to my mind, inevitably, permanently, naturally, ultimately, irreducibly, and absolutely coincide with some particular set of identities that grew at the end of European trading activities. I don't really believe that.

So my emphasis falls on what I tried to call, when I invoked Ian Hacking last night, a dynamic nominalism. It's a dynamic nominalism. It's dynamic. It involves a complex interplay between the naming and the named, institutionally mediated, historically specified, that interplay. Once this naming has happened, the named engage with that name and the institutions of that name and the histories of suffering and resistance and sex and music and art and all that other stuff. And shopping and Blackberries and iPhones, all of that. This interplay, this *dynamic* interplay because we're dealing with *dynamic* nominalism. A dynamic nominalism! And we're moving from, hopefully, a sense of a political ontology, in the name of nationality, national statecraft, and so on into a sense of historical ontology. Historical ontology and dynamic nominalism.

John Ribo: Recently you returned to the importance of love in Bob Marley's work and you pointed to the likes of The Streets and Billy Bragg as examples of alternative ways in which Britishness, in particular, is being articulated after empire. Obviously, music is important to your personal and intellectual life. Could you tell us about one of your recent projects, which I know is related to music? Could you also tell us about other musicians on the contemporary cultural scene that you consider to be among the most compelling, and why?

Paul Gilroy: Music, you know, teaches important lessons. And I've always been very influenced by Ernst Bloch, actually, because it seems to me that in the tradition of European modernism that I'm obliged to privilege over every other human creation—which I duly do—that Ernst Bloch is a person who thought most extensively, who was positioned to think most compellingly, about the relationship between music and utopia. And about the special dynamics of sound and what they tell us about the "yet to come." About the "not yet." I can't remember if I sent you the essay that I wrote about Hendrix and the "not yet," which is sort of where my book ends up because it concludes with a consideration of the relationship between diplomacy, war, and sound, and what it means to turn the music of Jimi Hendrix into a weapon of war, as happened in Fallujah not so long ago. I'm interested in the "not yet," the yet to come that I find in the work of musicians—not just the memory-work that we spoke about earlier but also a reaching for something in the future. One of the musicians who's influenced me most, actually, in the last fifteen or twenty years is a guitar player in New York, called Wayne Krantz, who plays in a trio with Anthony Jackson, the great bass player who wrote the bass line to The O'Jays' "For the Love of Money" when he was seventeen. Anthony plays with Wayne, and there's a drummer called Keith Carlock who's a very, very good drummer. I think he plays in the pit band of one of the TV chat shows you have here. Well, anyway, Anthony and Keith and Wayne—they improvise. Wayne is somebody who's influenced me a lot, and he has reinvented how to play the electric guitar, which interests me a lot, too. His license for that, his passion for that creativity, I take to be a philosophical inclination, which accords with the things I find in Bloch. Wayne says this: That what most people do when they sit down to play a piece—and this is again, a noble activity and it may correspond to memory-work and so on—they play an existing vocabulary. If someone gives me a guitar—I can play a piece of bebop and if I can do it well, you'll like it because you already know that you like bebop. So we affirm a vocabulary that we already know. Well I think that one thing that great musicians do is that they don't affirm an already existing vocabulary. What they do is give up the vocabularies they love; they throw away the things they love. They throw away the bebop, they throw away funk. They throw away all those great vocabularies that they love, in order to be people who can create something that is yet to come—something that points to new human possibilities. And if you are a great improviser—and think Wayne and Anthony and Keith and the others in their scene are, actually—you can bring your audience into the emergent truth of that common moment through improvisation.

Wayne is interesting for two other reasons. One, because he's tried to revive the sort of Renaissance notions of patronage in the way that he engages his fans and supporters—that failed terribly. But the other thing he did was, he discovered he didn't have to work in Kinko's anymore if he could record his band every week and put up a couple of sets on the web, and then he would sell the sets for five dollars a set or something, and if you wanted to listen to his music—you could do so. So, bypassing certain corporate forces, retaining a greater degree of control of his art, and pointing to a range of other possibilities that correspond to a world in which the idea of copyright is in crisis and the corporate management of the overall architecture of the music business is being, thankfully, I'm happy to say, destroyed and replaced by something more interesting. So, in the same way that I don't want to be compared to Edward Said, I don't want to be compared to Wayne either. I think that these are great, creative people of vision and energy and they're rare. And I think that to actually summon the future and to commit oneself to throwing away everything that has shaped you, formed you, and given you joy as a condition of your own creativity—that's the kind of thing to which I aspire. I'm not for one moment saying that I succeed. Please don't misunderstand. That would be worse than being a champagne anarchist.

TAMARA EXTIAN-BABIUK: In *'There Ain't no Black in the Union Jack,'* you use images as part of your analysis of race and politics in Britain. Your newest book, *Black Britain*, is devoted entirely to a visual exploration of blackness in Britain. I'm wondering whether you could talk about this work and to discuss some favorite images from the volume.

PAUL GILROY: Before I speak about the images in the book, I'd like to say just a couple of other things. I do wish Mark Anthony Neal were still here because in discussing the changing significance of popular culture, I wanted to ask him to tell us about the development of Ice Cube's career. I was really struck by him saying that, how can I put it?. . . that hip hop was really still only, was like the ghetto CNN, was all about communicating experience—and that was the role of reporting and translating. I myself don't believe that's a credible argument. Against it, I want to cite Ice Cube's development. Ice Cube's always sort of challenged me, after I saw "Dangerous Ground," with Liz Hurley and Ice Cube together. I think Ice Cube stands as a kind of cipher for the questions that can put some grit into that account. This connects to a bigger question about the currency of African American culture in the world, which corresponds to the global celebrity of Ice Cube. I want to emphasize that although you may think that the distribution and the local take-up and the development of Quaito in South Africa, or of the hip hop records that come out of Brazilian jails, means that African Americans are absolved of any particular responsibility, apart from the propriety claim that began that network of cultural dissemination, I don't believe that and I don't think the people in your government believe it either. If you look at what's going on in the state department division of cultural diplomacy and if you read Jared Cohen and these other people who are doing work with hip hop and around hip hop and Radio Sawa and all these things that are designed to intervene with the ways that Muslim youth and African youth are radicalized and how they're selling them "brand America," you know, I think that is an important thing and that Penny Von Eschen, bless her, did some of that important work in her book, *Satchmo Blows Up the World*. It corresponded to the Cold War and certain phases of that and if you think that worldly work has stopped—you are deluding yourselves. If you honestly think that there are not people—powerful, influential, well-funded people—who are alive to the value of African American culture and in projecting America into the rest of the world, you are deluding yourselves. You have to pay attention to this, and a good place to start is with Jared Cohen's book, *Children of Jihad*. He's a fluent Swahili speaker, Rhodes Scholar—Stanford, Oxford, you know, very confident. Much more open, actually, than many academics that I've met about these questions that are very troubling and are part of the reinscription of colonial order in the world. It's come back with a vengeance.

On art, there are a lot of people who've done very interesting work on black people in the British countryside. I would particularly suggest that you look for the work of the artist and photographer Ingrid Pollard, a neighbor of mine. We used to look after her hamster when she went away into the country to pose her companions in sort of Wordsworthian locations and take photographs. I think there was a book published here of her fantastic photographs and it's a very magical and interesting set of projects that she's done. There are many other people, I think, inspired by her that attempt to address the founding question of the black figure in the English landscape.

Now when I said that about Chaka Khan and Mary J. Blige . . . that I said that I couldn't think that Mary J. Blige—I don't want to sound defensive, but you really, you called me out on this and I have to say—I have to respond to that, right? . . . I'm sorry, I'm so sorry, but I have to say something about this. When I said that—it was 1995. Okay? It was 1995. And the point that I was trying to make was about a culture of simulation. Now, I think that one of the characteristics of postmodern culture, in general, is that we are required to address issues of simulation in a way that "the work of art in the age of mechanical reproduction" wasn't able to do. There are new questions of simulation that arise from thinking the work of art in the age of digital reproduction. All I am trying to say is that, for me, the category of simulation is relevant to understanding the difference between the work of art in the age of mechanical production and the work of art in the age of digital simulation. I still think, even though I've had to revise my opinion of Mary J. somewhat in the intervening fourteen years, that there are issues of relevance with regard to the question of simulation and, you know, actually, it corresponds somewhat to what I said earlier on about playing with an old vocabulary and what it is to just repeat a vocabulary that already exists and that we know gives pleasure. It may refer us to memory, but it may also, in that repetition, deny us the opportunity to develop. I'm not accusing her of that. I'm just saying that it's not a problem that goes away when we reinstate Chaka. Chaka interests me for a number of other reasons. She interests me because she comes from Chicago. She interests me because she was raised as a Catholic. She doesn't come out of a church tradition of singing—she comes from a completely different place. She interested me because she was involved in Black Nationalist politics in the South Side. She interested me because she took that name. She interested me because her life was as damaged as any of these other people by drugs and alcohol and violence and all the rest of it. Her autobiography, I don't know if you've read it, is a bit of a disappointment. Another one, really, that proves that autobiographies are sort of the last place you can really find anything interesting about anybody. She interested me too, of course, because although she had a mixed back-up band, the band that made her a star was a mixed band. I don't know how many of those you see around here these days—not so many. So, that's just a way of underlining the fact that each of these works—and I know that the nature of this occasion, which, I repeat, I find humbling, and embarrassing in many, many ways, is to look at this work as a body of work and, in a way, it isn't really a body of work, you know. It's just a bunch of stuff that happened. My favorite line from *The Simpsons*: A bunch of stuff that happened. Each of those bits of stuff is addressed to a moment and those remarks were addressed to a moment in which I was struggling with the transformation of a sound-centered black culture into a primarily visual one. When you said that you wanted us to do something—you said we should go look at a video. You didn't say, go buy a Mary J. Blige record. Go and watch a video. In a way, that makes it clear. There is a shift there and we have to address it, we have to be prepared to address that difference.

On the *Black Britain* book—there's a nice picture. I'll talk about this one [a young, sharply dressed black man in tall top hat]. I like this picture and why it comes very early in the book is because I like the fact that there's nothing behind him. I like the fact that he has his beaver topper there. I like the fact that he is posed in that way and that he is in some sense, I think, trying to negotiate the tone and terms in which that photograph is being taken. We don't know the name of this young man; we don't know who took the picture. We assume from the way it's posed and the mode of portraiture that this is something that he wanted to do. But it is captioned: "A Young Dandy." "A Young Dandy." And the question of style, we'll talk, perhaps, more on that tomorrow. I mean that's just one.

Maybe there are a couple of others I can just share with you, if you wouldn't mind looking. This is, again, a cropped picture—I'm so sorry about that—of soldiers from the West Indian regiment at the crossroads in Amiens in 1916. Getting ready to go and die for the butcher's apron, the Union Jack. The British presence in World War I. These are, as I said, Caribbean soldiers. My great uncle Hubert Answick was one of them. This was, I think, shortly before they were infected with the virus of Bolshevism and mutinied at Taranto. I'm sure you know that story, their mutiny. They were very brutally put down by the Brits as a result of their imagined Bolshevism, and the Brits didn't really want Bolshevism to spread to the colonies so they were pretty ruthless with the questioning of the regiment after the mutiny. And that's why they didn't fight in World War II because they weren't judged to be reliable. The people who controlled the army were worried that they might adapt the political morality of the inter-European War to the struggle with the colonies. Of course, that is my point about Fanon and Senghor and about Kemathi and the others. I'm sure many of you will be reading Biyi [Bandele-Thomas]'s book, *Burma Boy*, about the West African regiment fighting the Japanese in Burma and, you know, there's a sense when these histories are going to become more important now.

One of my rules in selecting the pictures was to take as many images of people with cups of tea as possible. [Image of man in doorway of rock shelter with tea pot—laughter from audience.] And this gentleman, George Dixon, was, I found, a retired circus performer who had been a sword swallower. One thing I did not want to do was to produce an overly London-centered story in these images, in this history. I was very struck by this picture of George Dixon, the unemployed sword swallower, living in a hut, a stone hut, in the valleys of South Wales, Pontypridd. George has his tea pot there and he seems to be a dignified character whose face and body are hewn from the kind of stone from which the dwelling is also made. I just found it a very poignant picture. Something about the way his hand, his left hand, hangs; something about his life in the entertainment industry as a swallower of swords, now unemployed, which struck me with great force when I discovered it. It's not a picture that people know—it's a wonderful *lieu de mémoire*. These were young people, again cropped on [a bus]; this is a picture from 1933. These young children are going off to a seaside outing, from an urban area where they live, to get some fresh air in their lungs. It's a picture that came from *The Keys*, which was an independent black magazine of a sort of Pan-Africanist stripe from the 1930s. There are a lot of images of children. One of the questions I tried to engage in the text I wrote alongside the pictures was, what work are these images of children doing?

Here, more tea drinking going on. [Soldier women drinking tea.] These women are WAACs from the Caribbean who've come to fight in the army, in London. Again, you know, something about their carriage and their bearing, and the way that the memory of the war is recovered and so on that just seems to make it a very—never mind the sort of civilizationist interaction that turns around the biscuits and the tea changing hands—I think it's terribly important for our younger people at home to have some idea of what people looked like and what they wore and their presence. There's something about the make-up. I just really wanted to recover as much of the texture of those sorts of everyday dimensions of life as possible. Similarly, with this, you know, this is the iconic Spitfire, this is the battle of Britain moment and these are, again, Caribbean airmen. [Two men are on a Spitfire plane, looking up.] Again, a very posed picture but you get the idea of its subversive character. This is a good one to end with, and, unfortunately more cropped on screen here than it is in the picture. [Three people sitting at conference table in front of audience.] This is from the Pan-African conference in Manchester—I'm sure some of you will know these pictures. I wanted to include this because I get a lot of shtick for my planetary humanism and all the rest of it, but, actually something like that is part of the rhetoric of this project. I thought I was recycling. I thought recycling was good, obviously it's not to everyone's taste here, but look: "Freedom for all subject peoples. Oppressed peoples of the world unite." Here, you can't see this one clearly, but it says: "Jews and Arabs Unite! Against British Imperialism." You don't hear that very often these days. All I'm trying to do is a bit of recycling. Just to feed some images back into the sorts of conversations that people have about our own history, and our own identity, and to invite them to take possession over it.

This is a nice black Atlantic picture of these kids with their phonograph. One of my friends is a teacher, and he brought a phonograph into his lecture theater, put it up on the podium, and put the record on and nobody knew what it was. They didn't know what a phonograph was—they didn't know what these large black CDs were. [Laughter from audience.] They couldn't understand why there was no electricity involved in generating the sound.

This is Claudia Jones. [Picture is of a woman reading a book.] She's someone else who, I guess, might have fit into the answer to your first question about women and the black Atlantic. Carole Boyce Davies has finally published her book about Claudia[4]—I haven't seen it yet. This is a picture of her that isn't a widely known one, and I really just love the expression on her face. No doubt you know about her expulsion from the United States for advocating the overthrow of your government by force and she's reading *Pages from a Worker's Life* in this beautiful portrait. I love her suit and I love her sort of sense of peace that comes with that picture. I'm really going to stop now 'cause I'm getting sick of the sound of my own voice. [Applause.]

Notes

1. Paul Gilroy, "Multiculture and the Negative Dialectics of Conviviality," chapter 4 in this volume.
2. In preparation for the conference, participants submitted prepublication versions of their papers so that all conference attendees, including Professor Gilroy, could read them before the conference convened. It is to these papers that Gilroy refers here.
3. Professor Gilroy refers to Wolf's essay, "Fascist America, in 10 Easy Steps," *The Guardian* 24 April 2007, G2: 4.
4. The book is Carole Boyce Davies's *Left of Karl Marx: The Political Life of Black Communist Claudia Jones* (Durham: Duke University Press, 2008).

Afterword

"The Right to Address the Future"

Utopian Thinking and Paul Gilroy

JOHN McGOWAN

> [M]y own desire to see the end of raciology means that I, too, have invoked the unknowable future against the unforgiving present. In doing this, I urge a fundamental change of mood upon what used to be called "anti-racism." It has been asked in an explicitly utopian spirit to terminate its ambivalent relationship to the idea of "race" in the interest of a heterocultural, postanthropological, and cosmopolitan yet-to-come.
>
> —Paul Gilroy, *Against Race*[1]

That Paul Gilroy's work is driven by "an explicitly utopian spirit" is hardly news. The appeal to "the conspicuous power of the slave sublime" to enable a "politics of transfiguration" in *The Black Atlantic*;[2] the celebration of "the forms of conviviality and intermixture" found in the "ordinary multiculture of the postcolonial metropolis" in *Postcolonial Melancholia*;[3] and the attempts to adumbrate a "planetary humanism" in *Against Race* and a rehabilitated discourse of human rights in *Darker than Blue* all mark different planks of Gilroy's utopian project. When I read the essays collected in this volume—both Gilroy's contributions and those of his readers—I process them as meditations on the problem of getting there, "the unknowable future," from here, "the unforgiving present." And I read them, also, as expressions of the troubled status of utopian thinking in our time, a time when we desperately desire alternatives but in which, on all sides, even the tamest suggestions that it could be otherwise are dismissed as wishful thinking. In the name of being serious or realistic, we constantly disavow what we desire: societies not built on racial and economic hierarchies.

May I begin by expressing some frustration with the current discourse around these matters? Part of me cannot help but see the debates unfolded in this book as yet another round of the endless and mostly fruitless wrangles to which the Left seems addicted. Like a set of diplomats fighting over word choices in a communiqué, leftists often appear convinced that choices before enactment are determinative. Unless we get the ideas, the structures, the formulas, the plans (in short, the theory) right, all will go horribly awry. So the other guy's version of utopia must be subjected to relentless critique, the deficiencies in his analysis made clear, and the extent to which he fails to address the problem at its fundamental roots exposed. The unforgiving present of interminable critique obliterates the effort to imagine a different future. I am more inclined to John Dewey's experimentalism and fallibilism. I submit that we cannot really know if something will work—and whether it will advance justice, equality, democracy, and other desired goods—until we have put it into practice. And a key political virtue—both for actors and for institutions—is the ability to respond to failure by changing course. Such an approach has the advantage of recognizing that specific circumstances matter greatly. What worked just fine over there may not work here. That's one reason why it is well nigh impossible to know what will work by engaging in thought experiments. We will not get to utopia by imagination and theoretical assessment of those imaginings alone. We need instead to be alert to forms of sociality in the imperfect present that indicate possible paths to the future—and think about how those forms can be encouraged, expended, and continually revised in response to the concrete feedback provided by ongoing social interactions.

Skepticism about intellectual disputes does not mean, however, that careful attention to the past and present has nothing to offer the attempt to create a better future. In *Darker than Blue*, Gilroy writes about the ways in which "history can furnish contemporary discussions with interpretive and ethical resources which we can use to orient ourselves."[4] That remark reminds us (Gilroy's readers) how dependent all his work is upon the inspiration he derives from other writers and artists. As Richard King astutely notes, Gilroy's use of his sources is creative; when he introduces us to the "counter-discourse of modernity" that he names "the black Atlantic," Gilroy is both uncovering a lost past *and* calling an imagined alternative into being. He assembles his utopian vision out of what the figures who inspire him provide.

To focus in this way on "resources" offers, I think, the most fruitful way to engage the essays in this volume. I want to invite you (my readers) to consider them as participating with Gilroy in the effort to find resources from our past and present that can serve utopian desires.

It might seem paradoxical that an orientation to the future generates an intense examination of the past. Why not just say "good-bye to all that" and start afresh? In fact, Gilroy's desire to transcend "race thinking" sometimes leads readers to believe that he simply wants to banish the category of "race" from our linguistic and theoretical toolbox. (That his American publishers changed the title of *Between Camps* to *Against Race* encouraged this misunderstanding.) If Gilroy's contribution to this volume does nothing else, I hope it at least makes it clear that he insists we cannot understand the past or the present without attending to "racial hierarchy." But, equally clearly, he does not believe that "race" as an indication of a settled identity for any individual or group is politically or strategically useful in the battle against racial hierarchy today. He fully accepts that it was useful in the past but offers various arguments for why he thinks antiracists are better off abandoning it in the present "conjuncture." While the specific reasons he offers are not well enough known (or, in some cases, not well enough attended to), the resistance to his position is fairly familiar by now. Worries about belonging and about solidarity based on shared identity motivate the attachment to racial categories. I will not rehearse these debates here because I think the contributors to this volume are mostly disinclined to revisit that (tired?) argument.

Rather, the contributors are more interested in thinking with Gilroy about how to get to utopia. What resources can help us overcome "the pessimism of the intellect" that says that you cannot get there from here? If we agree that "racial hierarchy" has been a central architect of the societies we aim to transform, then are other inherited concepts—like "human rights" and "humanism"—useful tools for that work of transformation? Questions of space as well as time, of means as well as ends, arise. Utopia is, literally, no place. Is utopia always only an imagined site from which the deficiencies of the present arrangements can be registered, or can utopia be given "a local habitation and a name"? Temporally, what kinds of discontinuities are required to deliver a future that is not just more of the same, not just a repetition of history's all-too-familiar, all-too-human, injustices? Can any of that history's components be repurposed as aids to transformation? What specific means are available? And how are we to articulate the ends that need to serve as guideposts and as motivations for our journey? These questions animate the worries, insights, analyses, and recommendations found in this volume's essays.

Ranu Samantrai asks us to attend to both geography and temporality in imagining utopia. She worries that Gilroy's celebration of urban conviviality privileges the city over the country, thus reproducing a hierarchy characteristic of a certain modernist aesthetic she thinks inadvisable to embrace unreservedly. Furthermore, the dissociation of racialized, nonwhite others from rural settings mirrors conservative fantasies that locate national purity, virtue, and strength in a racially homogenous countryside. Heteroculture, she wants to say, cannot be spatially confined to particular locales in any utopia worth having. The no place of utopia must be in every place equally.

Even more fundamentally, Samantrai is disturbed by the connection between utopian thought and the destructive temporalities associated with such features of the modern as capitalism, urban renewal, "development," and a modernist aesthetic of "making it new." The "modern" as an idea has often been used to relegate various communities and practices to the dustbin of history, condemned as outmoded. Either get with the program or we modernizers will get you out of the way. Doubtless, I am pushing Samantrai's argument further than she does, but the echoes of this suspicion of utopian politics, of the ways that such politics have justified mass killings, are there in her essay for me. Truer to the explicit argument she makes would be to say that she unpacks a set of intertwined associations between cities, cosmopolitanism, and change that is contrasted to the backwardness of rural settings and rural peoples. She wants to caution us against the stark binaries utopian dreams can posit between the desired future and the hated obstacles in our present that frustrate efforts to reach that future. She implies that an aesthetic of repurposing, of recycling, is to be preferred to one that aims to discard what the past and present gives to us. We need to imagine how to occupy the spaces available to us differently, not imagine how we will replace those spaces with the no place of utopia. Thus, Samantrai lovingly describes the cover photo of Gilroy's *Black Britain* as an emblem of such transformative occupation. She only longs for a complementary image of nonwhites occupying a rural place.

Dennis Dworkin also takes up issues of space and temporality. He locates Gilroy's work in the context of a persistent "narrative of decline" in post–World War II Britain. Of course, Gilroy addresses this narrative most directly in *Postcolonial Melancholia*, but Dworkin shows how the obsession with Britain's lost national glory helps situate Gilroy's work as a whole. Gilroy's utopianism means that he rejects any notion that the best was in the past and is irrecoverable. Gilroy finds that melancholic stance deeply objectionable since it rests on a denial of the great, foundational wrongs upon which the British Empire rested. He also fights against the persistent association of Britain's debased present with the increased presence of nonwhite Britons by reminding his fellow countrymen that colonialism was "raced" through and through. The notion of some completely white past is a dangerous fantasy made possible only by the denial of persistent, ever-present, white violence against nonwhites. Only a full recognition of the raced bases of Britain's former power will allow a movement into a better future. And, as Dworkin indicates, Gilroy often turns to the African diaspora, the black Atlantic, as the locus of that better future. Yet, Dworkin argues, Gilroy at times wants to deploy the resources of the black Atlantic to transform Englishness/Britishness. Even as (in the wake of America's militaristic response to the attacks of 9/11) Gilroy has become increasingly disenchanted with American and African American culture, he has increasingly attempted to come to better terms with his native country. An abiding allegiance to his identity as a "black Briton" sits alongside Gilroy's use of the diaspora and the transnational to loosen the binds of identity. Gilroy acknowledges this tension in the interview found in this volume: "strongly held group identity can't and shouldn't be wished away. . . . [T]hat is like trying to tell the snow not to arrive." Dworkin suggests, instead, that Gilroy aims to make race (as one marker of group identity, one marker of the group's difference from other groups) "ordinary." Conviviality means, among other things, that racial differences are no big deal, just a fact of daily life, always to be navigated through but never elevated into barriers we cannot cross or categories we cannot redefine. Narratives of decline remain attached, in ways they cannot acknowledge, to the power achieved through a violence that maintains racial barriers, that makes race a terrible, phobic fact, not an ordinary one. Utopia becomes a world where ordinary human decency replaces the imperial need to subjugate—and the use of race as a tool of subjugation.

During the conference in Chapel Hill from which this volume derives, Gilroy stressed "dynamic nominalism" more than "ordinariness" as the way to address the hardening of racial categories. Jay Garcia's essay has the great virtue of showing how these two strategies for undoing the spell race has cast are connected. Dynamic nominalism calls us to recognize that "race" is not a "natural kind" but a social fact created by acts of naming that establish terms of relation between one human and another. That race is discursively produced does not mean that it is unreal. Race has real effects: emotional, political, institutional, and historical. We cannot just wish race away, either by outlawing it or by changing its name. Race is a way of thinking, a way of processing the world, with an intersubjective weight that makes it, like any cultural practice, deeply embedded in selves and social institutions.

But—and here is the dynamic part of dynamic nominalism—race as a category, as a component of identity, and as a social position is not stable. It is constituted by acts of naming and thus changes in ways analogous to the ways that languages change over time. Most such changes are inadvertent, the byproducts of daily use. The ordinary makes its presence felt here. Race is a category used every day, and it changes through those usages. But some changes are purposive, as when a group seizes the initiative to name itself. "Negroes" become "African Americans," "colored people" become "black," through deliberate acts of naming—and racial signifiers shift as a result. These acts have consequences because how we name things (nominalism) has real effects. Garcia provides a meditation on this means toward a better future by juxtaposing Alain Locke's work with Gilroy's. Dynamic nominalism is important because it provides a theoretical tool for the analysis of race in our history or in any particular locale. But it also—and crucially—points the way toward an "interventionist cultural politics" by indicating that racial categories are not fixed, not immutable, and by outlining the means (imaginative renamings) toward change.

I return to cultural politics at the end of these remarks but turn first to questions about the ends toward which Gilroy's utopian thinking strives. Jonathan Boyarin, Anthony Alessandrini, and Tavia Nyong'o all devote their essays to thinking about the implications of adopting "planetary humanism" as the end toward which utopia aims and to mobilizing a repurposed notion of "human rights" to support that humanism. For Boyarin, the political and ethical objectives that motivate Gilroy's work are admirable. Better, we might even say that Gilroy's work is so important, so exemplary, because it addresses the crucial issues of our time. One way to characterize those issues would be the conundrums arising from efforts to achieve solidarity across the whole species while also honoring intraspecies differences. Boyarin is not convinced that appeals to humanism, to some commonality shared by the whole species, can work, can avoid being naïve, sentimental, or too abstract to gain much purchase in actual encounters between different groups. How is our shared humanity to be identified? By a bodily vulnerability to pain and psychic vulnerability to suffering? Boyarin objects that such an image of "bare life" is as rhetorical, as much a product of dynamic nominalism, as any other categorization. More broadly, Boyarin argues that it is hardly self-evident that there is something humans share that is more fundamental, or lies beneath, what differentiates them from one another. If we grant difference ontological equality with commonalities, then it is not clear what "planetary humanism" could mean. Similarly, if we do not privilege the common over the different, then it is not clear that allegiance to our fellow humans will have priority over allegiance to one's tribe. (History, of course, seems to indicate that tribe loyalty is much more common than attachment to any broader group of the "human" per se.) Since, Boyarin insists, markers of difference have been as persistent and ever present in human societies as intimations of shared humanity, the effort to create a "planetary humanism" has a steep hill to climb.

Alessandrini ends his essay by making a similar point but cast in a much more positive register. Humanism, he tells us, cannot be "built upon . . . the prior assumption that 'we' share a common humanity that transcends specific contexts." Rather, "this shared humanity . . . will emerge precisely in the struggle against 'the alienated sociality that absorbs the cries of those who suffer by making them sound less than human.'"[5] On one level, humanism is fellow feeling created by people working together, "acting in concert" to invoke Arendt's phrase, to create the world they inhabit. But, on another level, this humanism emerges in a process of "working through" that reminds us of Freud's use of that term. It is Fanon the psychoanalyst who proves a vital resource for Gilroy, especially in *Postcolonial Melancholia*, with its focus on how to reach a better future by coming to terms with the past. "The capacity to address the future" (*AR*, 336) must be achieved not simply by gaining the political standing to participate in a society's ongoing formation but also through a process of "dis-alienation," a "recovery from the alienating and corrupting antisociality of 'race'" (*AR*, 336).

We might say that each individual scarred by racism's creation of the "infrahuman" must discover his own humanity as part and parcel of bringing a "planetary humanism" into being. The scarring of racism, our poisoned legacy, touches everyone; since racism is played out as much in the *relations* between selves as in its individual embodiments, this work of "dis-alienation" is communal, not personal. It entails the rewriting of social relations in ways that will shift everyone's identity because identities are constituted through designations of difference. Thus, an interest in the psychological effects of racism—which include both pathological self-hatred and pathologies of melancholic denial—does not mean some kind of individualized therapeutic process is favored over political action. Racism is a social pathology and must be confronted socially. Alessandrini is very clear about Fanon's and Gilroy's preference for collective action over "scholastic reflections," "liberal pieties," or other apolitical palliatives. The creation of a translocal Palestine solidarity movement, as Alessandrini shows, provides a crucial example for Gilroy of what a planetary humanism created through collective action might look like. "Translocal, multicultural, and anti-imperial activism" (*PM*, 56) does not only wage a battle against racism but also begins to establish the alternative social relations that limn the utopian future.

Nyong'o's essay tackles head-on Gilroy's determination to mobilize a repurposed concept of human rights in service of his liberatory project. At first blush, the deployment of a vocabulary of rights can seem an effort to hoist the West on its own petard. The gambit is to call the West to account for its blatant breech of its own self-proclaimed ethical standards. But for many non-Westerners such a strategy entails adopting Western notions of "the human" and "the universal" too toxic to be handled with impunity. These two concepts, like that of "the modern," have been used to dismiss non-Western cultures as not up to standard—and, hence, to justify remedial actions that have destroyed the indigenous. Given this history, it is no surprise that anything resembling universal human rights has proved anathema to many anti-imperialist and antiracist activists.

For Nyong'o, this "realistic" approach to human rights must be paired with a "utopian" orientation that can somehow overcome the depredations of the past in order to open up a path to "futurity." Unlocking the radical potential in the idea of rights becomes central to imagining the future we desire. Similarly, Nyong'o believes this embrace of the utopian impulse will enable a different relationship to the past. The "history of black and radical contestations" on the terrain of human rights now becomes available as resources for a reconfiguration "that points to an absent in the present arrangement, gesturing in turn toward the future as the 'not-yet-present.'"

It is a mistake to understand "human rights" as a stable concept, with preordained results wherever it is utilized. (We are back on the terrain of dynamic nominalism here.) Wholesale condemnations of human rights are too abstract and foreclose possibilities in how appeals to rights can function in specific contexts. The institutional prestige of rights, their affective power for many people, and their utopian appeal to a notion of "the human" can prove highly effective resources in particular struggles. No concept, no legal term, no institution comes with a guarantee that the actions it enables will always be good ones. But to cede the concept of human rights to the neoconservatives makes no more sense than abandoning a desire for democracy because George W. Bush used that term in attacking Iraq. The deployment and meaning of such vital terms will be continually contested; their vitality and power are what make them worth trying to use. But we shouldn't expect the terms to fight the battles for us, to win the contest for the good guys even before the contest is waged—for once and for all. Human rights, in other words, are not a salvation device that will miraculously protect us from violence imposed by states—or by nonstate actors. Rather, human rights, as Nyong'o so eloquently shows, are one site where utopian desires are located, a site where we can probe the strength of those desires and their lineaments. Where specific societies—or the United Nations—have articulated a set of rights, they have articulated their image of the good society that they aspire to be. Of course, we should continually call attention to how far short of that image every society falls. But it would be foolish to think that human rights, even when legally established, can do the work of making the utopia they gesture toward a reality. That is work only we can do, in the everyday effort to make rights prevail.

Richard King helps us to focus on this work by calling attention to Gilroy's ambivalence when it comes to formal politics. On the one hand, Gilroy (especially in *Against Race*) has insisted that fascism remains a constant threat, even a constant fact, in our own times. King shows that Gilroy, following Arendt, understands fascism as antipolitics, as the destruction of the public sphere in which citizens can relate to each other without the mediation of the state and, through those relations, form opinions and associations that contest state power. In *Darker than Blue*, Gilroy takes this portrait of fascism as isolating the individual from others, placing him only in relation to the state, as analogous to the isolation of selves in consumer society, where the intense focus on building a career and accumulating possessions displaces social ties. (Here, Arendt's analysis of Eichmann's careerism already suggests this connection.) So, at least by negation, Gilroy appears to advocate a kind of Arendtian politics, one in which equals acting in concert create a common world, a "space of appearances" in which relations are primary since the self is realized precisely in and through its manifestation to others. And, periodically, Gilroy does gesture toward "more solid and supple forms of democracy" (*PM*, 147) as what is needed.

On the other hand, as King makes clear, for the most part Gilroy's energies are directed toward describing and celebrating "the carnival of heteroculture" (*PM*, 147). This carnival, like Bakhtin's, exists over, against, and outside of formal political and legal orders. And when Gilroy describes the work of transforming "the unforgiving present," that work also generally takes place outside the halls of power and even apart from organized political action within normal democratic channels. This neglect partly reflects Gilroy's rather despairing description of contemporary "society" (at least in America) as one "in which consumerism has largely superseded the rights and responsibilities of citizenship, and in which politics itself affords few meaningful possibilities for either redress or progress" (*DB*, 8).

We should not expect a writer to do everything. If Gilroy finds "politics itself" unpromising at present, he obviously needs to find the resources he needs elsewhere. I share King's wish that Gilroy would devote some more attention to "politics itself," if only because I believe that the strong light of Gilroy's utopian thinking would unlock potentials in formal politics that we currently cannot see. But writers need to do the work that energizes them, to converse with the living and dead who afford them, to use Wittgenstein's phrase, the means to "go on." In the interview in this volume, Gilroy is eloquent about his continual return to music—and what he is given in that encounter. "[O]ne thing that great musicians do is that they don't affirm an already existing vocabulary. . . . They throw away all the great vocabularies that they love, in order to be people who can create something that is yet to come—something that points to new human possibilities." Clearly, for Gilroy, his utopian project makes a connection to the arts, and the preference of cultural to formal politics, absolutely central. He is inspired by the new, by visions of what has never been but is possible. He counts on artists to provide such visions and to inspire our attachment to those visions. Not surprisingly, the avenues from an encounter with a possibility in an artwork to its instantiation in the world are hard to map. Just how an artist might move an audience to action defies any strict account, and Gilroy accepts that his position can seem "idealist" in the sense that it emphasizes changing people's ideas and feelings. He is impatient—and I think rightly so—with an old-line Marxist scorn for any politics that does not work on the economic "base." His own cultural politics does not entail saying the economic, the material, is unimportant; it only entails insisting that culture, that ideas and desires, are also important—and identifying that terrain as the one where Gilroy himself feels he can make his most useful contribution. Envisioning and naming what we want the future to be like is an essential ingredient in bringing that future into existence, especially now that the Left should know, from bitter experience, that the "contradictions" in the current order are not going to transform that order all by themselves.

In my opinion, Gilroy takes a huge step in *Darker than Blue* toward putting some flesh on what can too often be the pious hopes of cultural politics. Understanding that programmatic statements about the radical effects of art are usually self-congratulatory blather, Gilroy instead focuses on specific cases where art points a way forward. One instance is Harriet Beecher Stowe's *Uncle Tom's Cabin*. Gilroy confronts Stowe's critics—from James Baldwin to Costas Douzinas—and wonders what so many of them have invested in declaring the prospect of "any authentic human connection across . . . supposedly impermeable lines of absolute and always singular 'identity'" (*DB*, 66) a sentimental delusion. Instead, Gilroy suggests, we might consider ways of mobilizing sentiment to enable "heteropathic identification" (*DB*, 66). Stowe's book changed the course of history, its "structure of sentimental feeling was instrumental in the formation of a moral collectivity and in winning recognition of the suffering humanity of the slave, whom it was no longer possible to dismiss as a brute" (*DB*, 66). The charge of sentimentalism, I would suggest, signals one's embarrassment at acknowledging deep desires that the world, "serious people," deem foolish. Gilroy wants us to have the courage of those desires—and, furthermore, to mobilize the affects that accompany them. He believes art can do that work of making hard-to-acknowledge desires manifest—and of enlisting audiences into a community that shares those desires by enabling (midwifing, we might say) processes of identification. Gilroy's moral psychology here is akin to that of Adam Smith and David Hume; what he adds is an attention to the ways that art can generate and mobilize the moral sentiments of sympathy, indignation, and identification.

Gilroy's extended discussion of Bob Marley provides another occasion for thinking of art's contributions to the utopian project. Marley offers, Gilroy tells us, a "vernacular view of human rights" (*DB*, 87), illustrating for us the affective attachment to notions of human dignity and justice that can get expressed through a celebration of rights. Giving full credit to the complexities attending the music business and to Marley's ability to use celebrity to avoid pressures that constrain many others, Gilroy still insists that we should attend to the "alternative, postracial identity based not on some automatic or pregiven sameness, but on will, inclination, mood, and affinity" found in Marley's music and life. Even if that life is not yet available to all, the fact that Marley lived it proved such a life is possible. He embodied an alternative—and he provided a challenge because his music says that, "contrary to even the most awful appearances, you do rule your destiny" (*DB*, 92). This insistence on the "will," on the ability to make meaningful choices, is shocking in our times, when the Left is committed to uncovering the hand of power everywhere. Gilroy knows that the privilege accorded a celebrity like Marley is hardly general. But Gilroy is also committed to a vision of art as providing a space—even if it is a play space—in which alternative possibilities are not simply imagined but actually lived. And those alternatives both pose a challenge to our normal "unforgiving present" and "bring a novel solidary network into being" (*DB*, 92), a "solidarity that trumped the power of sameness"

(*DB*, 103). Art imagines new possibilities—and brings new communities into existence—because it attends to "the processes and mechanisms of identification" (*DB*, 114).

Interestingly, Gilroy claims that Marley's utopia has no particular locale. The no place of utopia returns here in Gilroy's thought as something in its favor because it avoids the territorial imperative of having and holding against threats from some invader or immigrant or alien. Marley breaks from the tradition in black thought in which "the alternative, utopian location was identified with a return to Africa" (*DB*, 113). Instead,

> rather than fixing Africa in the frozen time of the prediasporic past, this emergent option would allow it into the present and the future. The memory of slavery and the history of race hierarchy would remain extremely important, but this diasporic consciousness could not be confined by or responsible for them. If this can be accomplished in Marley's memory, he will be commemorated as a world figure whose willingness to dream forward revealed his unfashionable attachment to the idea of a better world. (*DB*, 115)

The fact that Marley's "life and work continually overflowed" (*DB*, 114) all the prevailing structures—race, nation, unitary culture—could be called dynamic nominalism in action. He resisted containment in the present and thus lit a path to the future. Paul Gilroy's work does the same.[6]

Notes

1. Subsequent references to Paul Gilroy, *Against Race* (Cambridge: Harvard University Press, 2000), are abbreviated *AR*, with page numbers given in the body of the text.
2. Paul Gilroy, *The Black Atlantic* (Cambridge: Harvard University Press, 1993), 36.
3. Paul Gilroy, *Postcolonial Melancholia* (New York: Columbia University Press, 2005), 124. Subsequent references are abbreviated *PM*, with page numbers given in the body of my text.
4. *Darker than Blue* (Cambridge: Harvard University Press, 2010), 72. Subsequent references to this work are abbreviated *DB*, with page numbers given in the body of my essay. Here's another instance in which Gilroy uses the notion of "resources": "Any lessons that can be derived from the

histories we have made can furnish resources for the future of this planet" (*PM*, 56).

5. See Anthony Alessandrini's essay, chapter 3 in this volume.
6. I want to thank Rebecka Rutledge Fisher for helpful suggestions for revision of this essay's first draft.

Contributors

Anthony Alessandrini is assistant professor of English at Kingsborough Community College, New York. His research interests include postcolonial literature and theory, with specific interests in diaspora studies; contemporary Arabic, Middle Eastern, and South Asian literature and culture, poetry and poetics, and critical theory. He is the editor of *Frantz Fanon: Critical Perspectives*, a collection that addresses Fanon's extraordinary, often controversial writings, and examines the ways in which his work can shed light on contemporary issues in cultural politics, as it offers new directions for cultural and political thought in the postcolonial era. His book, *Finding Something Different: Frantz Fanon and the Future of Cultural Politics*, is forthcoming.

Jonathan Boyarin is The Leonard and Tobee Kaplan Distinguished Professor of Modern Jewish Thought at the University of North Carolina at Chapel Hill. He is the author of numerous books and articles, including *From a Ruined Garden: The Memorial Books of Polish Jewry* (1983 and 1998), which served as an introduction for younger, English-speaking Jews to first-hand accounts of Jewish life in Eastern Europe. This was followed by *Polish Jews in Paris: The Ethnography of Memory* (1991), based on his dissertation fieldwork in Paris, and by a volume on the life history of Yiddish scholar Shlomo Noble. Further ethnographic and critical essays, including some dealing with the contemporary Lower East Side in New York, were published in *Storm from Paradise: The Politics of Jewish Memory* (1992) and *Thinking in Jewish* (1996). He edited and contributed to *The Ethnography of Reading* (1993) and *Remapping Memory: The Politics of TimeSpace* (1994). With his brother, Daniel Boyarin, he coedited

Jews and Other Differences: The New Jewish Cultural Studies (1997). His interest in Zionism, the Israeli/Palestinian conflict, and revaluation of diaspora in contemporary Jewish life is reflected in *Palestine and Jewish History* (1996) and (again with Daniel Boyarin) *Powers of Diaspora* (2002). His recent books include, *Jewishness and the Human Dimension* (2008), *The Unconverted Self: Jews, Indians, and the Identity of Christian Europe* (2009), and *Mornings at the Stanton Street Shul: A Summer on the Lower East Side* (2011).

Dennis Dworkin is an intellectual and cultural historian of Britain and Ireland and teaches at the University of Nevada, Reno. His most recent book, *Class Struggles* (2007), develops and extends themes elaborated in *Cultural Marxism in Postwar Britain: History, the New Left, and the Origins of Cultural Studies* (1997). The earlier book is a history of an unorthodox intellectual tradition that is both specific to Britain and part of a more general twentieth-century European development—Western Marxism. British cultural Marxism has been responsible for launching the interdisciplinary field of cultural studies; its impact on the social sciences and the humanities has been felt internationally, and, Dworkin shows in much of his work, it has been pivotal to the development of peoples' history or "history from below" and the "new social history." Edited and introduced by Dworkin, *Ireland and Britain, 1798–1922: An Anthology of Sources* (2012), presents fifty-six original sources, many of which have never been reprinted, to trace the origins and development of the conflict during the years of the legislative union between Britain and Ireland—years shaped by the rise of, and British and Irish Unionist responses to, Irish nationalism.

Rebecka Rutledge Fisher is associate professor of English and comparative literature at the University of North Carolina at Chapel Hill. Her work has appeared in the journals *Modern Fiction Studies*, *CR: The New Centennial Review*, *ESQ: A Journal of the American Renaissance*, and in the collection *Race and Ethnicity: Across Time and Space* (2004). Much of her research has been in the area of African American literature and literary theory, and centers on the thought of W.E.B. Du Bois. As a comparatist, she is interested in transnational, African American, and American studies, and has conducted various sorts of graduate and undergraduate seminars having to do with matters of cross-cultural representation and the philosophy of literature. Her introduction and notes for a recent edition of *The Interesting Narrative*, by the eighteenth-century autobiographer Olaudah Equiano, was published by Barnes and Noble Press in December 2005. She is the author of *Habitations of the Veil: Metaphor and* *the Poetics of Black Being in African American Literature* (2014). It examines the use of philosophical metaphors of knowing and being through discussions of canonical works that have been published across nearly two hundred years of African American literature.

Jay Garcia is associate professor of comparative literature at New York University. He is the author of *Psychology Comes to Harlem: Rethinking the Race Question in Twentieth-Century America.* He teaches seminars on American literature in global contexts, theories of racial formation, and the history of American studies. He is working on a book on transnationalism in twentieth-century U.S. writing.

Paul Gilroy is the first holder of the Anthony Giddens Professorship in Social Theory at the London School of Economics. His intellectual background is multidisciplinary and he has extensive interests in literature, art, music, and cultural history, as well as in social science. He is best known for his work on racism, nationalism, ethnicity, and his original approach to the history of the African diaspora in the Western hemisphere. His many works include *There Ain't No Black in the Union Jack* (1987), *Small Acts* (1993), *The Black Atlantic* (1993), *Between Camps* (published in the U.S. as *Against Race*, 2001), and, most recently, *Darker than Blue: On the Moral Economies of Black Atlantic Cultures* (2009).

Richard H. King is professor emeritus of American intellectual history at the University of Nottingham in the United Kingdom. He is the author of *Civil Rights and the Idea of Freedom* (1992), and the editor, with Helen Taylor, of *Dixie Debates: Perspective on Southern Cultures* (1996). His other books include *A Southern Renaissance* (1980), *Race, Culture and the Intellectuals, 1940–1970* (2004), *Hannah Arendt and the Uses of History: Nation, Race, Imperialism and Genocide* (with Dan Stone, 2007). He was a fellow at the Woodrow Wilson International Center for Scholars in 1997–1998. In King's edited collection, *Obama and Race: History, Culture, Politics* (2012), academics from both sides of the Atlantic analyze the confluence of a politician, a process, and a problem—Barack Obama, the 2008 U.S. presidential election, and the "problem" of race in contemporary America.

John McGowan is Ruel W. Tyson Jr. Distinguished Professor of the Humanities at the University of North Carolina at Chapel Hill. His work aspires to follow in the footsteps of John Ruskin, William James, John Dewey, Kenneth

Burke, and Hannah Arendt, all figures who are not quite philosophers, political theorists, or cultural critics, but some mixture of the three. His first book, *Representation and Revelation: Victorian Realism from Carlyle to Yeats* (1986), explores the theory and practice of representation in seven Victorian writers. His *Postmodernism and its Critics* (1991) considers the philosophical antecedents to contemporary theory; offers an account of the work of Derrida, Foucault, Lyotard, Rorty, Said, and Jameson; and presents an alternative political vision (based in a theory of democracy) to that found in postmodern thought. *Hannah Arendt: An Introduction* (1998) and *Hannah Arendt and the Meaning of Politics* (1997), edited with Craig Calhoun, continue exploring the resources of democratic theory through an engagement with Arendt's work on the public sphere, judgment, and storytelling. McGowan is one of the editors of the massive (2500 pages) new *Norton Anthology of Theory and Criticism* (2001, 2010). His *Democracy's Children: Intellectuals and the Rise of Cultural Politics* (2002) collects essays on the shifting roles of the intellectual and of the university in our time. In response to the shifts in American politics over the past thirty years, *American Liberalism: An Interpretation for Our Time* (2007) tries to articulate a liberal vision drawn from Madison and Dewey that can animate contemporary American politics. In *Pragmatist Politics: Making the Case for Liberal Democracy* (2012) McGowan provides a history of democracy as a way of life to show how pragmatism can be an inspiring alternative to the despair that seems to dominate contemporary American politics. McGowan is a founding and active member of UNC's Program in Cultural Studies and currently serves as the director of UNC's Institute for the Arts and Humanities.

Tavia Nyong'o is associate professor of performance studies at New York University, where he teaches black studies, queer studies, and cultural history. His first book, *The Amalgamation Waltz: Race, Performance, and the Ruses of Memory* (2009), won the Errol Hill Award for best book in African American performance studies. Nyong'o has published articles on music, digital media, film, and performance art in venues such as *Radical History Review*, *American Literary History*, *TDR: The Journal of Performance Studies*, *Women Studies Quarterly*, *The Nation*, and *n+1*. He is coeditor of the journal *Social Text*.

Ranu Samantrai is associate professor of English at Indiana University. Her book, *AlterNatives: Black Feminism in the Post-Imperial Nation* (2002), takes as its occasion the Black British feminist movement in London in the 1970s and '80s. She uses moments of conflict between, for instance, antiracist and feminist politics to articulate a theory of the radical potential of a democratic community that thrives on heterogeneity, conflict, and dissent. Samantrai coedited *Interdisciplinarity and Social Justice: Revisioning Academic Accountability* (2010) with Joe Parker and Mary Romero. Her current project, *Country People: Diaspora Aesthetics and Postcolonial Theory*, investigates the modernist investments of postcolonial and diaspora theory to ask how viable a frame they provide for the visual and literary arts of post-settler generations.

Index